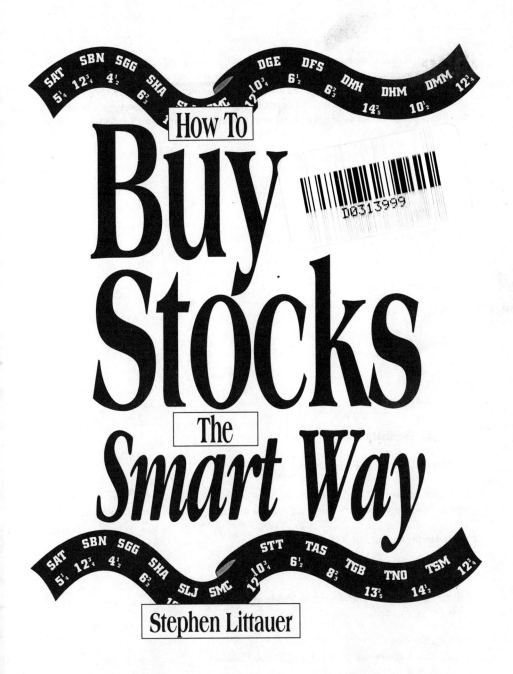

How To
Buy
Stocks

The
Smart Way

Stephen Littauer

Dearborn
Financial Publishing, Inc.

GREG HORVATH

While a great deal of care has been taken to provide accurate and current information, the ideas, suggestions, general principles and conclusions presented in this text are subject to local, state and federal laws and regulations, court cases and any revisions of same. The reader is thus urged to consult legal counsel regarding any points of law—this publication should not be used as a substitute for competent legal advice.

Publisher: Anita A. Constant
Editor-in-Chief: Caroline Carney
Senior Associate Editor: Karen A. Christensen
Managing Editor: Jack L. Kiburz
Editorial Assistant: Stephanie C. Schmidt
Interior Design: Lucy Jenkins
Cover Design: S. Laird Jenkins Corporation

Published by Dearborn Financial Publishing, Inc.

Printed in the United States of America

95 96 97 10 9 8 7 6 5 4 3 2 1

Library of Congress Cataloging-in-Publication Data

Littauer, Stephen L.
    How to buy stocks the smart way / Stephen Littauer.
        p. cm.
    Includes index.
    ISBN 0-7931-1090-4 (pbk.)
    1. Stocks. 2. Investments. I. Title   94-33695
HG4661.L567 1995   CIP

★ *Books by Stephen Littauer*

Grow Rich with Mutual Funds Without a Broker

How To Buy Stocks the Smart Way

How To Buy Mutual Funds the Smart Way

CONTENTS

INTRODUCTION

Most of us invest to provide ourselves with a financially secure future. But we have to make complex choices. What are we looking for? Current income? Capital growth? Future income? Where should we invest our money? Stocks? Bonds? Money market instruments? In what combination?

The securities markets are volatile. Successful long-term investing depends on sensible portfolio planning. You may well be asking yourself the question What kind of investment portfolio makes the most sense for *my* needs? This book is dedicated to helping you invest the smart way. It provides commonsense principles of intelligent investing plus information essential to building your investment portfolio on a firm foundation.

SELECTING AN OBJECTIVE

Before taking the first step on any journey, you need a clear destination. What are your objectives? The four most common objectives are financial security, retirement planning, income to meet living expenses and a child's education. You may be seeking one, a combination or perhaps entirely different ones. Whatever your objectives are, they should establish a destination, as well as a chart for measuring your progress. At times, securities markets will turn, and you will be tempted to change direction abruptly. Your objectives should serve as a road map for managing your investment program.

Investment returns generally are made up of some combination of growth and income. Investments fall into three major categories:

1. *Equity investments,* such as common stocks, have the potential for capital appreciation and are expected to provide a variable but generally rising income stream. In the short term, you may see substantial price volatility.

2. *Fixed-income investments,* such as corporate and government bonds, offer a rate of interest that tends to provide a stable flow of income over time. The principal value rises and falls as interest rates go down and up.

3. *Fixed-dollar investments,* such as bank deposits, U.S. Treasury bills (T-bills) or money market funds, usually provide a relatively low yield that rises or falls depending on the level of short-term interest rates. Note: While bank deposits are guaranteed up to specified limits by the Federal Deposit Insurance Corporation (FDIC) and T-bills are backed by the full faith and credit of the U.S. government, there is no guarantee that money market funds will maintain a stable net asset value (NAV).

According to Ibbotson Associates, the long-term historical return on common stocks has been the highest of the three investment categories. Over a 60-year period, beginning in 1932, the average annual return for T-bills was 3.8 percent; for corporate bonds, 4.8 percent; and for common stocks, 12.0 percent. Actually, the average interest rate return for bonds was 5.4 percent, but investors incurred an average annual principal loss of 0.6 percent as a result of changing interest rates. The 12.0 percent average total return for stocks was comprised of 4.8 percent from dividends and 7.2 percent from capital appreciation.

So if you have a relatively long time to accumulate capital, and if maximum return is your only criterion, common stocks obviously would be the investment choice—if you could be sure that the past is a forecaster of the future. Because the future is uncertain, however, risk must be considered along with return. It is the basic risk/return trade-off that is the essential challenge of investing. Chapter 9, "Keys to Successful Investing," discusses risk in-depth.

ACHIEVING FINANCIAL INDEPENDENCE

The long-term results of your investment program depend primarily on your determination and ability to hold to a true investment course. Equally important, you must develop *your own* portfolio, one that permits you to pursue your personal objectives by relying on your own judgment as you build your portfolio.

For long-term investment success in the stock market, here are six basic ingredients that will help you.

Knowledge

Knowledge is power. Learn about the economy and the financial markets. Look at investments from a long-term historical perspective, taking into account rewards, risks and fundamental investment characteristics. Evaluate the objectives and strategies of any company you may consider, as well as its management, its reputation and the stock's performance in up and down markets. Part One of this book, "Tools To Get You Started" will help get *you* started.

Consistency

Develop your own basic investment plan—and stay with it. Short-term fluctuations in the markets may tempt you toward *market timing*—selling stocks when they are high and buying them back when they are low. This is a lot easier said than done, and entails its own risks if you are wrong. Build your portfolio by investing in stocks or bonds systematically so that you will be practicing *constant dollar investing,* rather than committing all your money at a single time. See Chapter 5, "A Time-Tested Investment Technique for Successful Investing," for a full explanation of this.

Balance

A prudent way to hedge against uncertainties of the future is to hold a balanced portfolio of stocks, bonds and cash reserves. Add foreign investments through American depository receipts (ADRs) for further diversification. There is no single answer to determining the best balance. Your age may provide a clue regarding how your assets can be best allocated. The following illustration offers four examples of balanced portfolios, based on different age ranges:

Your Age	Stocks	Bonds	Money Market
30	75%	15%	10%
40	65	20	15
50	50	35	15
60	40	40	20

This simple chart is meant to stimulate thought rather than be a definitive recommendation. It raises additional questions. Should you purchase stocks primarily for growth or income? Should bonds be safe U.S. Treasuries, or lower-quality corporate bonds? Should you be looking for taxable or tax-free bonds? Finally, the balance you choose in your 40s while building capital for retirement may not be appropriate when you are retired and need a generous and continuing income stream. In Part Two of this book, "Investment Strategies," you will find many ideas to help answer these and other questions.

Diversification

Whichever investment balance you settle on, prudence dictates that you diversify your investments among large numbers of stocks and bonds. It is impossible to forecast with any precision the risk or reward of any single stock or bond. Diversification improves the safety of your portfolio by significantly reducing the risk. Again, see Chapter 9, "Keys to Successful Investing," for information on how diversification reduces risk.

Low-Cost Investing

Whatever investment costs you incur represent a reduction in the return you receive. The major costs involved in maintaining an investment program are brokerage commissions, which are paid when you buy and when you sell stocks and bonds. See Chapter 7, "How Much Should You Pay Your Broker?," for how you can get the service you need at the least amount of cost.

Healthy Skepticism

Crowd psychology can be tempting. Watch out for the seductiveness of market "gurus," the allure of market timing and the "conventional wisdom" of all the experts. Never simply assume that past returns guarantee the same in the future. There are no easy answers in the complex world of investing.

REINVESTING DIVIDENDS

One of the difficult decisions facing long-term investors is what to do with the dividends that companies pay out to shareholders. Most individual investors cannot buy additional shares in the same company on the open market simply because buying a few shares at a time is too costly. Fortunately, there is an easy and inexpensive solution. More than 750 companies offer automatic *dividend reinvestment plans* (DRIPs). Under this arrangement, instead of sending participating investors cash dividends, the company uses those dividends to purchase additional shares of company stock.

This gives investors several advantages: Dividend payments are put to work, transaction costs are eliminated or kept to a minimum, and the additional shares are purchased gradually over time, an easy-to-implement form of constant dollar investing. Chapter 6, "DRIPs—Reinvesting Dividends Automatically," explains the benefits of automatic reinvestment plans and how they work. In addition, Appendix B, "Companies with Dividend Reinvestment Plans (DRIPs)," lists most companies offering this plan.

GETTING CURRENT INVESTMENT INFORMATION

Serious investors need timely and comprehensive information to make wise investment choices. Chapter 4, "Buy, Sell or Hold?—Information Sources That Can Help You Find the Answers," provides information on a number of investment services that have consistently produced accurate, in-depth information for stock market investors.

SUMMARY

Most of us invest to provide ourselves with a financially secure future, but we have complex choices to make. Are we looking for current income, capital growth, future income or some combination? Should our money be invested in stocks, bonds or money market instruments? Successful long-term investing depends on sensible portfolio planning. This book is dedicated to helping you invest the *smart* way. It provides commonsense principles of intelligent investing plus information that is essential to building your investment portfolio on a firm foundation.

PART ONE

Tools To Get You Started

CHAPTER 1

Stock Market Opportunities

The proliferation of state lotteries across the country and the media attention focused on the huge jackpots are ample evidence of our desire to get rich quickly. But the chances of an individual to cash in big are remote.

In the Florida Lottery, for example, one lucky player won $30 million. But the odds of winning the grand prize are a remote 1 in 13,983,816!

Fortunately, your chances of getting rich in the stock market are better, *a lot better*. The main requirements are using common sense and patience. Part of using common sense is understanding that the stock market is not a get-rich-quick scheme. You can get rich if you have a clear objective, concentrate on the long term, develop a diversified portfolio of securities and stick with your plan.

This chapter is designed to give you a guided tour through some of the investment opportunities offered by the New York Stock Exchange (NYSE), the American Stock Exchange (AMEX) and the National Association of Securities Dealers Automated Quotations (Nasdaq) national market system.

GETTING STARTED

You always should base your investment decisions on your own particular financial position, risk comfort level and goals. Remember, no one is as interested in you and your financial situation as you are. So listen, learn and consult with people you trust. But in the end, make your own decisions. If you do not understand a finance or investment term, consult the extensive glossary in this book.

You will want to consider three basic factors before making any investment decision:

What Is Your Investment Objective?

Is your objective capital appreciation? Then you will seek out investments that will grow in value to produce capital gains. Along with the appreciation of the asset's value, you will want to take into consideration the reinvestment of dividends and interest.

Is your objective income? Then you will want to identify investments whose primary feature is to provide regular income. You will want to know if it produces an income of fixed payments, or if you can expect an income stream of gradually increasing payments.

How about inflation? If the value of an investment can be expected to rise at the same rate or at a rate higher than the rate of inflation, the investment is said to be inflation-sensitive.

Are there tax considerations? Are you looking for an investment to be included in a tax-deferred retirement account? Such accounts include individual retirement accounts (IRAs), Keogh plans for self-employed individuals, 401(k) plans and other qualified pension or profit-sharing plans.

Can you borrow against it? This question involves the general value of an investment as collateral for a loan. Borrowing can be a way of raising cash when an investment cannot readily be sold or when it may not be the right time to sell. An investment also can be used in a margin account with a broker. This gives you leverage, the ability to control a greater value of securities than the amount of cash you have available.

How Much Risk Can You Tolerate?

The answer to this question is subjective and varies widely among investors.

Principal Risk   You want to know what assurance you have of getting your full investment back. This involves two types of risk. The first is *market risk* and involves fluctuations in value because of forces operating in the market system, such as the optimism or pessimism of investors, changes in the economy or unexpected events occurring in the national or international arena. The other type of risk is financial or *credit risk*. This is the risk that an issuer of a debt security will default on a contractual obligation or an equity investment will lose value because of the bankruptcy or financial difficulty of the issuer.

Income Risk   If you have an investment that produces income, you want to know the probability that the issuer will be able to continue the flow of dividend or interest payments.

Are Taxes a Consideration?

Dividend or interest payments are subject to income tax liability, while profits taken when a security appreciates in value may be subject to a lower capital-gains tax. These factors may influence how long you hold an investment and whether you buy stock in a company that reinvests its earnings or pays out a substantial portion in dividends.

STOCK MARKET INVESTMENT ALTERNATIVES

In addition to investing in stocks, you also can choose a number of investment alternatives traded in the securities markets and available through a broker. The major categories, with a brief description of each are as follows:

Closed-End Funds

A closed-end fund is a type of mutual fund with a relatively fixed amount of capital, whose shares are traded on a securities exchange or in the over-the-counter (OTC) market. The value of a closed-end fund's shares rises and falls in the marketplace based on the value of the fund's portfolio as well as investor confidence and other market factors. Shares of closed-end funds usually sell at a premium to or discount from the value of their underlying portfolios.

If you are seeking an investment that will grow in value, select a fund having appreciation as its primary objective. Bond funds generally have an objective of providing income. *Dual-purpose funds* have two classes of stock, with common shareholders benefiting from all the capital gains and preferred shareholders receiving all the interest and dividend income.

Common Stocks

For total return (capital gains and dividend income), no publicly traded investment offers more potential over the long term than common stock.

Common stock represents the basic equity ownership in a corporation. A shareholder normally is entitled to vote for directors and in other important matters and to share in the wealth created by the corporation's business activities. Shareholders participate in the appreciation of share values and in dividends declared out of earnings that remain after debt obligations and preferred stock dividends are met.

The market values of shares in publicly held corporations are based primarily on investor expectations of future earnings and dividends. These expectations and the resulting stock values often are influenced by forecasts of business activity in general and by so-called investor psychology, which reflects the current business and economic environment. The relationship of market price to a company's actual or expected earnings is called the *price-earnings (PE) ratio,* or *multiple.* For example, a stock selling at $60 a share with earnings of $5 a share is said to be selling at a PE ratio of 12 times earnings, or a multiple of 12.

Stocks of young, rapidly growing companies tend to be volatile, have a high PE ratio and usually carry a high degree of risk. Such companies seldom pay dividends. Instead, dividends are reinvested to finance growth. As opposed to these growth stocks, stocks of older, established companies with histories of regular earnings and dividend payments tend to have more price stability and low PE multiples. Some of these stocks would be characterized as *blue chips;* those paying out substantial dividends are called *income stocks.*

Convertible Securities

Some bonds (debentures) and preferred stocks are convertible into common stock, usually of the issuer. These convertible securities offer both fixed income and capital appreciation potential. They pay a fixed dividend or rate of interest and are convertible into common stock at a specified price or conversion ratio. The yield on convertibles normally is less than that of nonconvertible bonds or preferreds, and the potential for capital gains is less than with a common stock investment.

Convertibles usually offer less credit risk and market risk than common stock while providing an opportunity for an investor to participate in the future success of the corporation into whose common shares they can be exchanged. Convertible bonds and convertible preferred stock have the same priority of claim on the earnings and assets of a corporation as regular bonds and preferreds. In terms of priority in claims against the corporation's earnings and assets, bonds take precedence over preferred stock, and both take precedence over common stock.

Convertibles have an investment value and a conversion value. *Investment value* is the market value the security would have if it were not convertible. *Conversion value* is the market price of the common stock multiplied by the number of shares into which the bond or preferred stock is convertible. This is called the conversion rate or ratio.

Consider buying a convertible security if your investment objective is capital appreciation and if you want the greater yield and safety of bonds and preferred stocks. Remember, though, because growth is a key feature, yield is less than on a straight bond or preferred stock. Convertibles tend to rise in value with increasing common stock prices, so they also represent a hedge against inflation.

From a risk perspective, convertibles will not sink in value below the market value that the same investment would have without the convertible feature. But like any interest-rate-sensitive investment, the investment value of convertibles varies inversely with interest rates. Prices rise when interest rates decline, and they go down when interest rates go up.

And as with regular corporate bonds and preferred stock, convertible bonds have priority over convertible preferreds in claims against the corporation's earnings and assets, and convertible preferreds have priority over the common shares. Assuming the issuer is financially strong and has dependable earnings, you do not have to be concerned about much credit risk.

Corporate Bonds

A corporate bond is a debt security of a corporation that requires the issuer to pay the bondholder the par value at a specified maturity date and to make scheduled interest payments. The general attractions of corporate bonds are their relative safety and the higher yields they pay than government bonds. Unsecured bonds are called *debentures* and have a claim on the assets of the issuing corporation. Secured bonds usually are backed by mortgages against specific assets of the corporation. The creditworthiness of corporate bonds are closely monitored by the major bond rating services. Interest on corporate bonds is fully taxable.

A *bond* is a contract between a borrower (the issuer) and a lender (the bondholder). The face amount of a bond (par value) is normally $1,000, except for baby bonds that have par values of $500 or less.

Bonds can trade in the market at a premium or discount to their par values so that their yield is in line with current interest rates. There is an inverse relationship between bond prices and interest rate movements. When interest rates rise, bond prices decline, and vice versa. Bond prices also vary with the time remaining to maturity. Generally, the longer the maturity, the higher the yield will be and the lower the price of a bond. This is because time means risk and more risk requires a higher yield.

Another factor that affects bond prices is safety. This relates to credit risk, the borrower's ability to pay interest and principal when due. The financial strength of the corporation is reflected in the ratings assigned to its bonds by the major credit services. These ratings affect yield, which is adjusted by changes in a bond's price.

Bonds usually are issued in minimum amounts of $5,000 and are traded by brokers in round lots of 10 or 100 bonds ($10,000 or $100,000). Odd lots often are available at higher commission rates or dealer *spreads* (the difference between what a dealer buys and sells a security for).

You generally should buy bonds when your investment objective is income. Capital appreciation, however, is possible when bonds can be bought at a discount or when declining interest rates cause bond prices to rise.

Foreign Stocks

You can take advantage of opportunities occurring where economies or industry sectors may be growing faster than those in the United States by investing in foreign stocks. These are securities of foreign issuers denominated in foreign currencies. Total returns can be increased through profits on currency movements; but remember, this also means additional risk.

American depositary receipts (ADRs) provide a convenient way to invest in foreign stocks. These negotiable receipts are issued by U.S. banks and represent actual shares held in their foreign branches. ADRs are traded actively on the major stock exchanges and in the OTC market. There still are currency risks and foreign withholding taxes, but the depositary pays dividends and capital gains in U.S. dollars and handles splits, stock dividends and rights offerings. Trading inconveniences and custodial problems that exist with trading in foreign stocks are eliminated with ADRs.

You also can buy foreign stocks through your broker in foreign markets. Depending on the issue and the market, problems include inadequate financial information and regulation, high minimum purchase requirements, higher transaction costs, taxes, possible illiquidity, political risk and possible currency losses. Unless you are able to take big risks and are sophisticated in the ways of international interest rates and foreign exchange, this avenue of investment may not be a wise one for you to take. International diversification can be readily achieved on a much lower level of risk by investing in closed-end or open-end mutual funds.

Most foreign stock shares traded through ADRs represent solid, established companies, and volatility has tended to be low. Thus, these foreign equities on average may normally be safer than many domestic issues. Adverse currency fluctuations, however, introduce an added element of risk.

If your investment objective is growth of capital, foreign stocks offer you the potential for both capital and currency appreciation. From an income perspective, foreign stocks generally have lower dividend yields than U.S. stocks, and exchange-rate fluctuations are a factor in expected returns.

Put and Call Option Contracts

An *option contract* gives the owner the right, for a price, called a *premium,* to buy or sell an underlying stock or financial instrument at a specified price, called the *exercise* or *strike price,* before a specified expiration date.

A *put* is an option to sell, and a *call* is an option to buy. Option sellers are called *writers.* If they own the underlying security, they are called *covered* writers; they are called *naked* writers if they do not.

Options are traded on national stock and commodity exchanges and also in the OTC market. Those listed on the exchanges have greater visibility and are less expensive than those traded over the counter, which are individually negotiated and less liquid. Listed options are available on stocks, stock indexes, debt instruments, foreign currencies and different types of futures.

Options make it possible for an investor to control a large amount of value with a much smaller amount of money at risk. Options provide leverage, so a small percentage change in the value of a financial instrument can result in a much larger percentage change in the value of an option. Thus, large gains and losses are possible. Options usually are bought and sold, then allowed to expire without ever being exercised. They are financial instruments with lives of their own.

Option prices are determined mainly by (1) the relationship between the exercise price and the market price of the underlying security, (2) by the time remaining before the option expires and (3) by the volatility of the underlying security.

Consider using options only if you are interested in speculating. Because a small change in a stock price causes a higher percentage change in a related option price, options can give you a substantial amount of leverage. Profits can be great, but losses can mount quickly if the underlying stock does not move in the right direction. Income in the form of premiums you receive from the sale of covered options can add to your income return on the underlying investment. Remember that if you write (sell) an option on a security you own, you may be forced to sell the underlying security if the price moves in the wrong direction.

Preferred Stocks

Preferred stock is an equity security that includes features of both common stocks and bonds. Because it is not debt, however, it is riskier than bonds.

The dividends on preferred stock are usually a fixed percentage of par value or a fixed dollar amount. Thus, share prices are interest-rate-sensitive. Like bonds, prices go up when interest rates go down and vice versa. Preferred dividends, however, are not a contractual expense of the issuer. Although they are payable before common stock dividends, they can be skipped if earnings are low. Again, if the issuer goes bankrupt, although the claims of preferred shareholders come before common shareholders, they do not share in assets until bond-holders are paid in full.

Preferred issues are designed for insurance companies and other institutional investors that, as corporations, benefit from an 80 percent tax exclusion on dividends earned. For individuals, though, their fully taxable yields are not much better than that of comparable bonds, and they lack the greater degree of safety bonds afford. Another negative aspect of preferred stock is that trading often is inactive. This means less liquidity and higher transaction costs for the small investor.

Preferred stock comes in several varieties, of which *cumulative preferred* is the most common. Dividends, if missed (not paid by the company), accrue, and common stock dividends cannot be paid until all missed dividends on the preferred have been caught up.

Other types of preferred stock include:

Convertible preferred, mentioned earlier in this chapter, is convertible into common shares and so offers growth potential plus fixed income.

Participating preferred is issued by companies having difficulty in raising capital. Shareholders participate in profits with common shareholders in the form of extra dividends declared after regular dividends are paid.

Adjustable rate preferred has the dividend adjusted quarterly to reflect money market rates. It is marketed mainly to corporate investors seeking higher after-tax yields (remember their 80 percent tax exclusion on dividends) together with market price stability. For the individual investor whose dividends are fully taxed, a money market fund is generally a better choice.

Normally, you should invest in preferred stock only if your objective is income, although appreciation is possible if shares are bought at a discount from par or redemption value, or prior to a decline in interest rates. But unless you are a corporation, you probably are better off with a comparable corporate bond, which is less risky in terms of both principal and income.

SUMMARY

When selecting investments, always consider your own particular financial position, risk comfort level and goals. Remember, no one is as interested in you and your financial situation as you are. So listen, learn and consult with people you trust, but in the end make your own decisions. Before making any investment decision, evaluate your investment objective, how much risk you are able to tolerate and how your tax situation will be affected. You can choose from a wide range of stock investment choices as well as stock alternatives.

CHAPTER 2

Major Market Indexes

Market indexes show the general direction of fluctuations in the securities markets and reflect the historical continuity of security price movements. While this information will not necessarily tell you whether the stocks in your portfolio are up or down, it is useful to understand how the indexes work for they are commonly used as benchmarks for judging the performance of individual stocks. So-called market "averages" are not really averages anymore. The term *index* is more appropriate, because the numbers given, usually called *points* should not be mistaken for dollars-per-share prices of stocks. Points refer to units of movement in the average, which is a composite of weighted dollar values.

Indexes track stocks in particular industry sectors, in specific markets or of a certain capitalization. For instance, one index tracks gold stocks. Another tracks stocks of companies engaged in the distribution and transmission of natural gas. An index exists for each of several exchanges where stocks are traded, including indexes for stocks that trade on the NYSE, the AMEX and OTC. One index tracks small capitalization stocks, one tracks large capitalization stocks and another tracks all stocks traded in the United States. This chapter describes the more widely known indexes.

DOW JONES INDUSTRIAL AVERAGE (DJIA)

The best known and most widely quoted index is the Dow Jones Industrial Average (DJIA), often referred to simply as "the Dow," published by Dow Jones & Company. You can hardly avoid hearing the Dow's progress as newscasters comment daily on radio and television news programs.

For nearly 100 years, industrial stocks have proliferated, and the industrial average has come a long way. It easily has become the best known and most often quoted of all the averages. It is also the most widely used stock market indicator, although Standard & Poor's 500 Stock Composite Index (S&P 500) has become an important standard for many.

The DJIA is simply a statistical compilation that reflects combined, not individual, performances. The two great advantages of the industrials are simplicity and continuity. The present high level of the average is a result of its continuity. Its base never has changed, because to do so would, in effect, start a new average.

A problem of the Dow Jones Industrials is that the average exaggerates market movements. This is because it is described in "points" and runs about 50 times the straight average price of industrial stocks. Over the years, stocks have been split, but the industrial average has not. It has been suggested that the publisher of the index split the industrials one-for-ten or move the decimal one place to the left. The general opinion, however, is that the average has gone to its lofty height and moves up and down strictly according to arithmetic. If the arithmetic were changed, continuity would be lost—and continuity is the average's greatest advantage.

Keep in mind that the market "averages" really are not averages anymore. They were originally and still are referred to as such. Although they are useful measures of the overall movement of the stock market, the numbers themselves should not be mistaken for dollar-per-share prices of stocks. This applies not only to the Dow Jones Industrials but to all stock averages, or *indexes,* as many now are called.

The reason for the disparity is *stock splits,* which occur when a company believes that the per-share price of its stock is too high for broad investor appeal. The company then arbitrarily splits the high-priced shares, creating more lower-priced shares. For example, if a stock selling for $100 is split two-for-one, the new price will be $50, other factors remaining unchanged. Of course, each owner of each share of the old $100 stock must be given an additional share of stock so the value of his or her holding will not be reduced.

Stock splitting, which occurs year after year, would distort the averages unless statistical market value-weighted adjustments were not also made to compensate for them. Thus, the Dow Jones averages are not dollar averages of current market prices but movement indicators, kept essentially undistorted by stock splits over nearly 100 years.

The DJIA, originally consisting of 12 stocks in 1896, was increased to 20 in 1916 and then to 30 in 1928. Whenever any particular component stock for any reason becomes unrepresentative of the American industrial sector, a substitution is made and the average adjusted, just as when a split occurs.

Critics sometimes charge that the DJIA includes only 30 companies and so fails to reflect the movement of hundreds of other stock prices. But these 30 securities are chosen as representative of the broad market and of American industry. The companies are major factors in their industries, and their stocks are widely held by both individuals and institutions. Changes in the components are made rarely, often as a result of mergers, but occasionally, they may be made to effect a better representation.

TODAY'S *OTHER* WIDELY USED MARKET INDEXES

The DJIA is a price-weighted average of 30 actively traded blue chip stocks consisting primarily of industrial companies. The components, which change from time to time, represent between 15 percent and 20 percent of the market value of NYSE stocks.

The DJIA is calculated by adding the closing prices of the component stocks and using a divisor that is adjusted for stock splits and dividends equal to 10 percent or more of the market value of an issue, as well as for substitutions and mergers. The average is quoted in points, not dollars. In March of 1994, the Dow Jones Industrials consisted of the following companies:

Allied Signal Company
Aluminum Company of
 America
American Express Company

American Telephone &
 Telegraph (AT&T)
Bethlehem Steel
Boeing Company
Caterpillar, Inc.

Chevron Corporation	International Paper Company
Coca-Cola Company	McDonald's Corporation
Disney (Walt) Company	Merck & Company
DuPont de Nemours, E. I. &	Minnesota Mining &
Co.	Manufacturing (3M)
Eastman Kodak Company	Morgan (J. P.) & Company
Exxon Corporation	Philip Morris Company, Inc.
General Electric (GE)	Procter & Gamble Corporation
Company	Sears, Roebuck & Company
General Motors (GM)	Texaco Incorporated
Corporation	Union Carbide Corporation
Goodyear Tire & Rubber	United Technologies Company
Company	Westinghouse Electric
International Business	Corporation
Machines Corporation (IBM)	F. W. Woolworth & Company

Over time, especially in recent years, the number of market averages—now widely called indexes—has proliferated. Dow Jones & Company itself now publishes an average for 20 transportation stocks, one for 15 utility stocks and a composite average of all 65 stocks. In addition, market indexes have been developed by investment services firms, an industry association and even mutual fund companies. Some of the more widely known indexes are presented in the following section.

American Gas Association (AGA) Stock Index   The AGA Stock Index contains approximately 107 publicly traded stocks of companies engaged in the natural gas distribution and transmission industry. The industry is composed of gas distribution companies, gas pipeline companies, diversified gas companies and combination gas and electric companies.

AMEX Major Market Index   This indicator is a price-weighted average, meaning that high-priced issues have more influence than low-priced issues. It is composed of 20 blue chip industrial stocks and is designed to replicate the DJIA in measuring representative performance of the stocks of major industrial corporations. It is produced by the AMEX but consists of stocks listed on the NYSE, 15 of which also are components of the DJIA.

AMEX Market Value Index   This index is a capitalization or market value–weighted index. In other words, the impact of a component's price change is proportionate to the overall market value of the issue. It was introduced at a base level of 100.00 in September of 1973 and adjusted to half that level in July of 1983. It measures the collective performance of more than 800 issues that represent all major industry groups trading on the AMEX. ADRs and warrants, as well as common stocks, are included. Cash dividends paid by component stocks are assumed to be reinvested and are reflected in the index, a characteristic unique to the AMEX Market Value Index.

Benham North American Gold Equities Index   This index consists of 28 stocks of North American companies engaged in exploring for, mining, processing, fabricating or otherwise dealing in gold.

Dow Jones Transportation Average (DJTA)   This index is a price-weighted average of the stocks of 20 large companies in the transportation business, including airlines, railroads and trucking. From 1897 to 1969, this indicator was called the Dow Jones Railroad Average. The transportation average contains the following components:

Airborne Freight Corporation
Alaska Air Group, Inc.
American President Companies
AMR Corporation
Burlington Northern, Inc.
Carolina Freight Corporation
Consolidated Freight
   Corporation
Consolidated Rail Corporation
CSX Corporation
Delta Airlines

Federal Express Company
Norfolk Southern Corporation
Roadway Services, Inc.
Ryder System, Inc.
Santa Fe Southern Pacific
   Company
Southwest Airlines
UAL, Inc.
Union Pacific Corporation
USAir Group
Xtra Corporation

Dow Jones Utility Average (DJUA)   This is a price-weighted average composed of 15 geographically representative and well-established gas and electric utility companies. The utilities average consists of the following components:

American Electric Power
Company
Arkla, Inc.
Centerior Energy
Commonwealth Edison
Company
Consolidated Edison Company
Consolidated Natural Gas
Company
Detroit Edison Company
Houston Industries

Niagara Mohawk Power
Company
Pacific Gas & Electric
Company
Panhandle Eastern Company
PECO Energy
Peoples Energy Corporation
Public Service Enterprise
Group
SCE Corporation

Dow Jones 65 Composite Stock Average   This average consists of the 30 stocks in the Dow Jones Industrial Average, the 20 stocks in the Dow Jones Transportation Average and the 15 stocks in the Dow Jones Utility Average. This average is significant because it is a combination of the three blue chip averages and, therefore, gives a good indication of the overall direction of the largest, most established companies.

Lehman Brothers Aggregate Bond Index   This index measures total investment return (capital changes plus income) provided by a universe of fixed-income securities, weighted by the market value outstanding of each security. More than 6,000 issues (including bonds, notes, debentures and mortgage issues) are included in the index. The securities generally have an effective maturity of not less than one year, an outstanding market value of at least $25 million and investment-grade quality (rated a minimum of Baa by Moody's Investors Service, Inc., or BBB by Standard & Poor's Corporation).

Morgan Stanley Capital International Europe (Free) Index (MSCI-Europe (Free))   MSCI-Europe (Free) is a diversified, capitalization-weighted index comprising approximately 575 companies located in 13 European countries. Three countries—the United Kingdom, Germany and France—dominate MSCI-Europe (Free), with 40 percent, 14 percent and 14 percent of the market capitalization of the index, respectively. The "Free" index includes only shares that U.S. investors are "free to purchase." It excludes restricted shares in Finland, Norway, Sweden and Switzerland.

Morgan Stanley Capital International Pacific Index (MSCI-Pacific) This is a diversified, capitalization-weighted Pacific Basin index consisting of approximately 525 companies located in Australia, Japan, Hong Kong, New Zealand and Singapore. The MSCI-Pacific is dominated by the Japanese stock market, which represents about 85 percent of its market capitalization.

Morgan Stanley Capital International Europe, Australia and Far East (Free) Index (EAFE Free) EAFE Free is a broadly diversified international index consisting of more than 1,000 equity securities of companies located outside of the United States.

Nasdaq National Market System Composite Index This is a market value–weighted index composed of all the stocks traded on the National Market System (NMS) of the OTC market, which is supervised by the National Association of Securities Dealers (NASD). The companies in this index are generally smaller growth companies.

New York Stock Exchange (NYSE) Composite Index This index is market value–weighted and relates all NYSE stocks to an aggregate market value as of December 31, 1965, adjusted for capital changes. The initial, or base, value of the index in 1965 was $50, and point changes are expressed in dollars and cents.

Russell 2000 Small Stock Index This is a broadly diversified, small capitalization index consisting of approximately 2,000 common stocks. As of September 30, 1993, the average capitalization (number of outstanding shares times the market price per share) of stocks in this index was about $360 million.

The Schwab 1000 Index This index is composed of the common stocks of the 1,000 largest U.S. corporations (excluding investment companies) as measured by market capitalization. A particular stock's weighting in the index is based on its relative total market value divided by the total market value of the index. As of December 31, 1993, the aggregate market capitalization of the stocks constituting the index was approximately $4 trillion.

Standard & Poor's 500 Composite Stock Price Index The S&P 500 Index measures the *total investment return* (change in market price plus income) of 500 common stocks, which are chosen by Standard & Poor's Corporation on a statistical basis. The 500 securities, most of which trade on the NYSE, represented about 67 percent of the market value of all U.S. common stocks as of December 31, 1993. Each stock in the index is weighted by its market value. Because of its market-value weighting, the 50 largest companies in the S&P 500 Index currently account for about 50 percent of the index. Typically, companies included in the S&P 500 are the largest and most dominant firms in their industries.

Standard & Poor's 40 Stock Financial Index   This market value–oriented index is composed of 40 large financial institutions, such as banks and insurance companies.

Standard & Poor's 20 Transportation Stock Index   This market value–oriented index is made up of 20 large transportation companies in the airline, trucking and railroad businesses.

Standard & Poor's 40 Utilities Stock Index   This market value–oriented index consists of 40 large and geographically representative electric and gas utilities.

Standard & Poor's 100 Composite Stock Index   This market value–oriented index is made up of the 40 stocks in the S&P Financial Index, the 20 stocks in the S&P Transportation Index and the 40 stocks in the S&P Utilities Index.

Standard & Poor's 400 Industrial Stock Index   This is a market value–weighted index comprising 400 large, well-established industrial companies, most of which are traded on the NYSE. The S&P 500 Index is made up of the S&P 400 Index plus the S&P 40 Utilities, the S&P 20 Transportation companies, and the 40 financial institutions indexes.

Standard & Poor's/BARRA Value and Growth Indexes   To construct these indexes, Standard & Poor's Corporation semiannually ranks all common stocks included in the S&P 500 Index by their price-to-book ratios. The resulting list then is divided in half by market capitalization. Those companies representing half of the market capitalization of the S&P 500 Index and having lower price-to-book ratios are included in the S&P/BARRA Value Index; the remaining companies are incorporated into the S&P/BARRA Growth Index.

On December 31, 1993, the S&P/BARRA Value Index consisted of 310 common stocks in the S&P 500 Index, while the S&P/BARRA Growth Index consisted of the remaining 190. Each index represented half of the market capitalization of the S&P 500 Index. Typically, the stocks included in the S&P/BARRA Value Index exhibit above-average dividend yields and lower price-to-book ratios. By comparison, the stocks included in the S&P 500/BARRA Growth Index exhibit below-average dividend yields and higher price-to-book ratios.

Value Line Composite Index   This equally weighted geometric average is composed of the approximately 1,700 stocks tracked by the *Value Line Investment Survey* and traded on the NYSE, AMEX and OTC market. It is particularly broad in scope, because Value Line covers both large industrial companies and smaller growth firms.

Wilshire 4500 Index   This index consists of all U.S. stocks that are not in the S&P 500 Index and that trade regularly on the NYSE and AMEX as well as in the Nasdaq OTC market. More than 5,000 stocks of midsize and small capitalization companies are included in the Wilshire 4500 Index.

Wilshire 5000 Index   This index consists of all regularly and publicly traded U.S. stocks; it provides a complete proxy for the U.S. stock market. More than 6,000 stocks, including large, medium-size and small capitalization companies, are included in the Wilshire 5000 Index. It represents the value, in billions of dollars, of all NYSE, AMEX and OTC stocks for which quotes are available. This index is used to measure how all stocks are doing as a group, as opposed to a particular segment of the market.

Wilshire Small Cap Index   This index consists of common stock of 250 companies with an average market capitalization of $400 million, and it is designed to accurately reflect the general characteristics and performance profile of small capitalization companies. Stocks in the index were chosen on the basis of market capitalization, liquidity and industry group representation.

SUMMARY

While market indexes will not necessarily tell you whether the stocks in your portfolio are up or down, understanding how the indexes work is useful because they are commonly used as benchmarks for judging the performance of individual stocks. Securities market indexes give a general rather than precise idea of fluctuations in the securities markets and reflect the historical continuity of security price movements. So-called market averages really are not averages anymore. The term *index* is more appropriate, and the numbers given, usually called points, should not be mistaken for dollars-per-share prices of stocks.

CHAPTER 3

Tools the Pros Use

HOW TO READ THE TICKER TAPE

No longer does an investor have to journey to a broker's office to "watch the tape." Today cable television allows investors access to the stock ticker tape continuously throughout the business day in the convenience of their own homes. What you see on such stations as CNBC and CNN "Headline News" is the same report of trading activity displayed on the floors of the major stock exchanges. To give stock exchange members an advantage, the tape is transmitted with a 15-minute delay.

The ticker tape is a running report of trading activity on the stock exchanges. The name comes from machines used years ago that printed information from punched holes in a paper tape, making an audible ticking sound as the tape was fed through. The ticker tape today is a computer screen and the term refers to the consolidated tape, which shows the stock symbol, latest price and volume of trades on the exchanges for securities as they are traded. It also refers to news ticker services, which pass along the latest economic, financial and market news developments. This information is distributed to investors all over the world.

But unless you are an investment professional or work for a broker-age firm, the figures and symbols that pass constantly across the lower portion of the television screen may need explanation. The purpose of this section is to take the mystery out of the tape.

Consolidated Tape

This is the most frequently seen display. It is a combination of two cable networks, A and B. Network A reports all NYSE issues traded on the NYSE and other identified markets, including five regional exchanges, and the OTC market. Network A also reports special markets such as Instinet, a computerized market in which large institutional blocks are traded. Network B reports all AMEX issues traded on the AMEX or other identified markets. Nasdaq OTC quotes are presented separately in the lower band.

During each business day, while the exchanges are open, the consolidated tape reports actual transactions. Here is an explanation of the elements of the tape:

Stock Symbol

The first letters are the stock ticker symbol: for example, T for American Telephone and Telegraph Company, DIS for Walt Disney Company and BA for Boeing Company. The prefix Q is added to the symbol when a company is in receivership or bankruptcy.

The ticker symbol may be followed by an abbreviation designating a type of issue, such as Pr to signify preferred stock. This, in turn, may be followed by a letter indicating a class of preferred. Thus, CMBPrJ means Chase Manhattan Bank's preferred stock series J. If Chase Manhattan Bank's preferred stock series J were convertible, the abbreviation .CV would be added to read CMBPrJ.CV. Common stock classes are indicated by a period plus a letter following the ticker symbol. For example, Playboy Enterprises Class A common would be designated PLA.A.

Other abbreviations placed after the ticker symbol when required are rt for rights, wi for when issued, .WD for when distributed, .WS for warrants and .XD for exdividend.

Market Identifiers

When the information about the stock is followed by an ampersand (&) and a letter, this indicates that the transaction took place in a market other than the NYSE if you are looking at Network A, or the AMEX if you are looking at Network B. Letters used to identify the various markets are as follows:

A = American Stock Exchange
B = Boston Stock Exchange
C = Cincinnati Stock Exchange
M = Midwest Stock Exchange
N = New York Stock Exchange
O = Other markets (mainly Instinet)
P = Pacific Stock Exchange
T = Third market (mainly Nasdaq)
X = Philadelphia Stock Exchange

Volume

The number of shares traded is the next portion of the transaction information provided on a ticker tape. It may appear below or to the right of the stock symbol and market designation. But if the trade is in a *round lot* of 100 shares, which is usually the case, no volume is indicated and the tape just shows the issue and the price. Therefore, IBM 55½ means that 100 shares of IBM were traded at $55.50 a share.

When larger round lot transactions occur, the number of round lots is indicated by the letter s followed by the price. So, IBM 5 s 55½ means that 500 shares were traded at $55.50. Twelve hundred shares would be IBM 12 s 55½ and so on. When the volume is 10,000 shares or more the full number is given: for example, IBM 13,500 s 55½.

Odd lots (quantities other than multiples of 100, or whatever other unit represents the round lot) do not appear on the ticker tape unless approved by an exchange official. If approval is given, odd lots of 60 shares and 160 shares of IBM would be displayed this way: IBM 60 SHRS 55½ and IBM 160 SHRS 55½.

A small number of issues, mostly inactive stocks or higher priced preferred stocks, trade in round lots of less than 100 shares. Such round lots are always 10 shares on the NYSE, but on the AMEX they can be 10, 25 or 50 shares. A transaction in these special round lots is designated by a number showing how many lots were traded followed by the ticker symbol. When one of these transactions refers to a stock traded on the AMEX, you would not be able to tell from the tape whether the lot involved was 10, 25 or 50 shares. Instead, you would have to consult a stock guide.

Procedures in an Active Market

Shortcuts are implemented when heavy trading causes the tape to run more than a minute behind. The measure most often taken to cope with heavy trading is signified by the tape printout DIGITS AND VOLUME DELETED. This means that only the unit price digit and fraction will be printed, except when the price ends in zero or is an opening transaction. Thus, 55½ becomes 5½. Volume information will not be deleted when trades are 5,000 shares or more, a threshold that can be increased if necessary.

A second common practice is to announce REPEAT PRICES OMITTED. This means that successive transactions at the same price will not be repeated. Another procedure is MINIMUM PRICE CHANGES OMITTED: Trades will not be displayed unless the price difference is greater than ⅛ of a point. These last two procedures do not apply to opening transactions or to trades of 5,000 shares or more. When market activity returns to a more normal level, the tape will read DIGITS AND VOLUME RESUMED with similar indications for the other procedures.

Other Abbreviations

A number of other abbreviations are used in the following special circumstances.

CORR indicates that a correction of information follows.

ERR or CXL indicates a print is to be ignored.

OPD signifies an opening transaction that was delayed or one whose price is substantially different from the previous day's close.

When a transaction is reported out of its proper order, the letters .SLD will follow the symbol. For example, IBM .SLD 5s 55½.

If the price is followed by SLR, then a number, it indicates seller's option and the number of days until settlement.

RATIOS THE PROS USE

For professional investment analysts and individual investors alike, financial ratios are an important tool in the process of selecting stocks for purchase or sale. This section explains the principal ratios, what they signify and how you can use them to increase your chances for success in personal investing.

Ratios indicate relationships, so by themselves, their meaning can be limited and even misleading. Other considerations, such as dollar amounts, the overall size of a company and industry characteristics also are needed in your analysis. Ratios have their greatest significance when used in comparison with industry information or to make year-to-year comparisons to determine trends. Composite ratios for different industries are published by the Federal Trade Commission, Dun & Bradstreet, Standard & Poor's Corporation and Robert Morris Associates.

To illustrate several commonly used ratios, Figure 3.1 shows a sample summary income statement and balance sheet from an annual report of "ABC Corporation" in the apparel industry. On December 31 of the company's fiscal year shown in the figure, the stock traded at $18 per share and paid dividends during the year totaling $.50 per share.

RATIOS USED TO MEASURE
STOCK VALUES

Price-Earnings Ratio

This ratio, one of the most widely used and quoted, reflects the value put on a company's earnings and its prospects of future earnings by the securities marketplace. This is important to individual investors because it represents the value of their investments. It also is important from the corporation's point of view because it indicates the price it could expect to receive if it were to issue new shares, that is, its cost of capital.

By itself, a PE ratio may have little meaning. It must be looked at in the context of how it compares with the PE ratios of other companies in the same industry. Over the years and through market cycles, the PE ratio for a particular company can change dramatically. Changes can

FIGURE 3.1   Sample Summary Income Statement and Balance Sheet

ABC Corporation

Consolidated Statement of Income and Retained Earnings

This statement is a summary of the company's operating performance for one fiscal year. It shows sales and expenses that result in net income. Sales are from the sale of services and products to customers of ABC Corporation. Expenses include costs of services and products; depreciation; and selling, general and administrative expenses. Taxes also are a major expense category.

Net Income

(Dollars in thousands, except per-share amounts)

	For the year ended December 31, 199X
Net sales	$346,206
(minus) Cost of products sold	259,344
Gross profit	$ 86,862
(minus) Selling, general and administrative expenses	66,555
(plus) Restructuring	(2,800)
Operating income	**$ 23,107**
Other income (expense):	
(minus) Interest expense	$ (797)
(plus) Interest income	1,022
(plus) Royalty income	3,110
(plus) Minority interest in loss of subsidiary	108
(plus) Miscellaneous income	67
Other income - net	$ 3,510
Income before taxes (operating income plus other income)	26,617
(minus)Income taxes	10,881
Net income	**$ 15,736**
(plus) Retained earnings at beginning of year	164,263
(minus) Cash dividends per common share	(7,362)
Retained earnings at end of year	$172,637
Net income per common share	$ 1.08

FIGURE 3.1   Sample Summary Income Statement and Balance Sheet
(Continued)

ABC Corporation
Consolidated Balance Sheets

(Dollars in thousands, except per share amounts)

	December 31, 199x
Assets	
Current assets	
Cash and cash equivalents	$ 21,129
Accounts receivable	24,425
Inventories	92,752
Prepaid expenses and other current assets	2,185
Deferred income taxes	5,819
Total current assets	$146,310
Property, plant and equipment	72,312
Other assets	7,573
Total assets	**$226,195**
Liabilities and Shareholders' Equity	
Current liabilities	
Current maturities of long-term debt	$ 7,896
Accounts payable	11,096
Accrued liabilities	16,243
Total current liabilities	35,235
Long-term debt	1,293
Deferred income taxes	3,680
Employee benefit plan liabilities	10,834
Shareholders' equity	
Common stock, par value $.01 per share, issued and outstanding—14,585,800 shares	146
Additional paid-in capital	2,971
Retained earnings	172,036
Total shareholders' equity	175,153
Total liabilities and shareholders' equity	**$226,195**

result from how well or poorly the company is doing, or they may reflect whether the stock market is in a *bull* (upward) or *bear* (downward) trend. At times in the past, a PE ratio of ten times earnings per common share was considered normal for an established company. Earnings per share is calculated by dividing a company's net profits by the total number of common stock shares outstanding. As the stock market has climbed over the past few years, the PE multiple of many companies also has climbed. According to *Barron's,* the PE ratio for the DJIA was 37.1 times earnings on January 10, 1994. The ratio for the S&P 500 Composite Stock Index on the same date was 23.01 times earnings. In the late 1980s, when Japan's Nikkei 225 Stock Index was at its peak, its PE ratio was more than 60 times earnings.

Following below is an example of how a PE ratio is calculated for the ABC Corporation, whose common stock is trading at $18 per share and has earnings of $1.08 per share.

Price–Earnings Ratio

$$\frac{\text{Market price of common share}}{\text{Earnings per common share}} = \frac{18}{1.08} = 16.7 \text{ times earnings per share}$$

ABC Corporation's PE ratio is somewhat higher than average for its industry, which has been running in the range of 12 to 15 times earnings in recent years.

Dividend Payout Ratio

The dividend payout ratio indicates the percentage of earnings per common share that are paid out in dividends. Typically, young companies that are growing rapidly tend to reinvest their earnings to finance expansion, using them as sources of capital. So they will have low dividend payout ratios or ratios of zero. Established companies experiencing lower growth rates normally will have higher payout ratios.

In the example that follows, ABC Corporation has common stock earnings of $1.08 per share and pays out $.50 per share in dividends.

$$\frac{\text{Dividends per common share}}{\text{Earnings per common share}} = \frac{.50}{1.08} = 46.3\%$$

This dividend payout ratio of 46.3 percent by ABC Corporation is higher than typical for most companies in the apparel industry, which have averaged about 25 percent in recent years. In the case of ABC

Corporation, its high dividend payout ratio results from a sharp drop in annual earnings without a reduction in the dividend payout.

Market-to-Book Ratio

This ratio indicates the value the market places on the company as a going concern in relation to the value of its shares if the firm were liquidated and the proceeds from the sale of assets, after creditor claims have been satisfied, were paid to shareholders.

$$\frac{\text{Market price of common share}}{\substack{\text{Book value per share (total}\\ \text{assets} - \text{intangible assets} -\\ \text{total liabilities and preferred/}\\ \text{common shares outstanding)}}} = \frac{18}{12} = 1.5 \text{ times}$$

The market-to-book ratio for ABC Corporation indicates that the market values the company at half again as much as its value would be in liquidation.

RATIOS USED TO MEASURE PROFITABILITY

Operating Profit Margin

A key to measuring a firm's operating efficiency, this ratio is a reflection on management's purchasing and pricing policies, as well as its success in controlling costs directly associated with running the enterprise and building sales. It does not include other income and expenses, interest and taxes.

$$\frac{\text{Net operating profit}}{\text{Net sales}} = \frac{23.1}{346.2} = 6.67\%$$

To be useful, the operating profit margin should be compared with how the company has performed in previous years and how it compares with other companies in this industry. ABC's operating profit margin is substantially lower than that of other companies in its industry, which have been about 13 percent. ABC has been going through a difficult competitive environment.

Net Profit Margin

The net profit margin measures management's overall efficiency, not only its success in managing operations but also in terms of borrowing money at favorable rates, investing reserve cash to produce extra income and taking advantage of tax benefits.

$$\frac{\text{Net income}}{\text{Net sales}} = \frac{15.7}{346.2} = 4.5\%$$

The net profit margin of ABC Corporation is slightly below that of its industry peers, who generally have produced margins averaging just more than 5 percent. In previous years, ABC has enjoyed profit margins in the 8 percent to 10 percent range, well above that of its industry.

Return on Equity

This ratio measures the overall return the company has been able to deliver on shareholder equity. It is the bottom line profit measured against the money that shareholders have invested in the company.

$$\frac{\text{Net income}}{\text{Total shareholders' equity}} = \frac{15.7}{175.2} = 9.0\%$$

ABC Corporation's return on equity is below average for the apparel industry, reflecting the difficult business period it has encountered.

Numerous other ratios used in analyzing financial statements are listed as follows. They are not treated in detail because they are used mainly by professional analysts and by corporate financial officers.

RATIOS USED TO MEASURE LIQUIDITY

Ratio		Calculation
Current ratio	=	$\dfrac{\text{Current assets}}{\text{Current liabilities}}$
Quick ratio	=	$\dfrac{\text{Current assets} - \text{Inventory}}{\text{Current liabilities}}$

RATIOS USED TO MEASURE ACTIVITY

Ratio		Calculation
Inventory turnover	=	$\dfrac{\text{Net sales}}{\text{Inventory}}$
Average collection period	=	$\dfrac{\text{Accounts receivable}}{\text{Annual credit sales/360 days}}$
Fixed assets turnover	=	$\dfrac{\text{Net sales}}{\text{Net fixed assets}}$
Total assets turnover	=	$\dfrac{\text{Net sales}}{\text{Total assets}}$

SUMMARY

Today, investors with cable television can conveniently "watch the tape" throughout the business day in the comfort of their own homes. What is available is the stock ticker tape, the same report of trading activity displayed on the floors of the major stock exchanges. The only difference is that it is transmitted with a 15-minute delay.

Ratios can be very helpful to use as a tool in evaluating investment opportunities. By their nature, ratios indicate relationships and so must be used in conjunction with other information, such as dollar amounts, size of a company and industry characteristics. Ratios are most significant when used to make year-to-year comparisons for the purpose of determining trends and in comparing industry information.

CHAPTER 4

Buy, Sell or Hold? Information Sources That Can Help You Find the Answers

If you are like most prudent investors, you constantly will seek out securities that you hope will accomplish your objectives. And the best way to do that is to be informed. A host of services, newsletters and other sources of information is available to investors. Many publications are advertised regularly in *Barron's, The Wall Street Journal* and *Investor's Business Daily.* You can find a complete list of just about all the major publications that can help keep you informed about developments in the world of finance and investment in *The Finance and Investment Handbook* (Barron's Educational Series, Inc., 250 Wireless Blvd., Hauppauge, NY 11788; 800-645-3476) by John Downes and Jordan Goodman.

Many of the most popular and useful services are available at your local public library, which is a good place to start and where you can get a feel for which services will be of most value to you. Several of the most useful investment services and organizations are as follows:

American Association of Individual Investors (AAII)
625 North Michigan Avenue
Chicago, IL 60611-3110
312-280-0170

AAII is a nonprofit corporation recognized under Section 501(C)(3) of the Internal Revenue Code as a public educational organization.

Membership in the organization entitles you to the following partial list of benefits.

The *AAII Journal* (free to members)
Published ten times a year, the journal provides a continuing stream of information on investment theory and practice. Recent topics have included how you can use time to reduce risk; how to evaluate investment newsletters; how a living trust can help with your estate planning; the characteristics of stock market winners.

AAII Year-End Tax Strategy Guide (free to members)
An extensive guide to the tax-planning aspects of investment, the guide is based on the latest laws and rulings. It is released each year at the end of November.

AAII Quoteline (free to members)
AAII Quoteline lets you use your telephone to obtain real-time (not delayed) quotes on stocks, options and mutual funds. You also may establish a theoretical portfolio with a number of shares and receive the current value of each stock and the entire portfolio at any time.

Investment Seminars (at reduced cost)
More than 50 seminars are conducted in cities throughout the United States each year, introductory as well as advanced.

Study Programs (at reduced cost)
A wide variety of home-study materials is offered by AAII to its members, taking investors as far as they want to go from the basics to the concepts of a graduate-level course in investment theory.

Computer Users Newsletter ($30 a year to members)
AAII publishes a bimonthly newsletter aimed at the growing number of members who use computers in their investment decision making. The publication, *Computerized Investing,* evaluates software and explores a variety of ways to make the computer a more effective investment tool.

Dividend Reinvestment Plans (DRIPs)
Each June, AAII members receive a free listing of the hundreds of major corporations that allow you to buy additional stock with your dividends, without commissions and often at below-market price.

Stock Brokerage Survey
Each January, AAII sends members a free survey of the charges and services of brokerage firms. The survey also provides an analysis to help you choose the pricing system and service package that best meets your needs.

Local Chapter Membership
More than 50 AAII chapters are operating in metropolitan areas of the United States, and more are being added. Chapters offer the opportunity to meet with fellow members and to hear experts discuss a variety of investment topics.

The Hulbert Guide to Financial Newsletters
Dearborn Financial Publishing, Inc.
155 North Wacker Drive
Chicago, IL 60606-1719
800-322-8621

Mark Hulbert is editor and publisher of *The Hulbert Financial Digest,* which is widely recognized as an important source for objective performance comparisons of investment newsletters. Because investors can subscribe to literally dozens of investment advisory newsletters, they need a way to analyze which newsletters interest them. This book provides information on more than 100 newsletters and compares the performance of one portfolio of each newsletter to the Wilshire 5000 Index.

Morningstar Closed-End Funds
225 West Wacker Drive
Chicago, IL 60606
800-876-5005

Morningstar Closed-End Funds provides complete profiles on 284 of the most actively traded closed-end funds. Biweekly reports permit you to scan 12 years of premium/discount history with yearly market-price highs and lows, monitor each fund's portfolio, examine each fund's stated objective and keep abreast of how trends in the closed-end market can affect your investments.

Each fund is profiled in a single-page format that includes an analyst evaluation, net asset value and market-price returns, Morningstar's risk-adjusted rating, performance history, top-30 holdings and portfolio breakdown.

A three-month trial subscription is available for $35. The full-year cost is $195.

Securities Research Company (SRC)
101 Prescott Street
Wellesley Hills, MA 02181
617-235-0900

For investors interested in using technical analysis to predict future price movements, this company produces SRC Chart Books covering both listed and OTC stocks. Charts plot pure market performance. You get a picture of past price action and how it may repeat or break with prior patterns, resistance levels, turning points, major formations and volume of buying or selling. All Security Research charts are plotted on semilogarithmic scales, showing percentage changes rather than ordinary numerical changes.

The following chart books are available:

Monthly short-term *Red Book* of 1,108 listed stock charts,
Quarterly long-term *Blue Book* of 1,108 listed stock charts,
Monthly short-term *Brown Book* of 1,012 OTC stock charts and
Quarterly long-term *Orange Book* of 1,012 OTC stock charts.

Standard & Poor's Corporation
25 Broadway
New York, NY 10004
212-208-8000

Standard & Poor's Corporation's highly respected publications cover virtually the full spectrum of investor needs. A partial list follows. Some of these will be found in your local public library.

Analyst's Handbook
Blue List
Bond Guide
Called Bond Record
Corporation Records
Current Market Perspectives
Daily Action Stock Charts
Daily Stock Price Record
Dividend Record
Earnings Forecaster

Emerging and Special
  Situations
Growth Stocks Handbook
High Tech Stocks Handbook
High Yield Quarterly
Income Stocks Handbook
Index Services
Industry Surveys
Municipal Bond Book
Mutual Fund Profiles
OTC Handbook

OTC Chart Manual   *Statistical Service*
The Outlook   *Stock Guide*
P.C. Investor   *Stock Reports*
Register of Corporations *Stock Summary*

TeleChart 2000 (TC2000) Software Bundle
Worden Brothers, Inc.
4905 Pine Cone Drive
Durham, NC 27707
800-776-4940

TC2000 is a fully integrated technical analysis service designed to provide an advanced charting module and inexpensive toll-free price data 24 hours a day. This PC up-to-date multicolor charting software was developed in 1988. The service provides free daily information on symbol changes, company name changes, stock split dates and ratios, new issues and so on. As a new subscriber, you receive symbol guides containing more than 10,000 stock and mutual funds, alphabetized by both symbol and company name; ten stock and mutual fund historical data files; and $15 of free usage credit, letting you download and chart stocks you are interested in.

TC2000 requires an IBM-PC compatible, modem, hard disk, and EGA or VGA color monitor.

The Value Line Investment Survey
711 Third Avenue
New York, NY 10017-4064
800-833-0046

This service provides a complete 2,000-page loose-leaf reference book with full-page reports on all stocks under review.

Every week for each of 1,700 stocks, the *Value Line Investment Survey* in its Summary & Index presents the up-to-date

- rank for probable relative price performance in the next 6 to 12 months, ranging from 1 (highest) down to 5 (lowest);
- rank for investment safety (from 1 down to 5);
- estimated yield in the next 12 months;
- estimated appreciation potentiality in the next three to five years, showing the future "target" price range and the percentage price change indicated;

- current price and estimated PE ratio based on the past 6 months earnings plus future 6 months earnings and estimated annual earnings and dividends in the next 12 months; and
- the latest available quarterly earnings and dividends, together with year-earlier comparisons.

Ratings & Reports

A 2,000-page Investors Reference Library, this loose-leaf-bound volume of 1,700 stocks is the subject of a comprehensive new full-page Rating & Report once every three months. Each report includes 23 series of financial and operating statistics going back 15 years and estimated 3 to 5 years into the future.

Selection & Opinion

The weekly Selection & Opinion section gives Value Line's opinion of the business prospect, the stock market outlook and the advisable investment strategy. It also carries analyses of interesting industries and more extensive reports on one or two stocks that are favorably ranked for timeliness.

Value Line offers a special introductory trial offer. You can receive the complete Value Line Service for ten weeks for $55. The full-year cost is $525.

SUMMARY

Most prudent investors constantly seek out securities that they hope will accomplish their objectives. The best way to do that is to be informed. There is a host of services, newsletters and other sources of information available to investors. Many are advertised regularly in *The Wall Street Journal, Barron's* and *Investor's Business Daily.* Your public library will carry some of the most useful publications. A complete list of most major publications can be found in *The Finance and Investment Handbook,* by John Downes and Jordan Goodman. Your local public library is a good place to start, where you can get a sense of which services will be most useful to you.

CHAPTER 5

A Time-Tested Technique for Successful Investing

Few investment techniques have stood the test of time so well that one can confidently say, "This works." One such method is easy, it works and you can do it! It is called *constant dollar investing* (also known as *dollar cost averaging*) and is simply the practice of buying securities at regular intervals in fixed dollar amounts, regardless of price levels.

Many investors build up their security portfolios through such systematic purchases over long periods of time. These investors may add as little as $1,000 a year to their portfolios, or they may participate in company retirement plans that invest millions of dollars each year. Both take advantage of constant dollar investing, one of the simplest and most effective ways of building an investment portfolio that has ever been developed.

When this procedure is followed, more shares of stock are purchased at relatively low prices than at high prices. As a result, the average cost of all shares bought turns out to be lower than the average of all the prices at which purchases were made. The combination of buying shares at a variety of price levels and acquiring more shares at low rather than high prices has proven to be an efficient and cost-effective method of accumulating securities.

AVERAGE COST VERSUS AVERAGE PRICE

The arithmetic that illustrates how constant dollar investing works is simple. You need to remember only that by periodically purchasing shares with identical amounts of money, as long as there is any change in share prices at all during the investment period, the average cost of the shares you purchase will be less than the average of the prices paid. For example, assume you decide to invest that $280 every month. Your series of five purchases totaling $1,400 is made at prices varying between $10 and $5 a share. The number of shares bought for each $280 purchase would be as follows (commissions are not considered):

Price	Shares Purchased	Total $ Amount
$10	28	$ 280
8	35	280
7	40	280
5	56	280
8	35	280
	194	$1,400

Average cost of each share ($1,400 ÷ 194): $7.21
Average price of shares purchased: $7.60

The principle that makes this program work is that equal numbers of dollars buy more shares at low prices than at high prices. It is essential that purchases be made at low prices when they are available. If you contemplate constant dollar investing, you must take into account your emotional and financial ability to continue making new investments through periods of low price levels.

The use of constant dollar investing does not guarantee that investors always will have profits in their portfolios or that they never will incur losses. A stock accumulation program of this type should be used only for long-term purposes. An investor should feel strongly that he or she will not need the invested funds for a considerable number of years.

The risks inherent in securities investing are substantially reduced through constant dollar investing. This is because shares are bound to be purchased over the years at a variety of price levels—high, low and in between. That fact alone should provide a better income and capital-gains experience than haphazard investing or buying only when the outlook appears bright.

GROWTH IS NOT ESSENTIAL

Fluctuating security prices are more important to successful constant dollar investing than long-term growth alone. This surprising fact arises because it is actually during periods of declining prices that the investor gets his or her best opportunity to acquire a large number of shares.

Continuing with the previous example, assume that after you make the five purchases, the share price returns to $10, the level of the first purchase. The 194 shares already owned would have a value of $1,940. During the purchase period, note that a 50 percent decline in price was assumed to have taken place.

Now, instead of a drop in price, let's see what would happen if the share price had steadily advanced to an increase of 50 percent and the five equal purchases of $280 were made. For this example, we will assume that partial shares could be purchased.

Price	Shares Purchased	Total $ Amount
$10	28.00	$ 280
11	25.45	280
12	23.33	280
14	20.00	280
15	18.67	280
	115.45	$1,400

Average cost of each share ($1,400 ÷ 115.45): $12.13
Average price of shares purchased: $12.40

In this example, the process of constant dollar investing also results in an average cost that is less than the average price. But notice that after a 50 percent increase from the initial price of $10 per share, the total value of the 115.45 shares at $15 is $1,731.75, or about 10.7 percent less than the $1,940 that the 194 shares in the previous example were worth at $10.

Of course, investors have no control over the direction security prices will take once they start a constant dollar investing program. The main advantage of the plan is that in the long run it will work to an investor's benefit almost regardless of what the market does. This fact is particularly important to investors who fear starting an investment plan because they believe stock prices are too high. If an investor is right and the market does decline, the timing may be just right to begin constant dollar investing.

REINVESTING DIVIDENDS

Many investors who invest in stocks on a periodic basis can and do reinvest any dividends they receive. The effect in the beginning is minor, but as the program continues, the impact of compounding shares becomes more and more significant. The relative importance varies, of course, depending on the emphasis that a particular company places on paying dividends on its stock.

CONSTANT DOLLAR INVESTING AT WORK

To illustrate the value of a long-term investment program using constant dollar investing, Figure 5.1 shows the hypothetical results of investing $2,000 in the S&P 500 Index on January 1st of each year for 35 years, beginning in 1959 and continuing through 1993, assuming that all dividends are reinvested.

The annual amount of $2,000 was chosen because it is the maximum allowable IRA contribution for an individual participant under current law. With no income taxes required to be paid on dividends or capital gains accumulating in an IRA, the IRA is an ideal vehicle for a constant dollar investment plan.

The widely known S&P 500 Index has been used because it generally is recognized as representing overall price trends among a wide segment of well-known industrial common stocks. Because it is simply a list of the stocks of 500 large companies and is subject to no expenses or commissions, the index is not strictly comparable to the shares of any one stock or group of stocks.

The 35-year period represented in Figure 5.1 was one of widely fluctuating common stock prices in which there were years of both rapidly rising and falling markets. While the total value of the account was never less than the total amount invested, it is certainly possible.

BEGINNING CONSTANT DOLLAR
INVESTING IN A DOWNTURN

If the plan in Figure 5.1 had been started in 1973, as stock prices were declining, the account would have shown a substantial loss at the end of both 1973 and 1974. In 1973, the market (as measured by the

FIGURE 5.1   Example of Investing $2,000 Annually for 35 Years in the
              S&P 500

Year	Total Dollars Invested	End-of-Year Value of Investment
1959	$ 2,000	$ 2,238
1960	4,000	4,254
1961	6,000	7,937
1962	8,000	9,072
1963	10,000	13,597
1964	12,000	18,155
1965	14,000	22,675
1966	16,000	22,207
1967	18,000	29,993
1968	20,000	35,512
1969	22,000	34,361
1970	24,000	37,779
1971	26,000	45,427
1972	28,000	56,439
1973	30,000	49,848
1974	32,000	38,212
1975	34,000	55,131
1976	36,000	70,728
1977	38,000	67,492
1978	40,000	74,009
1979	42,000	89,994
1980	44,000	121,801
1981	46,000	117,734
1982	48,000	145,477
1983	50,000	180,660
1984	52,000	193,985
1985	54,000	257,916
1986	56,000	308,261
1987	58,000	326,394
1988	60,000	382,579
1989	62,000	501,260
1990	64,000	487,558
1991	66,000	644,210
1992	68,000	696,614
1993	70,000	769,174

Total value on December 31, 1993, of investing $2,000 annually at 10 percent
compounded rate without any up or down market fluctuations: $596,210.

S&P 500 Index) dropped 14.7 percent, and in 1974, it dropped 26.3 percent. At the end of 1973, with $2,000 invested, the account value would have been $1,706; and at the end of 1974, with $4,000 invested, the value would have been $2,731.

The investor who persevered, however, would have benefited by buying more shares at the lower prices. In 1975, the market rebounded 37.1 percent, and in 1976, it went up by 23.8 percent. By the end of 1975, with $6,000 now invested, the investor would have had a value of $6,486. And at the end of 1976, with $8,000 invested, the account would have been worth $10,506, and the investor would have achieved a 31.3 percent return on his or her money.

CONSTANT DOLLAR INVESTING IN ONE STOCK

Maybe you have personal knowledge of a company that you feel comfortable with and would like to invest in it. The company may be located in your area, perhaps it is your employer, or you like their products. Many companies are neither on their way to stardom nor to bankruptcy, but keep plugging along from year to year "doing their thing." In a sense, these companies are the backbone of the U.S. economy, providing thousands of people with steady work, but having their ups and downs as the health of the economy waxes and wanes. You can make a good return on your money buying stock in this type of company provided you have patience and enduring confidence in the firm.

KLA Instruments Corporation was founded in 1975. (Ticker Symbol: KLAC. The stock trades in the OTC market.) Headquartered in San Jose, California, the company designs, manufactures, markets and services automated optical inspection systems used primarily in the production of integrated circuits. KLA systems combine advanced optics with custom digital electronics and software to replace human eye-to-brain recognition and interpretation methods traditionally used for image technology, process control and testing. Foreign business accounts for about 62 percent of sales and 59 percent of operating profits. The company has 1,100 employees and 1,500 shareholders.

Over the ten years from 1984 to 1993, the stock has moved erratically. Its average price in 1984 was $16 per share, the average price in 1993 was $18.55 per share. The company pays no dividends. A $10,000

FIGURE 5.2   Example of Investing $5,000 Annually from 1984 to 1993
at the Yearly Average Price

Year	Average Share Price	Shares Bought	Total Shares	Total Value	Total Investment
1984	$16.00	314	314	$ 5,000	$ 5,000
1985	20.00	250	564	11,280	10,000
1986	18.65	268	832	15,516	15,000
1987	17.45	286	1,118	19,509	20,000
1988	15.25	327	1,145	22,036	25,000
1989	10.65	469	1,914	20,384	30.000
1990	9.15	546	2,460	22,509	35,000
1991	11.25	444	2,904	32,670	40,000
1992	9.90	505	3,409	33,749	45,000
1993	18.55	269	3,678	68,226	50,000
12/31/93	27.75	–	3,678	$102,064	50,000

investment in 1984 at $16 a share would have had a value of $17,343 on December 31, 1993, when the stock closed at $27.75 per share. This represents a 73.4% return on the original investment (calculated by dividing the $7,343 profit by the original $10,000 investment), or a compound annual return of a bit over 5.5 percent. Not very exciting. But a constant dollar investment program presents a different picture. Figure 5.2 shows the results of investing $5,000 each year from 1984 to 1993 at the average price the shares traded at during each year. Commissions are not considered.

The closing price of KLA Instruments on December 31, 1993, was $27.75 a share. With an ownership of 3,678 shares on that date, the investment had a value of $102,064. Figure 5.2 illustrates well the advantage of maintaining a constant dollar investment program through both the up and down years. When you get to the "light at the end of the tunnel," good things begin to happen.

OTHER HIGHLY REGARDED STOCKS

Figure 5.3 lists companies that are highly regarded by many analysts and might make ideal candidates for a constant dollar investment program. In some cases, the companies have traveled rocky roads in the past several years, but all are expected to experience growing

FIGURE 5.3 Ideal Companies for Constant Dollar Averaging

Company	Exchange Where Traded and Symbol	Share Value Growth Past Ten Years*	Yield	12/31/93 Price
Brunswick Corp.	NYSE/BC	107	2.3	18
Builders Transport	OTC/TRUK	– 5	Nil	15¾
Consolidated Freightways	NYSE/CNF	–22	Nil	23⅝
Federal Mogul	NYSE/FMO	34	1.3	29
Gaylord Entertainment A	NYSE/GET	N/A	0.9	28⅛
Integrated Device	OTC/IDTI	71	Nil	17⅛
KLA Instruments	OTC/KLAC	17	Nil	27¾
Lowe's Companies	NYSE/LOW	308	0.6	59½
Micron Technology	NYSE/MU	50	0.1	46½
Omnicare, Inc.	NYSE/OCR	20	0.6	32
Roberts Pharmaceutical	OTC/RPCX	N/A	Nil	39¾
Thor Industries	NYSE/THO	373	0.4	25¾
Unitrode Corp.	NYSE/UTR	–59	Nil	14½

*Based on average price of shares during each calendar year.

earnings in the years ahead. The stocks trade on the NYSE or in the OTC market.

SUMMARY

The widely used concept of constant dollar investing helps you assure favorable long-term investment results. Fluctuating market conditions actually enhance the performance of such a systematic investment program. The benefits of constant dollar investing depend on the assumption that the securities in which one invests will go up or down about as the general market does and sooner or later will rise in value. Persistence in continuing to buy shares regularly throughout periods of declining, as well as rising, prices is essential to produce the kinds of results that have been illustrated.

CHAPTER 6

DRIPs—Reinvesting Dividends Automatically

Long-term stock market investors who are in the accumulation phase of their investment plans always have faced the problem of how to handle income. Dividends received by most individual shareholders are insufficient to buy additional shares economically. And yet, to maximize long-term total return, buy-and-hold investors must continuously reinvest investment income. Happily, there is a simple solution. Today, more than 750 companies offer dividend reinvestment plans. You can find a list of most companies offering these plans in Appendix B.

Dividend reinvestment plans (DRIPs) are ideal for buy-and-hold investors and serve as a bonus for shareholders of companies with favorable long-term growth prospects. The plans are simple. Instead of sending cash dividends out to participating investors, the company applies the cash dividends to the purchase of additional shares of company stock.

Participants enjoy several advantages:

- Dividend payments are put to work.
- Transaction costs are eliminated or held to a minimum.
- The additional shares are purchased gradually over time, an easy-to-effect form of constant dollar investing (see Chapter 5).

Special Features

Some company plans have the following special features that make them even more attractive.

- You may make optional cash payments to purchase additional shares through the plan.
- Participants are permitted to receive cash dividends on some of their shares while reinvesting dividends on the remaining shares.
- Shares purchased under the plan are available at discounts, ranging from as little as 1 percent to as high as 10 percent.
- Brokerage costs and service fees for share purchases are paid for by the company rather than the participant.

Most DRIPs require that you own shares registered in your name, that is, that you are a shareholder "of record." That means your name must appear on the corporate records as the owner of the shares, rather than having the shares held in "street name" by the broker or bank that may have bought the shares for you and who may be holding them for you. If your shares are held in street name, just ask your broker to transfer the shares to your own name.

Usually, a company will send you a DRIP prospectus or description and an authorization card once you become a registered shareholder. You also can call the company's shareholder relations department or the DRIP agent to request these items. The prospectus or description will provide information relating to eligibility requirements, plan options, costs, how and when purchases are made, how and when certificates will be issued, and how you may withdraw from the plan.

A few corporations sell their shares directly to investors who do not yet own any stock, including Atmos Energy Corporation, Exxon Corporation, Johnson Controls and Texaco.

How the Plans Work

DRIPs are part of a corporation's overall shareholder relations effort and serve existing shareholders. Some companies, such as utilities, have large investor relations departments and administer their own DRIPs. Most companies, however, hire an outside agent to serve as the administrator for the plan.

The plan administrator maintains records, sends account statements to participants, provides certificates for shares upon request and liquidates participants' shares when they leave the plan. The agent also has the responsibility of buying company shares for the plan. When you join a plan, you sign a card that authorizes the agent to act on your behalf to purchase shares.

When shares are purchased under a DRIP, they are held by the plan and registered in the nominee name of the agent or plan trustee on behalf of the participants. An account is maintained for each participant under the plan. Most participants hold the company's shares in two places; your original shares will be held by you or in the custody of a brokerage firm or bank, and the shares purchased through the DRIP will be held by the plan.

Some plans permit participants to deposit certificates of shares registered in their own name into their DRIP account for safekeeping at no cost, or for a small fee. These shares then are treated in the same way as the other shares in the participant's account, making it possible to consolidate all your shares in one safe location.

Certificates for shares purchased under a plan normally are issued only on written request, but often at no charge. Certificates also are issued when a participating shareholder wants to terminate participation.

When companies have different kinds of stock outstanding, they may allow shareholders of several forms to participate. Reinvestment sometimes may be in stock of the same form; for instance, preferred reinvests in preferred. Or perhaps dividends from all forms may be reinvested into one form; for instance, all reinvestment is in common stock. The prospectus indicates where your dividends are being reinvested.

Options That Are Available

Full reinvestment on all shares of stock registered in the participant's name is standard under the basic DRIP. But under some plans, it is not necessary to reinvest all dividends. Instead, participants may reinvest dividends on a portion of their registered shares, while receiving cash dividends on the remaining shares. This often is referred to as a *partial reinvestment option.*

Many plans permit participants to buy additional shares by making cash payments directly to the plan, sometimes in large allowable amounts. Often referred to as *optional cash payment,* this option offers participants a low-cost way to build a sizable holding in a company.

The payments are optional, and participants are not committed to making periodic cash payments. However, there are minimums and usually a maximum for each payment made. Because interest is not paid on payments received in advance, you should find out approximately when the plan invests cash payments it receives.

Some companies also offer a *cash payment only option*. Registered shareholders are allowed to make cash investments without being required to reinvest dividends on the shares they are holding, although they may do so if they wish.

Under most, but not all, DRIPs, dividends paid on shares that are purchased and held under the plan are automatically reinvested.

Costs of DRIPs

In general, the cost of participating in a DRIP is low, especially when compared to the alternative of buying shares through a broker.

Service charges and *prorated brokerage commissions* are the two forms of costs that plan participants may encounter. Service charges cover administrative costs and generally are made on each transaction. Costs can be held down by a participant combining a cash payment with a dividend reinvestment transaction, for charges usually are capped at a maximum of $3 to $5. Brokerage costs paid by the plan when buying shares on the open market are at institutional rates, considerably lower than the rate an individual investor would pay.

Many companies cover all the costs for share purchases from both optional cash payments and reinvested dividends. Some companies assess service charges, others prorate brokerage costs, while still others charge participants for both. The plan prospectus or description spells out which of the many variations apply in your case.

When you terminate your participation, some DRIPs will sell plan shares for you if you wish, instead of sending you certificates. The cost to you is usually any prorated brokerage commissions, a lower-cost choice than selling through a broker. Some plans will sell some of your plan shares for you, even when you are not terminating. Again, check the prospectus or plan description.

Purchasing Shares

The plan prospectus or description spells out the source of share purchases under a DRIP.

The most common source is the *secondary market,* a securities exchange where the shares are traded or in the OTC market, or through negotiated transactions. In some cases, the source may be the company itself, using authorized but unissued shares of common stock or shares held in the company's treasury. An advantage to a participant when shares are purchased directly from the company is that there are no brokerage expenses to prorate.

For the company, DRIPs that purchase shares directly from the company provide an inexpensive source of financing. The proceeds often are used for general corporate purposes. From the point of view of investors, however, new issues dilute existing shares, which can have the effect of depressing share prices.

The plan prospectus or description specifies when shares are purchased by the agent. Normally, they coincide with the dividend payment date, but some companies that permit participants to make cash investments have additional investment dates.

When shares are purchased in the open markets, most plans give some discretion to the agent on his or her buying, for a large purchase made on a single date could affect the share price. Usually, it is required under the plan that all monies be invested within 30 days. The share price for any participant is an average price of all shares purchased for that investment period.

The prospectus or plan description describes how the share price is determined when shares are purchased directly from the company. Generally, it is based on an average of the high and low or the closing price for the stock as reported by a specified source.

Discounts on the share price sometimes are offered to participants in company plans, but with wide variations. In most cases, discounts are available only on shares purchased with reinvested dividends. But some companies permit discounts on shares purchased both with reinvested dividends and with cash payments. A few companies offer discounts only on newly issued corporate shares and not on shares that are bought in the securities markets.

Taxation and Reinvestment Plans

No special tax advantages are connected with reinvestment plans. A taxable event occurs whether you receive your dividends in cash or have them reinvested. If your dividends are reinvested, the IRS considers the taxable amount to be equal to the fair market value of the shares acquired with the reinvested dividends. That value is the price on the exchange or market where shares are traded, not any discounted price. In addition, any brokerage commissions paid by the company in open market purchases are considered as taxable dividend income to the participant.

At the time shares are sold, the tax basis is the fair market value as of the date the shares were acquired, plus any brokerage commissions paid by the company and treated as income to the participant. If you are a DRIP member, you will receive a 1099-DIV form each year from the company detailing dividends to be treated as income as reported to the IRS.

SUMMARY

More than 750 companies now offer DRIPS, solving the problem faced by long-term stock market investors of how to handle dividend income. The plans enable buy-and-hold investors to maximize long-term total return. DRIPs are ideal for buy-and-hold investors and serve as a bonus for shareholders of companies with favorable long-term growth prospects. Under the terms of a plan, a company applies the cash dividends of participating investors to the purchase of additional shares of company stock, instead of sending the dividends out in the form of cash. Thus, dividend payments are put to work, transaction costs are eliminated or held to a minimum and the additional shares are purchased gradually over time. The effect is an easy-to-implement constant dollar investment plan.

CHAPTER 7

How Much Should You Pay Your Broker?

Advertising by attorneys has become commonplace in many parts of the country, and the advertisements often are followed by a caveat such as "The hiring of an attorney is an important decision that should not be based solely on advertisements." This is sound advice and also applies to selecting a stockbroker. In choosing your broker, you need to consider a number of things. What services do you need from a broker? Which broker, or type of broker, can serve you best? And, finally, which broker can provide the services you need at the least cost?

Stockbrokers generally provide a variety of services for their customers, enabling them to buy and sell stocks, bonds, commodities, options, mutual funds, limited partnerships, certificates of deposits, annuities and other financial products. In addition, brokers may offer asset management accounts, combining a customer's holdings of stocks and bonds with a money market fund. The customer then can write checks against the account, which also may have credit-card features. Many brokers also offer individualized financial planning services. With the wide choice of products and services they have made available to the public, brokers today have a wide-ranging clientele, from novice investors to wealthy and sophisticated individuals.

WHAT CAN FULL-SERVICE BROKERS DO FOR YOU?

Full-service brokers offer investors far more guidance on what investments are appropriate for each client. Clients pay substantially higher charges for this guidance. Full-service brokers also may engage in investment banking, helping to raise capital for federal, state and local governments and for corporations. This involves underwriting new issues of stocks and bonds for corporations, as well as debt issues for governments, and distributing them to both institutional and individual investors.

TIPS: WHAT TO WATCH OUT FOR WITH FULL-SERVICE BROKERS

If you are with a full-service broker, be particularly careful about which account executive you deal with. These brokerage firm employees are paid on the basis of the amount of commissions they develop from customers. As a result, they are under constant pressure to "produce." This pressure to produce commissions often leads to various abuses.

One abuse to watch out for is an investment recommendation that is unsuitable for you but may be appropriate for a speculator with a high tolerance for risk. So-called *penny stocks,* which typically sell for less than $1 per share, or other very volatile securities might be recommended if the broker believes you are looking for something that will quickly move up in price. Or if you are seeking income, a risky speculative bond might be suggested.

Another abuse commonly employed by a hungry broker is churning, the excessive trading of a client's account. Churning increases a broker's commissions but usually leaves you worse off, or no better off, than before the activity occurs. Churning is illegal under Securities and Exchange Commission (SEC) and stock exchange rules but is difficult to prove. Clients who believe they are victims of churning or being sold inappropriate investments can sue or take their complaints to arbitration.

If you are going to deal with a full-service brokerage firm, ask for a person who has been in the business for at least five years. After you have been assigned a broker, discuss your financial situation and investment objectives. Be sure your broker knows how much risk you are willing to take. You must feel comfortable with your broker. Beware of a broker who constantly calls you with recommendations to move from one security to another. You may become a victim of churning.

WHAT CAN DISCOUNT BROKERS DO FOR YOU?

Prior to 1975, all brokers charged the same fixed commission rates. On May 1, 1975, known as May Day in the brokerage industry, the era of fixed commissions ended. Since then, brokers have been free to charge whatever they like. This resulted in greater competition within the industry and introduced to the public a new type of broker: the *discounter*. These brokers specialize in executing orders to buy and sell stocks, bonds, options and mutual funds. Usually, they charge commissions that are far less than full-service brokers but offer fewer services.

Discount brokers account for about 25 percent of all brokerage trades of stocks and earn roughly 15 percent of commission dollars. The *Big Three* are Charles W. Schwab, Fidelity Brokerage and Quick & Reilly. Together, they earn about 70 percent of the discount brokerage revenue. *Banks,* which mostly operate locally, account for 10 percent of the discount business. The balance goes to the approximately 90 *deep-discount* brokers. On average, the Big Three charge 58 percent less than the commissions charged by full-service brokers, such as Merrill Lynch, Pierce, Fenner & Smith (the largest in terms of number of account executives). According to Mercer, Inc., a New York research firm, the 30 deepest discounters charge 78 percent less than the rates typical of full-service brokers. The Big Three and banks usually charge by a transaction's dollar value, determined by multiplying the number of shares by the market price. Deep-discount brokers charge by the number of shares traded in the transaction. Some brokers offer both approaches. Nearly all discount brokers have at least a minimum transaction fee.

If you require less "hand holding," a discount broker may serve you just as well and at much less cost. In many cases, discounters offer more services than you might expect. Their objective is to offer an investing climate that is easy, convenient and inexpensive, plus a

FIGURE 7.1   Commissions Charged for Buying 100 Shares of Stock at $50 Each

	Commission
Full-Service Broker	
Typical charge	$106
Large Discount Brokers	
Quick & Reilly	$ 49
Fidelity Investments	54
Charles Schwab	55
Deep-Discount Brokers	
K. Aufhauser & Company	$ 25
Bidwell & Co.	29
Brown & Company	28
Kennedy Cabot & Co.	30
Pacific Brokerage Services	25
Security Brokerage Services	25

certain amount of the help you need to make informed decisions. When dealing with a discount broker, you should expect to pay less in commissions and account fees. The Big Three firms, mentioned previously, offer free investment guides and even seminars. Plus, you have a wide range of different investments to choose from, such as

- stocks—both listed and OTC;
- mutual funds—both load and no-load;
- government securities, including U.S. Treasury bills, notes and bonds; and
- municipal bonds, corporate bonds, government agency securities and other fixed-income investments.

COMPARING BROKERS' TRANSACTION FEES

There are substantial differences in transaction charges made by full-service brokers, large discount brokers and deep-discount brokers. But pricing in the industry can be complex. In addition to minimum fees, some brokers charge for postage, stock transfers and inactive accounts. Then there are discounts by certain brokers for electronically placed orders and rebates for monthly trading that exceeds a stated

FIGURE 7.2   Charles Schwab Commission Schedule for Stocks

Commission Schedule
Effective June 1, 1993

STOCKS

Overriding Minimum: $39 per trade

Transaction Size	Commission Rates
$0 – 2,500	$30 + 1.70% of principal amount
$2,500 – 6,250	$56 + 0.66% of principal amount
$6,250 – 20,000	$76 + 0.34% of principal amount
$20,000 – 50,000	$100 + 0.22% of principal amount
$50,000 – 500,000	$155 + 0.11% of principal amount
$500,000 +	$255 + 0.09%* of principal amount

OR the following minimums and maximums:

Minimum Charge: $0.09 per share for the first 1,000 shares, plus $0.04 per share thereafter for stocks below $5 per share or $0.05 per share thereafter for stocks $5 per share or greater.

Maximum Charge: $55 for the first 100 shares, plus $0.55 per share thereafter.

Stocks Costing Less than $1 per share: $39 plus 4% of principal amount. For purchases of stocks less than $1 per share, we require cleared funds in the account. When selling we require stocks in advance.

Large Block Transactions: Please contact your local Schwab office on orders of 10,000 shares or more or on orders over $500,000. These orders may be eligible for special handling and/or pricing.

MUTUAL FUNDS*

Overriding Minimum: $29 per trade

Transaction Size	Transaction Fees
$0 – 15,000	0.6% of principal
$15,000 – 100,000	0.6% on first $15,000
	0.2% on amount over $15,000
$100,000 +	0.6% on first $15,000
	0.2% on amount between $15,000 & $100,000
	0.08% on amount over $100,000

200 Mutual Funds are available without the above transaction fees. Call 1 (800) 2-NO-LOAD for a list of these funds.

To save money when switching among fund investments, place a simultaneous order to sell one fund and use the proceeds to purchase a new fund. You'll pay the standard fee on the sale and just $15 on the corresponding buy. (This policy does not apply to the SchwabFunds® or the other funds on which Schwab does not charge transaction fees.) Some funds may also charge sales and/or redemption fees. Please read the prospectuses for details. You can choose to buy shares directly from the fund itself or its principal underwriter or distributor without paying Schwab's transaction fees.

*Applies to open-end mutual funds only. For closed-end funds, refer to the stock schedule. Prospectuses are available for all Schwab customers.

Source: Reprinted by permission of Charles Schwab & Co., Inc.

FIGURE 7.2   (Continued)

OPTIONS

Options with Premiums of $0.50 or Under
Overriding Minimum: $39 per trade

Contracts	Commission per contract
0 – 49 contracts	$1.80 + 1.5% of principal amount
50 – 149 contracts	$1.10 + 1.8% of principal amount
150 – 499 contracts	$0.75 + 2.0% of principal amount
500 – 1,499 contracts	$0.60 + 2.0% of principal amount
1,500 + contracts	$0.60 + 1.5% of principal amount

Options with Premiums over $0.50
Overriding Minimum: $37.25 + $1.75 per contract

Dollar Amount	Commission per contract
$0 – 2,500	$29 + 1.6% of principal amount
$2,500 – 10,000	$49 + 0.8% of principal amount
$10,000 +	$99 + 0.3% of principal amount

Maximum Charge: $40 per contract on the first two contracts, plus $4 per contract thereafter.

Options carry a relatively high level of risk and are not suitable for all investors. Certain requirements must be met to trade options through Schwab. Please read the Options Disclosure Document titled "Characteristics and Risks of Standardized Options" before considering any option transaction. Call your local Schwab office or write Charles Schwab & Co., Inc. at 101 Montgomery Street, San Francisco, CA 94104 for a current copy. Cleared funds must be in your account before option orders are accepted.

FIXED INCOME

Corporate Bonds & Corporate Zeros
Overriding Minimum: $39 per trade

Transaction Size	Commission
0 – 25 bonds	$5 per bond
25 + bonds	$5 per bond on first 25 bonds
	$3 per bond thereafter

OR 1% of principal, whichever is less.

Large Transactions: Please contact our Bond Specialists on orders of more than 250 bonds which may be eligible for special handling and/or special pricing.

Municipal Bonds: Markup included in price. Schwab acts as principal.

Treasury Bills, Notes & Bonds: $49 fee per transaction. Schwab may act as principal.

Zero Coupon Treasury Bonds: Markup included in price. Schwab acts as principal.

Certificates of Deposit: No commission. Schwab receives a fee from the depository institution.

Unit Investment Trusts: Sales charge. Prospectuses available.

Schwab will not act as principal and agent simultaneously in the same transaction.

FIGURE 7.3   K. Aufhauser & Company, Inc., Commission Schedule

Commission Schedule A: US, Canadian, ADR, $24.99 minimum.

Shares	\$1.	\$5.	\$10.	\$20.	\$30.	\$50.	\$75.	\$100. +
				Price per Share				
1-399	\$24.99	\$24.99	\$24.99	\$24.99	\$24.99	\$24.99	\$24.99	\$24.99
400-499	\$34.99	\$34.99	\$34.99	\$34.99	\$34.99	\$34.99	\$34.99	\$34.99
500-599	\$40.99	\$40.99	\$40.99	\$40.99	\$41.99	\$41.99	\$41.99	\$41.99
600-699	\$41.99	\$46.00	\$49.00	\$49.00	\$49.00	\$49.00	\$49.00	\$49.00
700-799	\$41.99	\$47.99	\$49.99	\$50.99	\$50.99	\$52.99	\$52.99	\$52.99
800-899	\$41.99	\$53.00	\$59.00	\$59.00	\$59.00	\$59.00	\$59.00	\$59.00
900-999	\$42.00	\$53.00	\$59.00	\$63.00	\$63.00	\$63.00	\$63.00	\$63.00
1000	\$42.00	\$53.00	\$59.00	\$68.00	\$70.00	\$70.00	\$70.00	\$70.00

Each share above 1000 shares : . . . .   Add 2/3 cents per share OTC/Listed to 1000 share base.

Orders above 5000 shares: . . . .   2 cents OTC; 3 cents Listed.

Securities under $1.00 per share: . . . .   OTC $25 + 3%; Listed $25 + 3 cents.

FIGURE 7.3　(Continued)

Commission Schedule B:　2 cents per share, Listed or OTC, $34 minimum.

Indicate your choice of Schedule A or B when submitting your application. (Default is A.) You may occasionally change Schedules.　The following apply to A or B.

Exchange and Mailing Fee	$2.50 per executed order.
Bonds:	$5 per $1000 (min. $39).
No-Load Mutual Funds:	See verso.
Options:	$25 + $2.50 per contract　or $2　(10th or more).
Transfer and Ship:	Free (allow four weeks).
Checkwriting, Master Card	Free if equity > $10,000.　**Pro Cash Plus** Account.
Gold and Silver (metals account agreement required)	2% of principle. Minimum $75.　Storage: 1/4 % p.a.
Account opening fee	$20 (one time only, waived if initial equity > $10,000).
Option exercise;Short Sales (if less than 500 shares)	$.025/share; (Currency option:$250)
Late payment charges	$15 per event, plus applicable interest charges.
Returned Checks (any reason)	$20
Inactive fee: if less than 3 trades/yr. and we're custodian	$25.00 . Doesn't apply to ProCash Plus accounts.
Cxl/Replace limit if order <500 shares or 10 Contracts	20% surcharge.
Return of Securities not in deliverable form	$15
Outward money transfers (wire or express service)	**$20. (No charge for checks by regular mail.)**
IRA's set up or maintenance	$35 annually ($50 termination charge).
Bond Redemption/Call	$5/$20
Reorganization, Voluntary or Mandatory	$49
Foreign Securities Settlement (Not ADR's or Canadians)	$90.00/trade; $5/quarter/item custody.
Duplicate sending of confirms & statements	**Free if you notify us in advance, otherwise $5 per month.**
Change in Certificate Name/Account	$25.00/item (Legal , Gifts, Estates, Corporations).

(Effective 12/12/93)

minimum. Figure 7.1 lists the results of a survey made of a number of brokers in early 1994 that indicates the commissions you would be charged if you were to buy 100 shares of stock at $50 per share.

Like those at full-service brokers, customers' securities accounts at discount brokers are insured for at least $500,000 by the *Securities Investor Protection Corporation* (SIPC) a nonprofit company established by Congress in 1970.

To give you an idea of what commissions you would expect to pay one of the Big Three discount brokers for stock transactions, Figure 7.2 represents the commission schedule of Charles W. Schwab effective June 1, 1993.

Deep-discount brokers charge much less but of course deliver less in service. Figure 7.3 shows the commission schedule of K. Aufhauser & Company.

Some discount brokers permit you to trade directly via a touchtone telephone or by using your personal computer. AccuTrade, for instance, makes it possible for you to enter orders 24 hours a day; view your positions, balances and open orders; and receive stock quotes 24 hours a day. It charges three cents per share traded, regardless of stock price, with a $48 minimum commission. Always be sure to ask what other charges may be applicable.

It is almost impossible to determine who is the cheapest broker. The answer depends on your needs and the size and type of trade involved. To select the best broker for you, first determine what your average transaction size will be. Then shop around.

Fortunately, some researchers already have done the shopping for you. The American Association of Individual Investors (AAII 312-280-0170) annually calculates the fees for three typical trades—100 shares at $50, 500 shares at $50 and 1,000 shares at $5—charged by about 70 nonbank discount brokers. The report is inexpensive. Much more detailed information is available from Mercer, Inc. (800-582-9854) in its "Discount-Broker Survey," which features fees charged by most industry brokers for 22 different trades. The cost is a little more than $30.

It is likely that a discount broker is located near you. For a listing, check the yellow-page section of your telephone book under "Stock and Bond Brokers." It will list all the discount brokers, as well as the full-service brokers, in your area.

FIGURE 7.4   Discount Brokerage Firms

AccuTrade
4211 South 102nd Street
Omaha, NE 68127-1031
402-331-2526
800-592-3700

K. Aufhauser & Company, Inc.
112 West 56th Street
New York, NY 10019
212-246-9431
800-368-3668

Bidwell
209 S.W. Oak Street
Portland, OR 97204
503-790-9000
800-547-6337
800-452-6774

Brown & Company
20 Winthrop Square
Boston, MA 02110
617-742-2600
800-343-4300

Burke Christensen & Lewis
303 West Madison Street
Chicago, IL 60606
312-346-8283
800-621-0392

Fidelity Brokerage Services, Inc.
161 Devonshire Street
Boston, MA 02110
617-570-7000
800-225-1799

The R. J. Forbes Group, Inc.
150 Broad Hollow Road
Melville, NY 11747
516-549-7000
800-488-0090

Heartland Securities
208 South LaSalle Street
Chicago, IL 60604
312-372-0075
800-621-0662
800-972-0580

Kennedy Cabot & Co.
9470 Wilshire Boulevard
Beverly Hills, CA 90212
310-550-0090
800-252-0090

Lombard Institutional Brokerage
800-688-0882

Barry Murphy & Co., Inc.
270 Congress Street
Boston, MA 02210
617-426-1770
800-221-2111

Pacific Brokerage Services
5757 Wilshire Boulevard
Beverly Hills, CA 90211
213-939-1100
800-421-8395

Andrew Peck Associates, Inc.
32 Broadway
New York, NY 10004
212-363-3770
800-221-5873

Prestige Status, Inc
271-603 Grand Central Parkway
Floral Park, NY 11005
718-229-4500
800-STATUS 1

Quick & Reilly, Inc.
120 Wall Street
New York, NY 10005
212-943-8686
800-533-8161

Charles W. Schwab & Co.
101 Montgomery Street
San Francisco, CA 94104
415-398-1000
800-342-5472

Security Brokerage Services, Inc.
5757 Wilshire Boulevard
Los Angeles, CA 90036
800-262-2294

FIGURE 7.4   Discount Brokerage Firms (Continued)

Muriel Siebert and Co. 444 Madison Avenue New York, NY 10022 212-644-2400 800-872-0711	**Jack White & Company** 9191 Towne Centre Drive San Diego, CA 92122 619-587-2000 800-233-3411
Waterhouse Securities, Inc. 100 Wall Street New York, NY 10005 800-765-5185	**York Securities** 11 Wall Street New York, NY 10005 212-349-9700

Figure 7.4 is a partial list of discount brokers that operate nationally. You can contact them directly for complete information on their fees and the services they offer.

SUMMARY

With the extensive range of products and services they offer, stockbrokers today have a wide-ranging clientele, from novice investors to wealthy and sophisticated individuals. There are three kinds of brokers: full service, discounters and deep discounters When choosing a broker, you should first decide what services you need, then who can serve you the best and, finally, how much you are willing to pay. Generally, the less you pay, the fewer services you can expect to receive.

CHAPTER 8

How Securities Are Taxed

There is a price to pay for successful investing. You must pay taxes on certain income and realized capital gains to the IRS as well as to many state revenue collectors. To help you develop a tax-efficient investment strategy, this chapter explains the impact of federal taxes on income and capital gains under the provisions of current tax law, the Revenue Reconciliation Act of 1993.

CHANGES UNDER THE NEW TAX LAW THAT MAY AFFECT YOU

The 1993 Act includes a number of tax changes that can affect you as a securities investor. Let's take a quick look at some of the key changes.

Higher Top Rates

There are two new tax brackets for higher income individuals: 36 percent and 39.6 percent. These new brackets do not apply to net capital gains (long-term gains in excess of short-term losses), which still are subject to a top tax rate of 28 percent.

Higher Alternative Minimum Tax (AMT)

Under the new law, there are two AMT rates: 26 percent on AMT income of up to $175,000 and 28 percent on AMT income over $175,000. Previously, the AMT rate was 24 percent.

You may be subject to the AMT if you have deductions for accelerated depreciation and tax shelter losses, or if you have tax-exempt interest from private activity bonds. The AMT also may apply if you have substantial itemized deductions that are not deductible for AMT purposes such as state and local income taxes, certain interest expenses and miscellaneous deductions.

Capital Gain Rollover

You may defer taxable gains on publicly traded securities you sell, if the proceeds are rolled over into common stock or a partnership interest in a *specialized small business investment company* (SSBIC). An SSBIC is a small business licensed by the Small Business Administration (SBA). A tax-free rollover must be completed within 60 days of the sale of securities and is limited to $50,000 of gain annually when filing a joint tax return.

Investment Interest Deduction

In the past, capital gains realized on the sale of investment property were treated as investment income for purposes of figuring the "net investment income" ceiling for the investment interest deduction. Under the new law, if you claim the benefit of the 28 percent maximum rate for net capital gains you no longer can treat those gains as investment income to claim the interest deduction.

Gains on Market Discount Bonds

All bonds acquired after April 30, 1993, are subject to the market discount rules that treat gain on the sale of a bond as ordinary income rather than capital gain to the extent of the market discount. A market discount arises where the price of a bond declines below its face amount because it carries an interest rate that is below the current rate of interest.

Stripped Preferred Stock

Preferred stock pays dividends at a specified rate and has preference over common stock in the payment of dividends and the liquidation of assets. Buyers of stripped preferred stock after April 30, 1993, now are subject to *original issue discount* (OID) reporting rules. OID is the difference between the stated redemption price and the purchase price, a portion of which must be reported as interest income each year. Stripped preferred stock results when the stock and its stripped dividend rights are sold separately.

TAXATION OF INCOME

Publicly held corporations will tell you whether their distributions are taxable. Taxable dividends paid to you are reported to the IRS by the paying company on form 1099-DIV, a copy of which is sent to you. Taxable interest paid to you is reported to the IRS by the taxpayer on form 1099-INT. The IRS uses this information as a check on your reporting of dividends and interest.

Cash Dividends

Cash dividends you receive that are paid out of current or accumulated earnings of a corporation are subject to tax as ordinary income.

Dividends Reinvested in Company Stock

Some companies allow you to take dividends in cash or to reinvest the dividends in company stock. If you elect the stock plan and pay fair market value for the stock, the full cash dividend is taxable.

If the plan allows you to buy the stock at a discounted price, the amount of the taxable dividend is the fair market value of the stock on the dividend payment date, plus any service fee charged for the acquisition.

Stock Dividends and Stock Splits

If you own common stock and receive additional shares of the same company as a dividend, the dividend generally is not taxed. A stock dividend is taxed if you had the option to receive cash instead of stock, or if the stock is of another corporation. Preferred shareholders usually are taxed on stock dividends.

Stock splits resemble the receipt of stock dividends, but they are not dividends. If you receive additional shares as part of a stock split, the new shares are not taxable. Even though you own more shares, your ownership percentage in the company has not changed.

Investment publications such as Moody's or Standard & Poor's annual dividend record books provide details of dividend distributions and their tax treatment. These books are available at many public libraries.

Real Estate Investment Trust (REIT) Dividends

Ordinary dividends from an REIT are fully taxable. Dividends designated by the trust as capital-gains distributions are reported as long-term capital gains regardless of how long you have held your trust shares.

Return of Capital Distributions

A distribution that is not paid out of earnings is a nontaxable return of capital. Such a distribution can result from depreciation tax savings, the sale of a capital asset or of securities in a portfolio, or any other transaction not related to retained earnings. It is, in effect, a partial payback of your investment. The distribution will be reported by the company on form 1099-DIV as a nontaxable distribution.

Nontaxable distributions result in a reduction of the cost basis of your investment. Cost basis is the original price of an asset, used in determining capital gains. If your basis is reduced to zero by a return of capital distributions, any further distributions are taxable as capital gains.

Money Market Fund Distributions

Distributions paid to you by money market funds are reportable as dividends. Do not confuse these with bank money market accounts which pay interest, not dividends.

Interest on Corporate Bonds

Interest is taxable when you receive it or it is made available to you.

Interest on U.S. Treasury Obligations

Interest on securities issued by the federal government is fully taxable on your federal return. Interest on federal obligations, however, is not subject to state or local income taxes. Interest on bonds and notes is taxable in the year received.

On a Treasury bill held to maturity, you report as interest the difference between the discounted price you paid and the amount you receive on a redemption of the bill at maturity. If you dispose of the bill prior to maturity, taxable interest is the difference between the discounted price you paid and the proceeds you receive.

Market Discount on Bonds

When the price of a bond declines because its interest rate is less than the current interest rate, a market discount occurs. Gain on a disposition of a bond bought after April 30, 1993, is taxable as ordinary income to the extent of the accrued market discount, unless you reported it annually as interest income.

Original Issue Discount (OID) on Bonds

OID occurs when a bond is issued for a price less than its face or principal amount, and is the difference between the principal amount and the issue price. All obligations that pay no interest before maturity, such as zero coupon bonds, are considered to be issued at a discount. Normally, a portion of the OID must be reported as interest income each year you hold the bond.

Interest on State and Local Government Obligations

Normally, you pay no federal tax on interest on bonds or notes of states, cities, counties, the District of Columbia or a possession of the United States. Interest on certain state and city obligations is taxable, however, such as federally guaranteed obligations and private activity bonds.

Most states tax the municipal bonds of other states, but not their own. A few states and the District of Columbia do not tax the interest on any municipal obligations.

Taxation of Capital Gains and Losses

Net capital gains (capital gains less capital losses) are added to your other income and subject to regular tax rates if your top rate is 15 percent or 28 percent. If your top rate exceeds 28 percent, net long-term gains in excess of short-term losses are subject to a top rate of 28 percent. Capital losses are deductible from capital gains, and up to $3,000 of ordinary income, with a carryover for the excess over $3,000.

The taxable gain or loss realized from the sale of a security is calculated by deducting your cost from your net sales proceeds. Purchase expenses, such as commissions, are included in your cost.

How It Works

If your regular tax bracket for all income, including capital gains, is not more than 28 percent, net long-term capital gains are fully taxable at your regular rate. This is the same as for your short-term gains. If your regular tax bracket exceeds 28 percent, however, your tax should be computed on net capital gains using the 28 percent maximum rate. The 28 percent rate applies to net *capital gains,* (net long-term gains minus net short-term losses).

The period of time you own a security before its sale or exchange determines whether the gain is short term or long term. Gains or losses in 1993 and in later years are long term if the security was held more than one year.

Figuring the Holding Period

The period of time you own a security before its sale or exchange determines whether a gain or loss is short term or long term. The holding period for stocks purchased on a public exchange starts on the day after your purchase order is executed (trade date). The day your sale order is executed (trade date) is the last day of the holding period, even though delivery and payment may not be made until several days later (settlement date).

If you have purchased shares of the same stock on different dates and cannot determine which shares you are selling, the shares purchased at the earliest time are considered the stock sold first. This is the first-in, first-out (FIFO) rule.

SUMMARY

To develop a tax-efficient investment strategy, it is important to be generally familiar with how securities are taxed. For example, consider whether a security you want to invest in pays income that is taxable or is exempt from taxation by federal and/or state governments. Also consider how long you should hold a security before selling it. Holding it for at least a year may be an important way to reduce tax on a capital gain if your federal tax bracket exceeds 28 percent.

PART TWO

Investment
Strategies

CHAPTER 9

Keys to Successful Investing

According to the AAII, if you had been able to invest $1,000 in the S&P's 500 Composite Stock Price Index at the end of 1940, you now would have more than $400,000 (reinvesting dividends and excluding taxes). The figures are even more dramatic if the same investment had been made in small company stocks. AAII says your $1,000 would have grown to more than $2.5 million!

But individual investors do not have enough money to invest in all 500 companies making up the S&P 500, nor in the 2,000 companies in the Russell 2000 Small Stock Index. Instead, you must select stocks that you believe will accomplish your investment objectives. This is not always a simple task.

This chapter will help you understand some of the techniques used by successful investors to achieve their investment objectives. It shows how you can develop an investment strategy and explains important investment concepts and stock market approaches.

We start off with two widely discussed and controversial stock market theories, which provide an intriguing insight into the difficulty of trying to outguess the market.

THE RANDOM WALK THEORY

In 1900, a French mathematician named Louis Bachelier espoused the random walk theory. This theory, revived in the 1960s, holds that past prices are of no use in forecasting future price movements. Rather, stock prices reflect reactions to information coming to the market in a random way, so they are no more predictable than the walking pattern of a drunken person. Technical analysts sharply dispute the theory, saying that charts of past price movements enable them to predict future price movements.

THE EFFICIENT MARKET THEORY

The efficient market theory also contradicts the idea of being able to predict what the market or individual stocks will do in the future. This theory says that current market prices fully reflect the knowledge and expectations of all investors. Therefore, it is futile to seek undervalued stocks or to forecast market movements. Any new development is immediately reflected in a company's stock price, making it impossible to beat the market. This loudly disputed theory also claims that an investor who throws darts at a newspaper's stock listings has as good a chance to outperform the market as any professional investor.

An interesting sidelight to the dart-throwing claim is an experiment undertaken some years ago by NBC chief financial correspondent Mike Jensen and *Forbes* publisher Malcolm Forbes, Jr.

Forbes carefully selected five stocks, while Jensen threw five darts at an open newspaper page listing all stocks traded on the NYSE. At the end of five years, the random group of stocks substantially outperformed Forbes's selection.

In any case, most financial analysts agree that for total return over the long term, no publicly traded investment alternative offers more potential under normal conditions than common stock. But while the historical returns are high, the volatility of the market creates risk. Risk is the reason for the higher returns. If you want to earn more than is available from T-bills, you must assume risk.

DEVELOP AN INVESTMENT STRATEGY

Your investment strategy deals with the overall, long-term guidelines you set up in an attempt to ensure success in meeting your financial goals. Tactics are used to implement a strategy and relate to activities of shorter duration. This chapter focuses on strategy, the lifetime decisions you make in the course of managing your investment portfolio.

Long-term planning and decision making have two basic requirements:

1. You must have a clearly defined objective.
2. You must specify a time horizon.

For most investors, investing in the stock market goes through two general stages. The first is the *accumulation stage,* when your earnings exceed your expenses, and you are building wealth. The second stage begins when you start consuming your accumulated wealth. This is the *withdrawal stage.*

Key Points To Remember

When developing a long-term investment strategy, think in terms of a time horizon of at least five years. Only assets that you will not need for at least five years should be committed to your program.

Do not invest all your assets in common stocks. Unexpected events may require that you dip into savings, even while you still are accumulating wealth. Taking money out of the stock market at the wrong time can seriously hurt your long-term strategy. So keep enough liquid assets available for the inevitable emergencies that life confronts us with.

INVESTMENT CONCEPTS

To develop a successful long-term investment strategy, you need to understand how your strategy fits in with current stock market investment research and theory.

Managing Risk

Think of *risk* as the possibility that your investment will be worth less at the end of your holding period than it was at the time of your original purchase. Inflation can be taken into account by saying that risk is the possibility that your investment will be worth less in "real dollars" (inflation adjusted) at the end of the holding period. Another way to approach risk is to say that risk is the possibility that your investment will be worth less than if you had put it into a zero-risk investment, such as a money market fund or U.S. T-bill.

Many investors use statistics to provide a measurable definition of risk. This definition measures variability, the amount by which your investment return could vary around the expected average return. For example, suppose a five-year certificate of deposit has a guaranteed 6 percent return over the holding period. Because the 6 percent return is guaranteed, there is no other possible realized return and therefore no variability. The risk is zero.

Now you are presented with a second potential investment. Suppose that there is a 50 percent chance that this investment will return 40 percent and a 50 percent chance that a 10 percent loss will be realized over the holding period. The mathematically expected return on this second investment is 15 percent ($50\% \times 40\% + 50\% \times -10\%$). But the actual return may be different from the expected return of 15 percent. We see here the existence of risk. The greater the potential variability, the greater the risk.

Potential variability can be used to compare the riskiness of different investments and to make judgments about the suitability of a particular investment for your portfolio, taking into consideration your own level of comfort for risk. In practical terms, you often will determine the riskiness of a particular investment subjectively, using research and other information that is available to you.

However, comparing the 6 percent guaranteed investment with no risk to the second investment with an expected return of 15 percent, but having some risk, we are not able to say which is the better investment. Higher return means higher risk. The investment choice depends on the trade-off between risk and return that you are willing to make. Your objectives should be considered in terms of both reward and risk. In an efficient market, expected returns will be higher for securities that have higher degrees of risk.

How long you hold your securities has an important impact on the risk and return trade-off. For example, the risk and return trade-off for a one-year holding period will be different from the trade-off for a five-year holding period. Stock market risk tends to decline as the holding period lengthens. Therefore, setting a proper time frame is very important when making investment decisions.

Reducing Risk Through Diversification

In the stock market, two factors can cause a stock's return to vary. One relates to changes in the corporation or the way investors perceive the company. The other has to do with movements in the overall stock market. This means there are two components to the risk that an investor faces:

1. *market risk,* which is inherent in the stock market itself, and
2. *company risk,* which has to do with the unique characteristics of any one stock and the industry in which it operates.

About 70 percent of the risk you face as an investor is company risk. Fortunately, you can eliminate this risk by diversifying among different stocks. For example, you can invest in ten different stocks rather than just one.

Market risk is the other 30 percent of total risk and cannot be avoided by diversification, for all stocks are affected to some degree by the overall market.

The fact that you can almost entirely eliminate company risk simply by diversifying your portfolio is critical to the long-term success of your investment strategy. An investor who owns just one stock is taking on 100 percent of the risk associated with investing in common stocks, while an investor with a diversified portfolio has only 30 percent of that risk. Put differently, a single-stock investor has more than three times the risk of a diversified investor.

Investors who think of themselves as conservative but who invest in one low-risk stock actually incur more risk than investors who have a portfolio of ten aggressive growth stocks. In addition, the conservative investors are getting a lower expected return, for they are invested in lower-risk, lower-return stocks.

This brings us to an important investment concept. The stock market provides higher returns for higher risks, but it provides those higher returns only for *unavoidable* risk. Company risk is mostly avoidable through diversification. No matter what investment objective you may have, what your intended holding period is or what kind of stock analysis is performed: *If you do not have a diversified portfolio, you are either throwing away return or assuming risk that could be avoided (or dramatically reduced), or both.*

For adequate diversification, your portfolio should contain at least ten different stocks, with approximately equal dollar amounts in each. Select companies that appear to offer the greatest chance for future earnings expansion.

MARKET APPROACHES

Most strategies used to invest in the stock market fall into three general categories: *fundamental analysis, technical analysis,* and *buy and hold the market.*

Fundamental Analysis

This investment approach is primarily concerned with value. Fundamental analysis examines factors that determine a company's expected future earnings and dividends and the dependability of those earnings and dividends. It then attempts to put a value on the stock in accordance with its findings. A fundamentalist then seeks out stocks that are a good value, meaning stocks that are priced low relative to their perceived value. The assumption is that the stock market will later recognize the value of the stock and its price will increase accordingly.

Technical Analysis

The technical analyst attempts to predict the future price of a stock or the future direction of the stock market based on past price and trading volume changes. This approach assumes that stock prices and the stock market follow discernible patterns, and if the beginning of a pattern can be identified, the balance of the pattern can be predicted well enough to yield returns in excess of the general market. Most academic studies of this approach have concluded that investing based on purely technical analysis does not work.

Buy and Hold the Market

The buy-and-hold-the-market approach is the benchmark against which any other approach to the market should be measured. This strategy provides the returns that would be obtained by buying and holding the stock market, often defined as the S&P's Composite Index of 500 Stocks (S&P 500). Of course, no individual investor would buy all 500 stocks that make the index (although this can be achieved by buying shares in an S&P 500 Index mutual fund). By investing in a large number of well-diversified stocks, however, investors can build portfolios that closely resemble the S&P 500.

The buy-and-hold-the-market investment approach is used as a benchmark because no other investment approach based on analysis is valid unless it can outperform the market over the long run. When an investment produces a return that is above the market return with the same risk, the difference between the two returns is referred to as an *excess return*. The excess return represents the added value of the approach.

HOW EFFICIENT IS THE STOCK MARKET?

According to the efficient market theory described in the beginning of this chapter, stock prices in an efficient market reflect all publicly available information concerning that stock and so are extremely close to the true value of the stock. This does not mean that stock prices at all times reflect the stock's true value, but that stock prices on average reflect the true value. Variations about this average price may exist.

The random walk theory says that these variations are unpredictable; sometimes they are positive and sometimes they are negative. Because they are unpredictable, they cannot be used to obtain excess returns. This theory concerning random variation in prices purports to explain the short-term price fluctuations that occur seemingly without cause.

But the question remains: Is the stock market an "efficient" market? If it is, there would be no point in pursuing the fundamental approach that seeks to find stocks that are selling significantly above or below their value. The argument would be that stock prices vary randomly around their "true" value. Investors who believe the stock market is efficient would concentrate on developing the most efficient portfolio, rather than concentrating on specific stock selection. An efficient portfolio is one that provides returns closest to the market's return at a given level of market risk. The investor simply determines the amount of risk that he or she is willing to bear and then builds a portfolio accordingly.

Investors who believe the market is inefficient proceed on the assumption that variations in the way people receive and evaluate information cause the prices of some stocks to deviate significantly from their true value. Therefore, they see an opportunity for finding underpriced and overpriced stocks through diligent analysis, and being able to outperform a buy-and-hold-the-market strategy.

Based on substantial research evidence, many analysts believe that the market often is inefficient, and that there are opportunities for outperforming the market. The excess return potential appears to be in the range of 2 percent to 6 percent annually. Over a lifetime of investing, even a relatively small additional return can lead to substantially additional wealth.

THE EFFECT OF TRANSACTION COSTS

Do not ignore the impact of transaction costs when comparing the different approaches to investing. Take into account three important factors when trading stocks:

1. Commissions
2. The bid-ask spread
3. Taxes

Let's look at a typical transaction. You own 100 shares of stock in company A and decide to sell it and buy 100 shares of company B. Assume that the last trade on the exchange for each stock was for $25 a share. The overall cost of making the switch would look something like the following.

Commissions

The total commission cost for selling 100 shares of A and buying 100 shares of B would range from $50 (using a discount broker) to and $125 (using a full-service broker). This represents a commission of from 2 percent to 5 percent of your $2,500 investment. Of course, the percentage would be less for larger transactions.

Bid-Ask Spread

The cost of your switch is increased by the bid-ask spread, which is the difference between the price (bid) at which a stock can be bought and the price (ask) at which it can be sold. For example, for both company A and company B, the current spread may be $24⅞ (ask) to $25⅛ (bid). In this case, you would receive $24⅞ a share for selling A and pay $25⅛ a share for buying B. You have just suffered another 1 percent charge. The difference between bid and ask prices is the fee retained by the market maker or specialist. An actively traded stock will have a narrower spread than a stock that is thinly traded.

Taxes

If you enjoyed a profit on your sale of company A's stock, you will have to pay a tax. Of course, taxes would have to be paid eventually, but if they are deferred, you will continue to earn a return on the eventual liability. Comparing a one-year holding period with a ten-year holding period, the value of deferring taxes could be worth another 0.5 percent each year.

So switching can be expensive. You pay somewhere between 3 percent and 6 percent to switch from one stock to another. This does not mean it should not be done, just that the new stock must perform sufficiently better to overcome the setback. Investors who use investment techniques that result in turning over their entire portfolio several times a year must outperform the market substantially just to match a buy-and-hold-the-market approach.

SETTING YOUR OBJECTIVES

It is clear that a successful investor must set an objective in terms of what is to be achieved and what is the anticipated time frame in which to accomplish the objective. A useful way to approach this is to review the historical record, looking at what kinds of risks and rewards you can expect, based on what already has occurred. While history may not repeat itself, it can give you an idea of what you can reasonably

FIGURE 9.1   Range of Returns on Common Stocks (1926–1993)

Holding Period (Years)	Highest Returns for the Period	Lowest Returns for the Period
1	53.9%	–43.3%
5	23.9	–12.4
10	20.1	– 0.9
15	18.2	0.6
20	16.9	3.1
25	14.7	5.9

Source: *Stocks, Bonds, Bills and Inflation,* 1994 Yearbook, Ibbotson Associates, Chicago (annually updates work by Roger G. Ibbotson and Rex A. Sinquefield.) Used with permission. All rights reserved.

expect. Many potential investors make hypothetical stock purchases and then track the results to get a "full" for the market works.

Short-Term Versus Long-Term Risk

How long you hold an investment has an important effect on the degree of risk you undertake. In this context, consider risk as the likelihood that your capital will diminish from the time of your initial purchase to the end of the holding period.

Figure 9.1 illustrates that while the stock market can be risky in the short run, time has a moderating effect. The longer you hold a portfolio of stock market investments, the less are your chances of losing money and the greater are the odds of earning a return close to the long-term average.

A 1-year holding period for stocks can produce the most volatile returns, ranging from +53.9 percent to –43.3 percent. Over 10-year periods, the results change dramatically, with –0.9 percent for the worst 10 years to 20.1 percent for the best 10 years. There were no losing 15-, 20-, or 25-year periods. The numbers show that risk can be substantial over short periods, but your chances of losing money over longer time frames are substantially reduced.

Investment Classes and Risk

To create a successful long-term investment program, it is critical that you develop an asset allocation. How well you are able to achieve your objectives will be determined in large part by the balance you establish among the three common investment classes:

1. *Cash reserves* include money market funds, bank CDs and T-bills. They are securities that provide a stable investment value and current interest income.
2. *Bonds* are interest-bearing debt obligations issued by corporations, the federal government and its agencies, and state and local governments. Bonds typically offer higher yields than cash reserves, but their value fluctuates with market conditions.
3. *Common stocks* represent ownership rights in a corporation, usually pay dividends and offer the potential for capital growth. Stock market risk can be substantial.

As shown in the table below, studies indicate that investment returns depend mainly on how you allocate your money among these classes, not on the specific stock, bond or cash reserve investments you select.

Average Annual Rates of Return
from 1926 to 1993

Cash Reserves	3.7%
Bonds	5.0
Common Stocks	10.3

Over the long term, common stocks have delivered the highest average annual returns of the three investment classes. These returns reflect total return, income or yield plus any capital gain or loss.

The advantage of stocks is compelling when results are viewed over time. Over the past 30 years, an investment in stocks would have grown to more than twice the value of the same investment in bonds and nearly three times the value cash reserves would have produced. The numbers show clearly the power of compounding—the cumulative impact of investment returns over time.

Growth: What $10,000 Invested Would
Have Grown to from 1963 to 1993

Cash Reserves	$ 69,000
Bonds	84,390
Common Stocks	197,700

Stocks and bonds offer higher returns than cash reserves, but they also expose you to higher levels of risk. This is the risk-reward ratio: In order to pursue higher returns, you must be willing to assume additional risk.

Annual returns and growth figures reflect total return: income or yield plus any capital gain or loss. Taxes and transaction costs are not included.

As historical evidence shows, common stocks provide exceptionally high long-term returns compared to more conservative investments. The risk generally attached to common stocks becomes unimportant over long time periods.

Real Stock Market Risk

Because people do lose money in the market, what are the real risks of investing in the stock market? First, short-term investing is risky. As noted previously, an investor has about a 30 percent chance of showing a loss at the end of one year. This would happen more often if taxes and transaction costs are figured in. Second, many investors are not sufficiently diversified, taking on more risk and incurring more losses than the market as a whole. Third, many investors speculate ("play the market") in an attempt to make large short-term profits by trading their stocks frequently and by trying to predict short-term market swings (timing the market). Because of high transaction costs, most speculators lose money, even in a market with an overall upward trend.

SUMMARY

Investing in common stock offers an outstanding opportunity to accumulate wealth through growth at relatively low risk. The stock market is risky for short-term holding periods, and for speculators, but as an investor's holding period goes beyond five years, risk is greatly diminished. A successful investment strategy assumes that you have a clearly defined objective with a specified time horizon. Remember, though, that unforeseen circumstances can change an expected holding period, creating an extra element of risk. For this reason, always keep an adequate amount of assets in cash or liquid securities as a ready reserve.

CHAPTER 10

Investing for a Growing Income

Investors who seek current income that gradually will grow over the years as a way to offset the ravages of persistent inflation can easily put together a portfolio of common stocks that have a history of consistent dividend increases and that are expected to maintain the pattern in the future.

In early 1994, the median of estimated yields for all dividend-paying stocks was about 2.5 percent, according to the *Value Line Investment Survey*. This yield is near the bottom of what stocks have paid over the past ten years. Its low was 2.3 percent on September 4, 1987, when stock prices reached a peak (which has since been exceeded). The high yield of 7.8 percent occurred on December 23, 1974, when market prices were at a bear market low.

It is rarely possible, except by luck, to pinpoint when the market or the price of a particular stock has reached even a temporary high or low point. Many investors solve the problem of determining the best time to invest in common stocks by using the principle of *constant dollar investing* (investing a constant number of dollars at regular intervals. See Chapter 5 for a full discussion of this important concept).

You can put together a portfolio of stocks that will produce a regular income, with an expectation that the income gradually will grow through annual dividend increases. To do this, buy common stocks of high-quality, established companies that have a history of increasing their dividends on a regular basis over the years. This chapter describes one such corporation, Merck & Company, Inc., that appears to fulfill this requirement. Because diversification is desirable to effectively eliminate the problem of *company risk* (the risk of owning just one stock), you also will find information on a number of other solid dividend-paying companies to consider in your portfolio.

Merck & Company, Inc., my recommended stock for dividend income, is a good example of how the process works. If you had invested $10,000 in Merck stock in 1984 at the stock's average price during the year, you would have received an income in the first year of $348.72. As the company's earnings increased during the next ten years, it paid out a growing dividend stream. By 1993, your annual income from this one $10,000 investment would have grown to $2,112.82. Merck's sales, earnings and dividend payout are expected to continue growing in coming years.

★ *Recommended Company*

Merck & Company, Inc.
P.O. Box 100
Whitehouse Station, NJ 08889-0100
908-423-1000

Chairman & CEO: P. R. Vagelos
Number of shareholders: 161,200
Number of employees: 38,000
Where the stock trades: NYSE
Symbol: MRK

What the Company Does
Merck & Company, Inc., is a leading manufacturer of human and animal health-care products and specialty chemical products, including:

Vasotec, Prinivil:	angiotensin converting enzyme (ACE) inhibitor agents for high blood pressure and angina
Mevacor, Zocor:	cholesterol-lowering agents
Primaxin, Mefoxin:	antibiotics
Pepcid:	antiulcer agent
Recombivax HB:	hepatitis B vaccine
Prilosec:	gastrointestinal

International business accounts for about 46 percent of sales and 27 percent of pretax profits. The company spends 11.5 percent of sales for research and development. Its labor costs are about 26 percent of sales.

Comments

Merck's ongoing business increased 13 percent in 1993 over the previous year, with the fourth quarter showing a 17 percent increase over the same quarter in 1992. These gains are impressive in light of a 2 percent negative currency impact and no help from price increases. The improvement stems from rising unit volume, a cost-cutting program and a favorable product mix. Pretax profit margins were up by 2.9 percentage points. Sales of Proscar and Mevacor, two of Merck's important drugs, were up 22 percent, much better than some analysts had expected.

Merck acquired Medco Containment Company in November of 1993 for some $6 billion. Medco is a large marketer of discount prescription medicines. This acquisition is anticipated to dilute Merck's earnings by about 20 cents a share in 1994, to about $2.45 per share. This effect is the result of Medco's lower operating margins, an increase in depreciation and good well-related amortization, and an increase in the company's effective tax rate. But over the long term, the combination should pay off. Medco has a very strong growth rate. Its 1993 third quarter operating income was up by 56 percent. The merger has produced a strong, broadly diversified company, well-positioned to compete in the new health-care market that is increasingly dominated by managed-care firms. The combined concern has the ability to provide medicines covering a broad spectrum of therapeutic categories.

This top-quality company has the potential to generate substantial total returns over the balance of the 1990s. The company has a strong product group and a flow of new products in the pipeline. Drugs such as Proscar, for treating enlarged prostates, and Fosamax, for osteoporosis, are examples of new items that have tremendous growth prospects.

Investment Results

Over the years Merck has typically paid out about 42 percent to 44 percent of its profits to shareholders in increasing dividends. Figure 10.1 illustrates the annual income an investor would have received from declared dividends on a $10,000 investment made in Merck &

FIGURE 10.1   Annual Dividends Declared on a $10,000 Investment
in Merck & Company, Inc., Common Stock

1984	$348.72	1989	$1,128.20
1985	369.23	1990	1,312.82
1986	430.77	1991	1,579.49
1987	553.84	1992	1,887.18
1988	882.05	1993	2,112.82

Company, Inc., common stock in early 1984. It is assumed that the shares were purchased at 4⅞, the average price at which the shares traded in that year. The price has been adjusted for stock splits in 1986, 1988 and 1992. The cost of brokerage commissions paid in buying the shares has not been considered.

The next aspect to consider in owning shares in a successful company with a history of growing sales and earnings is what happens to the value of your investment. Figure 10.2 illustrates how the value of the same Merck & Company, Inc., shares purchased for $10,000 changed over the years from an initial investment in 1984. Calculation of the market value of the shares each year is based on the average price at which the shares traded during the year.

CREATING AN INCOME PORTFOLIO

Because diversification has such an significant impact on risk, it is important for you to hold at least ten stocks in your investment portfolio. Look for low-risk stocks that have solid records for dividend growth and that are expected to continue to increase their dividends at above-average rates. A number of good companies, such as Merck, have increased dividends by at least 10 percent each year over the past five years. While they may not be able to maintain such a rate, these companies have indicated a pattern of performance.

Look for stocks whose yields from dividend payouts generally are higher than those of most other dividend-paying companies and where the company's payout ratios are generous. A firm's *payout ratio* is the company's dividends as a percentage of its net profit. Also, add to your portfolio established companies that analysts have determined to be relatively safe and have strong financial ratings. They generally do better in hard times than more typical companies do.

FIGURE 10.2   Market Value of a $10,000 Investment in Merck & Company, Inc., Common Stock

1984	$10,000	1989	$46,872
1985	13,025	1990	54,051
1986	22,462	1991	85,128
1987	39,385	1992	99,692
1988	36,820	1993	74,564

Listed in Figure 10.3 is a group of companies that fit the criteria many prudent investors would want for a small portfolio of income-producing stocks. All are traded on the NYSE.

What the Companies Do

Anheuser-Busch Companies, Incorporated, is the largest brewer in the United States, shipping more than 40 percent of the industry's total product. Its brands include the Budweiser, Michelob and Busch families of beer. The company also markets the Natural Light, Classic Dark and O'Doul's brands. Anheuser-Busch operates 12 breweries with an annual capacity of about 87 million barrels. About 76 percent of its sales comes from beer, which also accounts for 93 percent of its operating profits. The company owns the St. Louis Cardinals baseball team. (The company has about 44,000 employees and 67,000 shareholders.)

H&R Block, Incorporated, operates and franchises more than 9,500 company-owned and franchised offices worldwide. The units are engaged in tax preparation, computer services and temporary personnel services. Tax-preparation activities account for about 48 percent of operating revenues and 65 percent of profits. The company acquired CompuServe in 1980, Access Technology in 1988, MicroSolutions, Inc., in 1990, Interim Services in 1991 and Mecca Software in 1993. (The company has about 3,600 permanent employees and 33,450 shareholders.)

Bristol-Myers Squibb Company manufactures proprietary medical products, ethical pharmaceuticals, diagnostics, infant formula, orthopedic implants and health and beauty aids. Its major brand names include Ban, Bufferin, Buspar, Capoten, Clairol, Comtrex, Enfamil, Excedrin, Isovue, Monopril, Nuprin, Paraplatin, Pravachol, Taxol, VePesid and Videx. International activities account for about 34 per-

FIGURE 10.3   Companies To Be Included in a Small Portfolio

Company	Ticker Symbol	Approximate Dividend Yield*	Payout Ratio	12/31/93 Price
Anheuser-Busch	BUD	3.1%	34%	49⅛
H & R Block	HRB	2.9	57	40¾
Bristol-Myers Squibb	BMY	5.0	68	58¼
Clorox Company	CLX	3.3	56	54¼
E-Systems	ESY	2.8	28	43⅜
First of America Bank	FOA	4.2	50	39¼
General Mills	GIS	3.1	49	60¾
Glaxo Holdings (ADR)	GLX	3.8	47	20⅞
John H. Harland	JH	4.6	57	21⅝
H. J. Heinz	HNZ	3.8	46	35⅞
Hong Kong Telecom (ADR)	HKT	2.9	69	62¼
International Flavors & Fragrance	IFF	3.0	55	113¾
Eli Lilly	LLY	4.2	46	59⅜
Merck & Company	MRK	3.0	44	34⅜

*The dividend yield is based on market price of the shares and latest dividends declared in mid-January 1994.

cent of sales and 24 percent of operating income. (The company has about 53,000 employees and 138,000 shareholders.)

Clorox Company is the biggest bleach producer in the United States. Products include Clorox 2, Liquid-plumr, Formula 409, Clorox Pre-Wash, Soft Scrub, Tilex, Pine-Sol, Combat insecticides, Kingsford and Match Light charcoal, K.C. Masterpiece barbecue sauce, Hidden Valley Ranch salad dressing and Fresh Step cat litter. (The company has about 4,700 employees and 12,900 shareholders.)

E-Systems, Incorporated, produces electronic products for use in defense, information gathering and processing, communications and aircraft navigation. Many of the company's military programs are classified. The firm also provides aircraft overhaul and maintenance services for the Air Force and commercial carriers. Sales to the U.S. Government account for 89 percent of the total, with foreign sales accounting for 9 percent and commercial sales 2 percent. (The company has about 18,600 employees and 10,800 shareholders.)

First of America Bank Corporation is a multistate bank holding company with 25 member banks and 550 offices located in Illinois, Indiana and Michigan. The company acquired Security Bancorporation in 1992. (The company has about 11,400 employees and 17,800 shareholders.)

General Mills, Incorporated, processes and markets consumer foods, which account for 66 percent of its sales and 81 percent of its operating profits. Its brands include Big G cereals, Betty Crocker desserts, Gold Medal flour, Gorton's seafood and Yoplait yogurt. The company operates more than 1,000 restaurants in the United States, Canada and Japan. The restaurants, which account for 34 percent of sales and 19 percent of profits, include Red Lobster, The Olive Garden and China Coast. (The company has about 121,300 employees and 33,800 shareholders.)

Glaxo Holdings PLC is Britain's largest drug company and ranks second worldwide. The company produces and markets ethical pharmaceuticals. Its principal products include Zantac, an antiulcerant; Ventolin and Beclovent, antiasthmatics; Zofran, an antiemesis; and Fortaz, Zinnat and Ceftin, antibiotics. Sales to Europe and North America account for 73 percent of the total, with the rest of the world accounting for the balance. (The company has about 40,000 employees and 123,000 shareholders, with 79,500 registered ADR holders.)

John H. Harland Company is the country's second largest financial stationer. It primarily is involved in printing checks and related items. The company's principal products are Magnetic Ink Character Recognition encoded checks, deposit tickets and related forms for financial institutions and their customers. Its market share of the industry is about 32 percent. The firm has about 68 plants. (The company has 6,700 employees and 8,200 shareholders.)

H. J. Heinz Company manufactures soups, catsup, baked beans, pickles, vinegar, baby foods and various condiments. Its brands include Star-Kist tuna, 9 Lives cat food and OreIda frozen potatoes. The company operates Weight Watcher programs and sells Weight Watcher and Alba low-calorie products. Foreign operations account for about 42 percent of sales and 52 percent of operating income. (The company has about 37,700 employees and 55,900 shareholders.)

Hong Kong Telecommunications Ltd. has exclusive franchises for local and international telecommunications services in Hong Kong to 1995. It has 2.82 million lines in service. All are digital. Its international calls account for 63 percent of revenues. Local calls, other telecommunications and equipment sales and other services account for the balance. (The company has about 15,800 employees and 25,400 shareholders.)

International Flavors & Fragrances is a leading creator and manufacturer of flavors and fragrances sold to consumer-products manufacturers around the world. Its products are used mainly in perfumes, cosmetics, soaps and detergents, prepared foods, beverages, dairy foods, pharmaceuticals, confectionery and tobacco products and animal foods. Fragrances account for about 60 percent of revenues, with flavors accounting for the balance. The company operates manufacturing plants in 23 countries. Foreign operations account for about 69 percent of sales and 68 percent of operating profits. (The company has about 4,200 employees and 4,400 shareholders.)

Eli Lilly and Company develops, manufactures and markets pharmaceuticals, medical instruments, diagnostic products and animal health products. The company sells its products in more than 120 countries. Among its brands are Prozac, an antidepressant; Axid, an antiulcer compound; Kefzol, Mandol, Ceclor and Lorabid, antibiotics; Dobutrex, a cardiovascular agent; Humatrope, a human growth hormone; and Humulin, human insulin. Forty percent of the company's sales come from international business. (The company has about 32,000 employees and 54,000 shareholders.)

SUMMARY

If you are seeing a current income that gradually will grow over the years as a way to offset the ravages of persistent inflation, put together a portfolio of common stocks that have a history of consistent dividend increases and that are expected to maintain that pattern in the future.

The solution for many investors to the problem of determining the best time to invest in common stocks is to use the principle of *constant dollar investing*.

CHAPTER 11

Investing for High Current Income

The steady decline of interest rates in the late 1980s and early 1990s has caused income-oriented investors to look for securities that are safe and yet produce a reasonably good income in today's economy. This chapter concentrates on highlighting income opportunities in closed-end funds that trade on U.S. stock exchanges and recommends two specific funds to consider.

The post-1990–recession recovery in the U.S. economy happened much faster than many economists expected. While business is not booming, corporations currently are experiencing a healthy improvement in cash flow, largely as a result of the aggressive downsizing that occurred during the last recession. Lower labor costs, and debt costs that were reduced by refinancing debt at lower interest rates, means that companies are able to spend more on capital goods, including machinery that will make them less labor-intensive.

Interest Rates and Bond Prices

Unlike stable cash reserves, bonds fluctuate in value as interest rates change. Generally, bond prices move inversely with interest rates. When interest rates go up, bond prices go down; when rates go down, bond prices go up. Furthermore, longer-maturity bonds experience greater price changes than bonds with shorter maturities in response to interest rate changes.

During the long rise in interest rates during the 1970s and early 1980s, when the economy was relatively stagnant and inflation soaring, bond prices were in a steep decline. Now, however, inflation is unlikely to climb at more than a slow rate. Part of the reason is an employment situation that probably will not improve much in the near-term. Layoffs will likely continue in many major industries. Companies have either permanently replaced labor with machinery or have moved production to low-cost foreign sites.

Some financial analysts predict that the interest rate on the 30-year U.S. Treasury bond will remain at or just under 7 percent through 1997, and good quality corporate bonds will remain under 8 percent. Broad values are expected to fluctuate within a narrow band. Thus, bond investors should not be faced with losses such as occurred in the early 1980s. The main problem of investors will be to time their purchases of bonds or bond funds so that they will buy when interest rates are at the top of the interest-rate span. You should find many such opportunities during the next five years or so. Older investors may yearn for the very high interest rates that were prevalent in the early 1980s. But their inability to achieve those rates will likely be compensated for by a low inflation rate.

Investment Climate

In early 1994, a surprising number of closed-end bond funds were trading at premiums to their net asset value (NAV)—total net worth of assets divided by total number of shares outstanding. This was despite the uncertainty in the bond market. Recognizing that the closed-end sector of the stock market tends to be inefficient (not necessarily reflecting true values), you generally should make commitments in bond funds when they are trading near or below NAV. Closed-end funds selling at a premium or a discount to NAV are listed separately each Monday in *The New York Times* and *The Wall Street Journal,* as well as weekly in *Barron's National Business and Financial Weekly.*

Investors in higher tax brackets will continue the substantial demand for tax-free municipal bonds. A heavy outpouring of new tax-exempt securities recently has kept their prices down, resulting in attractive yields. If you are looking for good buys with tax-free interest, there has been a widening of discounts from NAV among closed-end municipal bond funds. The Nuveen Municipal Value Fund, a value-oriented, multistate, tax-exempt fund, merits consideration.

For yields that may run as much as 200 basis points (two full percentage points) higher than those available in the United States, look at Global Yield Fund, an international bond fund that trades on the NYSE. This type of security carries a moderate amount of currency risk.

★ *Recommended Fund*

1838 Bond-Debenture Trading Fund
Five Radnor Corporate Center
100 Matsonford Road
Radnor, PA 19087
215-293-4300

President: John H. Donaldson
Investment Adviser: 1838 Investment Advisors, L.P.
Where the shares trade: NYSE
Symbol: BDF

Investment Objective
1838 Bond-Debenture Trading Fund seeks a high rate of return from interest income and trading activity. Income distributions are made quarterly.

1838 is a closed-end, diversified investment company with a portfolio of bonds. The fund may use bank loans to purchase bonds and may lend securities to brokers and other financial institutions in return for cash collateral that is invested in short-term debt. Investment income is distributed to shareholders quarterly.

Comments
1838 Bond-Debenture Trading Fund is a high-quality total-return bond fund, seeking both interest income and profits from trading activity. Its success as a total return fund was indicated when it became one of the first of 21 bond funds formed in the 1970s that was able to distribute a capital-gains payment, having used up all its tax-loss carryforwards. The tax-loss carryforwards resulted from portfolio losses that occurred during the rising interest rate environment prior to 1982. As long as tax-loss carryforwards are available to offset trading gains for tax purposes, funds will retain their realized gains.

FIGURE 11.1   Per-Share Performance of the Fund Through 1993

	NAV*	Income Dividends	Dividend Yield**	Total Return***
1984	$17.82	$2.00	12.3%	19.0%
1985	21.12	2.00	10.3	29.7
1986	21.25	2.00	8.8	10.1
1987	20.18	1.86	8.9	3.7
1988	19.75	1.86	9.5	7.1
1989	20.04	1.82	9.2	10.7
1990	20.27	1.87	9.3	12.6
1991	21.39	1.84	8.5	14.6
1992	22.27	1.83	8.1	14.2
1993	22.75	1.75	7.7	10.0

*NAV at the end of each year.
**Average dividend yield, based on average NAV during the year.
***Change in NAV plus dividend distributions.

1838 has consistently produced total returns above the average of the 21 funds in its peer group.

The fund's manager believes that 1838 will continue to perform well with its total return approach, even in an environment where interest rates are no longer in long-term decline. The fund has a long-standing policy of keeping its average maturity above 20 years, a portion of the bond yield curve where relatively more bond trading opportunities are available. 1838 has been working to reduce volatility in a period of low interest rates, taking a more conservative investment stance. As a way of lifting income somewhat, the fund reduced its holdings in the U.S. Government and highest quality corporate categories from 41 percent of assets in early 1993 to 31 percent of assets in late 1993. With an average credit quality bond rating of A, the fund still is considered high quality.

1838 Bond-Debenture Trading Fund looks good if you are seeking an investment that is considered a safe, high-income investment. As a bonus, diversification is built in.

Performance

As a result of the high regard in which it is held, the 1838 Bond-Debenture Trading Fund has typically traded at a slight premium to its NAV. Since 1985, the fund's NAV has remained quite steady, which is important for the investors who want high current income while maintaining the value of their assets. Figure 11.1 shows some key numbers relating to the performance of the fund for the ten-year period ending December 31, 1993.

1838 Bond-Debenture Trading Fund has historically outperformed the average of other closed-end bond funds. Figure 11.2 presents the total return–percentage change in NAV per share with all distributions reinvested for various periods ending March 31, 1994.

Dividend Reinvestment Plan (DRIP)

1838 Bond-Debenture Trading Fund has established a plan for the automatic investment of dividends and distributions that all shareholders of record are eligible to join. Dividends and distributions for participants in the reinvestment plan are made in the form of previously unissued fund shares, unless the NAV exceeds the market price plus commissions. In that case, the dividend or distribution proceeds are used to purchase shares of the fund on the open market for participants in the plan.

Portfolio
Large Bond Positions as of September 30, 1993

Security Issuer	*Maturities*
U.S. Treasury	2005–2021
FNMA Collateral Mortgage	2019–2021
Commonwealth Edison Company	2016
Texas Utilities Electric Company	2018 and 2020
CTC Mansfield Funding Company	2016
Hydro Quebec Company	2026
Union Camp Corporation	2011
Ford Motor Company	2022
Rohm & Haas Company	2021
Sprint Corporation	2022

AN INTERNATIONAL BOND FUND

As indicated earlier, if you can tolerate a certain amount of currency risk, income returns as much as 200 basis points higher than those available in U.S. bond funds sometimes are available in foreign bond funds. The *Global Yield Fund, Inc.,* is a nondiversified closed-end

FIGURE 11.2   Total Return–Percentage Change in NAV Per Share with All Distributions Reinvested[1]

	10 Years to 3/31/94	5 Years to 3/31/94	3 Years to 3/31/94	2 Years to 3/31/94	1 Year to 3/31/94	Quarter to 3/31/94
1838 Bond Fund[2]	238.63%	71.30%	38.90%	20.48%	4.65%	–3.92%
Average of 21 Other Closed-End Bond Funds[2]	210.54	64.79	37.50	19.42	4.38	–2.92
Salomon Brothers Bond Index[3]	258.56	73.26	36.25	19.89	2.38	–4.68

[1]This is historical information and should not be construed as indicative of any likely future performance.
[2]Source: Lipper Analytical Services Corporation.
[3]Comprised of long-term AAA and AA corporate bonds; series has been changed to include mortgage-backed securities.

Source: 1838 Bond-Debenture Trading Fund, Annual Report dated 3/31/94. Reprinted by permission of 1838 Investment Advisors, L.P.

investment company that owns non-U.S.–based debt securities. As a nondiversified fund, it has greater latitude under Securities and Exchange Commission (SEC) regulations regarding the percentage of assets it may invest in any single country. This is a good fund to consider when the shares trade near or below NAV.

Global Yield Fund aims to provide a higher yield than that available from U.S. dollar-denominated debt. Income distributions are made quarterly. Its major holdings as of June 1993 were in securities of issuers in the following countries.

Country	Duration	Percent of Assets
Australia	Long-term	6.8%
Canada	Long-term	10.7
Mexico	Short-term	5.1
United Kingdom	Long-term	9.7
United States	Long-term	15.6

Several years ago, when worldwide interest and inflation rates were higher, the fund's average maturity was less than three years, but by the end of 1993, maturities had lengthened to an average of about eight years. The lengthening of maturities reflects the fund's optimistic

FIGURE 11.3   Per-Share Performance of Global Yield Fund
Through 1993

	NAV*	Income Dividends	Dividend Yield**	Total Return***
1987	$ 9.95	$1.35	11.1%	18.0%
1988	9.41	.81	8.4	2.7
1989	8.57	.94	11.9	2.6
1990	8.96	.93	11.5	16.3
1991	8.99	.62	7.7	7.3
1992	8.10	.80	9.5	−1.0
1993	8.60	.72	9.3	15.0

*NAV at the end of each year.
**Average dividend yield, based on average NAV during the year.
***Change in NAV plus dividend distributions.

outlook toward European bonds and dollar-bloc countries other than
the United States.

As of the end of 1993, about 60 percent of the fund's assets were
invested in European bonds, with significant stakes in bonds originat-
ing in Holland, Germany, France and Spain.

The Global Yield Fund was issued in mid-1986 at $10 per share.
The fund presents a good illustration of why initial public offerings
(IPOs) of closed-end funds generally should be avoided. After the
initial sales promotion by broker-dealers that gave the shares early
price support, the shares traded later in the year on the NYSE at as low
as $8.25 per share. The lifting of broker-dealer support and the sales
fee built into the offering price often cause the share price of new issues
to drop from the offering price by at least the amount of the sales fee
within a few months of the issue date.

Figure 11.3 shows some key numbers relating to the performance
of the fund for the ten year period ending December 31, 1993.

OTHER HIGHLY REGARDED FUNDS

Investing in one closed-end bond fund gives you diversification in
terms of owning a portfolio of bonds from many different issuers. But
because the fund is under one investment adviser who has a particular
investment objective, it also may be prudent to diversify your invest-

ment into several funds. Following is a list of eight funds that some analysts feel are above average in safety and have a good history of dividend distributions.

Fund	Where Traded	1993 Yield	1993 Total Return
ACM Government Income Fund	NYSE	8.7%	19.1%
American Capital Bond Fund	NYSE	8.0	15.8
Duff & Phelps Utilities Income	NYSE	7.3	10.0
John Hancock Investors Trust	NYSE	7.7	13.5
Montgomery Street Income Securities	NYSE	8.0	15.0
Patriot Premium Dividend Fund I	NYSE	7.4	19.3
Pioneer Interest Shares	NYSE	7.5	11.5
TCW Convertible Securities Fund	NYSE	8.4	19.0

SUMMARY

Income-oriented investors who are looking for securities that are safe and yet produce a reasonably good income should consider the income opportunities available in closed-end funds that trade on U.S. stock exchanges. If you can tolerate a moderate amount of currency risk, yields on international bond funds sometimes run as much as 200 basis points (two full percentage points) higher than those available in the United States.

CHAPTER 12

Investing for Growth— Conservatively

Investors seeking capital growth generally are most interested in the "total return" of a stock rather than just the dividends or price appreciation. *Total return* is the sum of the dividend payout per year and the annual change in the market value of the stock. For example, a stock that has a dividend yield of 2 percent and rises 12 percent in value has a total return of 14 percent. The weight you give to dividends when selecting stocks depends on your particular need for income. If growth of capital is your objective, place your emphasis on the sum of annual dividends and price appreciation.

In putting together a portfolio of stocks for growth, it is useful to review the historical record of different categories of stocks. For instance, are you more likely to find success by investing in a group of the largest U.S. companies, or are medium-size or even small-capitalization companies likely to perform better? The past is not necessarily going to be repeated, but you may get some clues about what to expect. Figure 12.1 illustrates the average annual total returns for one-, three-, five- and ten-year periods ending June 30, 1993, for three representative market indexes.

This chapter focuses on financially strong companies that many analysts consider to have above-average potential for long-term price appreciation. In addition to my recommended company, information is presented on companies whose share earnings have compounded at

FIGURE 12.1   Average Annual Total Returns* for Periods Ended
June 30, 1993

	1 Year	3 Years	5 Years	10 Years
S&P 500 Index	13.61	11.43	14.17	14.35
Wilshire 4500 Index	21.62	14.16	12.75	15.34
Russell 2000 Index	25.96	13.46	11.15	8.71

*Includes the reinvestment of all dividends and any capital gains distributions.

a minimum 10 percent annual rate over the past five years and are expected to maintain a 10 percent growth rate over the next several years. Many growth stocks, including some with better historical and prospective appreciation potential, are not included because of their lower degree of financial strength or the volatility of their price movements.

Several stocks in this chapter are from the drug industry, hardly surprising given the high-growth, recession-resistant nature of the pharmaceutical sector. Though all the stocks listed here are of high-quality, established companies that have an excellent history, I strongly recommend investment diversification among at least ten companies to eliminate company risk.

Johnson & Johnson is my recommended stock for growth in a conservative portfolio. It is a good example of a financially strong company that has performed very well over many years and has a bright outlook for the future.

★ Recommended Company

Johnson & Johnson
501 George Street
New Brunswick, NJ 08903
908-524-0400

Chairman & CEO: Ralph S. Larsen
Number of shareholders: 69,900
Number of employees: 84,900
Where the stock trades: NYSE
Symbol: JNJ

What the Company Does

Johnson & Johnson is a leading manufacturer of health-care products. Product areas include consumer toiletries, first-aid products, hygienic and baby care; professional medical equipment, surgical products and apparel, and dental products; and pharmaceutical contraceptives, therapeutics and veterinary. Johnson & Johnson brands include Tylenol, Band-Aid, Stayfree, Modess and Reach, among many others.

International business accounts for about 50 percent of sales and 54 percent of operating profits. Some 8.2 percent of sales is spent for research and development.

Comments

International results of Johnson & Johnson have been under some pressure recently because of an appreciating dollar in foreign markets, a weak European economic climate and limited health-care reforms undertaken by some European countries. The company's domestic business, however, combined with streamlining of operations, has more than offset the foreign problems.

U.S. pharmaceutical sales are strong and have been helped by several new drugs released in 1993. One such drug is Prepulsid, a gastrointestinal product. The professional part of the business in the United States should continue to benefit from the rapid expansion of minimally invasive surgical instruments and further market penetration of Acuvue disposable contact lenses and the One Touch II glucose monitoring system. The growth from this market segment should more than make up for the sluggish demand for hospital supplies, due primarily to the trimming of inventories by hospitals to reduce costs. Johnson & Johnson's wide array of business has continued to expand faster than its expenses.

This top-quality stock should fit in well with almost any stock portfolio. While the details of future health-care reforms in the United States are uncertain, well-diversified Johnson & Johnson looks like a safe bet within its industry. It should do well in future years.

Investment Results

Over the past 15 years, Johnson & Johnson never has had a year in which its sales did not exceed that of the previous year. Earnings per share have kept pace. Only in 1984 and 1986 did per-share earnings fail to move forward. The company typically has paid out about 35 percent of its profits in dividends. A person who invested $10,000

FIGURE 12.2   Results of a $10,000 Investment in Johnson & Johnson
Common Stock in 1984

	Average Share Price	Annual Dividends	Shares Bought from Dividends	Total Shares Owned
1984	8⅞	$ 338	38	1,165
1985	11¼	372	33	1,198
1986	15	419	28	1,226
1987	20⅛	490	24	1,250
1988	19⅝	600	30	1,280
1989	25¼	716	28	1,308
1990	31⅜	863	27	1,335
1991	45⅜	1,027	22	1,357
1992	50⅞	1,207	23	1,380
1993	43	1,393	32	1,412

in Johnson & Johnson shares in 1984 (at the average price the stock traded at during the year), with dividends reinvested each year in additional shares, would own 1,412 shares with a value of $63,363 at the end of 1993. Brokerage commissions have not been considered. Figure 12.2 shows the ten years' results of a $10,000 investment in Johnson & Johnson common stock from 1984 to 1993.

The December 31, 1993, closing price of Johnson & Johnson common stock shares on the NYSE was $44.875. At the end of ten years, the original $10,000 investment had a market value of $63,363 and had paid dividends during 1993 of $1,393. In 1993, the yield on the original investment was nearly 14 percent. The value of the $10,000 had multiplied by more than six times.

Two interesting aspects of an investment in Johnson & Johnson can be seen in Figure 12.3. First, while the stock price did not pursue a continual upward move, the average yearly price dipped in 1988 and 1993, a patient investor benefited in those years because dividends bought more shares at lower prices than at higher prices. Second, the company increased its dividend payout every year.

Except for 1986, Johnson & Johnson has been able to produce an increasing stream of profits for its shareholders. Book value (assets less liabilities divided by number of shares) also increased in every year except 1986 and 1992. Note that the average price-earnings ratio (price per share divided by earnings per share) shows a fairly steady increasing trend over the years, moving from 12.5 times earnings in

FIGURE 12.3 Per-Share Financial Results of Johnson & Johnson From 1984 to 1993

	Earnings Per Share	Book Value	Average PE Ratio	Percentage of Profits Paid in Dividends	Average Price Per Share
1984	.69	$4.01	12.5	43%	8⅞
1985	.84	4.58	13.3	38	11¼
1986	.46	4.08	34.6	74	15
1987	1.21	5.06	17.9	33	20⅛
1988	1.43	5.26	14.2	34	19⅝
1989	1.63	6.23	15.4	34	25¼
1990	1.91	7.36	16.5	34	31⅜
1991	2.20	8.44	20.5	35	45⅜
1992	2.46	7.89	20.0	36	50⅞
1993	2.74	8.90	15.6	37	43

1984 to about 20 times earnings in the early 1990s. When the price of Johnson & Johnson shares dropped in 1993, the result was a lower PE ratio.

A high PE ratio indicates investor bullishness about a stock. Excessive optimism can lead to a price correction, both in a particular security and in the market as a whole. In early 1994, the median of estimated PE ratios of all stocks with earnings was 17.1. Shortly before the October 19, 1987, market collapse, the market hit a high on September 4. The PE ratio on that day was 16.9. On December 23, 1974, at the bottom of the 1973–1974 bear market, the PE ratio was 4.8! A high PE ratio may be a signal that a correction is near.

CREATING AN INCOME PORTFOLIO

To eliminate the risk that comes from having all your money in one stock, hold at least ten stocks in your investment portfolio. Seek the stocks of financially strong companies that have solid records of earnings growth and that are expected to continue to increase their earnings at above-average rates. Invest in companies whose share earnings have compounded at a minimum 10 percent annual rate in recent years and that can be expected to continue that performance.

For conservative investment portfolios, companies should exhibit characteristics of safety and good price stability.

Information on a number of top-quality companies that meet these criteria follows. As indicated earlier, many growth stocks that have had better past performance and appear to have brighter potential for the future are not included in this list because of their less-than-favorable financial positions or their volatile share price movements.

Following is a group of companies that fit the criteria many prudent investors would want for a small portfolio of growth stocks with low risk. The shares of these stocks are all traded on the NYSE.

Company	Ticker Symbol	1993 Percent of Profits Paid in Dividends	12/31/93 Price
Albertson's, Inc.	ABS	27%	26¾
American Cyanamid	ACY	39	50¼
American Home Products	AHP	60	25
American International Group	AIG	7	87¾
Bristol-Myers Squibb	BMY	65	58¼
Jefferson-Pilot Corp.	JP	35	46⅞
Johnson & Johnson	JNJ	37	44⅞
Merck & Company	MRK	43	34⅜
Sara Lee Corp.	SLE	43	25
Schering-Plough	SGP	42	68½
Warner-Lambert	WLA	48	67½

What the Companies Do

Albertson's, Inc. operates 655 retail grocery stores in 19 western and southern states. The store formats include some 235 combination food and drugstores with an average size of 58,000 square feet, 270 super-stores averaging 42,000 square feet, 105 conventional supermarkets averaging 27,000 square feet and 45 warehouse stores averaging about 40,000 square feet. The company operates ten full-line distribution centers that source 68 percent of the merchandise. The company is 40 percent unionized. (The company has about 75,000 employees and 14,700 shareholders.)

American Cyanamid Company manufactures pharmaceuticals, vaccines, health supplements and medical devices; herbicides, animal feed and veterinary products; and industrial chemicals and specialty chemicals. The company manufactures and distributes drugs through Lederle Laboratories. American Cyanamid operates 14 research laboratories and nearly 100 plants. The company merged with Praxis Biologics in November of 1989. Foreign operations account for about 40 percent of sales and 50 percent of profits. About 10.7 percent of sales is spent for research and development. (The company has about 32,800 employees and 43,400 shareholders.)

American Home Products Corporation is a leading manufacturer of prescription and ethical drugs, specialty foods and candies and proprietary drugs. Important brand names include Advil, Anacin, Ativan, Dimetapp, Inderal, Lodine, Norplant, Orudis, Premarin and Robitussin. The company acquired Sherwood Medical in 1982, A. H. Robins in 1989 and a 67 percent interest in Genetics Institute in 1993. International business accounts for about 32 percent of sales and 25 percent of operating income. About 6 percent of sales is spent on research and development. (The company has about 48,000 employees and 73,000 shareholders.)

American International Group, Inc., is a property and casualty insurance holding company. Domestic operations rank fourth in the United States based on premiums written. The company also sells individual and group life and health insurance and provides risk management and agency services. Foreign operations account for about 47 percent of total revenues. The company has more than $200 billion of life insurance in force. (The company has about 33,000 employees and 10,400 shareholders.)

Bristol-Myers Squibb Company manufactures proprietary medical products, ethical pharmaceuticals, diagnostics, infant formula, orthopedic implants, health and beauty aids. Important brand names include Ban, Bufferin, Buspar, Capoten, Clairol, Comtrex, Enfamil, Excedrin, Isovue, Monopril, Nuprin, Paraplatin, Pravachol, Taxol, VePesid and Videx. International operations account for about 34 percent of sales and 24 percent of operating profits. (The company has about 53,000 employees and 138,000 shareholders.)

Jefferson-Pilot Corporation is a holding company that owns Jefferson-Pilot Life, Jefferson-Pilot Communications, a title insurance company and two property and casualty insurance companies. Jefferson Standard and Pilot Life were merged to form Jefferson-Pilot Life in

1986. The communications subsidiaries include ten radio stations, two television stations and a broadcasting-services company. (The company has about 4,400 employees and 9,900 shareholders.)

Merck & Company, Inc., is a leading manufacturer of human and animal health-care products and specialty chemical products. Important brand names include Vasotec, Prinivil, Vevacor, Zocor, Primaxin, Mefoxin, Pepcid, Recombivax HB and Prilosec. Foreign operations account for about 46 percent of sales and 27 percent of pretax profits. The company spends about 11.5 percent of sales for research and development. For more complete information on Merck, see Chapter 10. (Merck has about 38,400 employees and 161,200 shareholders.)

Sara Lee Corporation (formerly Consolidated Foods) is a diversified international producer of consumer packaged goods with operations in coffee, specialty meats, frozen baked goods and food-service distribution. The food group brands include Douwe Egberts, Hillshire Farms, Jimmy Dean, Ball Park, Kahn's, Mr. Turkey and Sara Lee. The consumer products brands include Hanes, L'eggs, Kiwi, Aris, Bali, Champion, Isotoner, Playtex, Coach and Dim. Foreign operations account for about 35 percent of sales and 38 percent of pretax income. (The company has about 138,000 employees and 88,100 shareholders.)

Schering-Plough Corporation, formed by the January 1971 merger of Schering Corporation and Plough, Inc., is a worldwide manufacturer of prescription and over-the-counter drugs, animal health products, vision-care products, and sun-care and foot-care lines. Schering-Plough manufactures biotechnology products through 100 percent–owned DNAX Research Institute. Major brand names include Proventil, Vancenase, Afrin, Eulexin, Intron A, Scholl's and Coppertone. Foreign operations account for about 47 percent of sales. The company invests more than 12 percent of sales in research and development. (The company has about 21,100 employees and 32,200 shareholders.)

Warner-Lambert Company has three business divisions. Pharmaceutical products include Lopid, Dilantin and Accupril. This segment accounts for about 41 percent of sales and 62 percent of operating profits. Consumer division carries personal-care brands such as Halls, Listerine, Benadryl and Schick. This group accounts for about 21 percent of sales and 12 percent of operating profits. Confectionery products are mainly gums such as Trident, Chiclets and Dentyne; mints (Certs) and candy (Junior Mints). International operations account for about 50 percent of sales and 43 percent of profits. The company invests about 8.4 percent of sales in research and development. (Warner-Lamber has about 35,000 employees and 46,000 shareholders.)

SUMMARY

If you are seeking capital growth, you probably are more interested in the "total return" on your investment, rather than just the income you receive or price appreciation. In putting together a portfolio of stocks for growth, look at the performances of the largest medium-sized and even small-capitalization U.S. companies. Although the past does not necessarily repeat itself, you may receive some clues about who is likely to perform better. Select a portfolio of common stocks that have a history of consistent growth in earnings per share and are expected to maintain that pattern in the future.

CHAPTER 13

Investing for Growth— Aggressively

All investments involve risk. Aggressive investing generally means more risk. The important thing to remember is that the return you expect should correlate to the risk you expose yourself to. An investor willing to take on a higher degree of risk should expect a higher return on money invested. To properly manage your investment portfolio, decide in advance on the degree of risk you are prepared to accept.

The price sensitivity of a stock to market changes is measured by its *beta*. According to the *Value Line Investment Survey,* beta measures this sensitivity with values above and below 1.00. Any value above 1.00 indicates that a stock price tends to move more than the market. For instance, a stock with a beta of 1.10 tends to move 10 percent more than the market as a whole. A stock with a high beta can be expected to post larger-than-average declines when the market is falling and higher-than-average returns in a rising market. On the other hand, stocks with betas below 1.00 would tend to have price changes that fluctuate less than the general market. So low beta stocks typically realize below-average returns in a bull market and smaller-than-average declines during a bear market. A stock with a beta of 1.00 would be expected to have price changes that fluctuate about the same as the market.

The beta of stocks included in an aggressive growth portfolio are normally on the high side. For instance, the beta of Cardinal Health, Inc., is 1.15, so its price changes should fluctuate somewhat more than the market.

If your investment objective is capital appreciation and you want to pursue your objective aggressively, be prepared for a certain amount of risk. Diversify your portfolio into at least ten stocks to effectively eliminate company risk, the risk in owning just one stock. Following the recommended stock are a number of other highly regarded companies expected to perform well.

Cardinal Health, Inc., my recommended stock for growth in an aggressive portfolio., is a good example of a company of average financial strength that has performed very well over the past six years and that has a bright outlook.

★ Recommended Company

Cardinal Health, Inc.
655 Metro Place South
Dublin, Ohio 43017
614-761-8700

Chairman & CEO: Robert D. Walter
Number of shareholders: 1,200
Number of employees: 1,600
Where the stock trades: Nasdaq National Market
Symbol: CDIC
Beta: 1.15

What the Company Does
Cardinal Health, Inc., is the nation's third largest distributor of drugs, medical-surgical supplies and health and beauty aids to chain and independent drug stores, hospitals, clinics, mass merchandisers and supermarkets. The company operates 40 distribution centers, serving the entire continental United States. Cardinal acquired Marmac Distributors in 1988, Ohio Valley-Clarksburg in 1990, Chapman Drugs in 1991, Solomons in 1993, PRN Services in 1993 and Whitmire Distribution in 1994.

On January 27, 1994, the shareholders of Cardinal Distribution, Inc., voted to change its name to Cardinal Health, Inc. The merger of the company with Whitmire Distribution combined the strengths of two of the nation's leading superregional wholesale distributors. Cardinal Health estimates that total sales for the company will be about $6 billion in 1994.

Reason for Recommendation

Drug wholesaling remains a growth industry, expanding with the demographics of an aging population and increased consumption of pharmaceuticals. At the same time, demand for sophisticated services and some marginal pricing and excess capacity are driving a rapid consolidation in this industry. The industry that will emerge will be dominated by a handful of players that are leaner and larger in scale. Cardinal is building a market presence to solidify its role as an industry leader. The company is investing in innovative distribution technologies, information systems and marketing programs to further strengthen the services it offers to customer and vendor partners.

With the merger, Cardinal became the third largest distributor of drugs, medical-surgical supplies and health and beauty aids in the country, with annualized revenues exceeding $2 billion. Shareholders of Whitmire received about 8.4 million shares of Cardinal common stock in the deal. Despite the dilution, analysts believe that Cardinal per-share earnings should continue to climb.

Known for its commitment to making only nondilutive acquisitions, Cardinal already has seen synergies from the deal—new supply contracts with major hospital and managed-care customers. The company now has a national distribution system and additional agreements are expected to be signed. Also, benefits from classic efficiencies, such as eliminating of redundant sales, marketing, purchasing and operating expenses, should become increasingly noticed. Analysts expect per-share net earnings to continue a growth pattern of 20 percent per year in the near future.

With health-care reform in the offing, positive long-term industry trends are likely to benefit Cardinal's operations. Drug distributors are among the more efficient links in the system and stand to see additional business as costs are held to a minimum. Cardinal, with its recently improved competitive position, is likely to thrive on the increased business. Cardinal's recent purchase of PRN Services, the leading distributor of pharmaceuticals and medical supplies to oncologists and oncology clinics, should bolster Cardinal's presence in the lucrative alternative-care market, further assisting earnings growth in the years ahead.

FIGURE 13.1 Results of a $10,000 Investment in Cardinal Health, Inc., Common Stock Made in 1984

	Average Share Price	Annual Dividends	Value of Shares Owned	Total # Shares Owned
1984	5⅜	$ 37	$10,035	1,867
1985	6	56	11,256	1,876
1986	8½	56	15,997	1,882
1987	7½	75	14,940	1,992
1988	7⅛	79	14,342	2,013
1989	12	100	24,252	2,021
1990	17⅞	121	36,233	2,027
1991	29⅜	202	59,749	2,034
1992	28⅞	183	58,905	2,040
1993	36⅜	224	74,423	2,046

The common stock of Cardinal Health, Inc., seems to make sense for most investors. The Whitmire merger will be a strong help to future earnings, and Cardinal's strategy of external expansion through acquisitions should further its long-term growth.

Since 1984, Cardinal Health has been in a strong growth trend, with sales growing steadily from $320 million to some $3 billion in 1993. Earnings have grown from $3.7 million in 1984 to about $40 million in 1993, with per-share earnings going from $ .39 to $1.85.

Results of a $10,000 Investment

The share price of Cardinal Health, Inc., stock has moved generally upward since 1984, growing from an average price of 5⅜ in 1984 to 46⅛ in 1993. Prices have been adjusted to account for stock splits in 1990 and 1991 and 10 percent stock dividends each year from 1985 to 1988. The company has paid cash dividends to shareholders each year since 1983.

Figure 13.1 shows the ten-year results of a $10,000 investment in Cardinal Health, Inc., common stock from 1984 to 1993. It is assumed that the stock was purchased at the average of the high and low prices in 1984. A $10,000 investment would have purchased 1,860 shares in that year. Brokerage commissions are not considered.

The December 31, 1993, closing price of Cardinal Health, Inc., on the Nasdaq National Market was 47½. The value of the original 1984 $10,000 investment on that date was $97,185.

FIGURE 13.2   Per-Share Financial Results of Cardinal Health, Inc., From 1984 to 1993

	Earnings Per Share	Book Value	Sales	Average Price Per Share	Average PE Ratio
1984	$ .39	$ 3.40	$ 30.43	5⅜	13.8
1985	.36	3.96	40.80	6	16.7
1986	.38	4.43	61.91	8½	22.4
1987	.43	5.01	48.65	7½	17.4
1988	.65	6.19	63.92	7 ⅛	10.9
1989	.79	7.54	52.70	12	15.2
1990	1.01	10.28	62.98	17⅞	17.7
1991	1.26	11.66	87.59	29⅜	23.3
1992	1.53	13.38	102.93	28⅞	18.8
1993	1.85	11.35	95.25	36⅜	19.6

Historical Financial Data

Cardinal Health, Inc., has delivered a solid record of growth. From total sales of $320 million in 1984, the company's sales grew to nearly $1.2 billion in 1990 and about $3 billion in 1993. After the merger with Whitmire Distribution Corporation in early 1994, sales in that year were estimated to rise to approximately $6 billion. The company's earnings per share have moved steadily ahead, from $ .39 in 1984 to an estimated $1.85 in 1993 (see Figure 13.2). The fiscal year ends on December 31.

Over the past ten years, the PE ratio has fluctuated between a low of about 11 times earnings to as high as just more than 23 times earnings, a reflection of changing investor confidence about the future earnings growth of the company. Except for a dip in 1985, earnings per share have shown steady growth. Acquisitions in 1993 diluted share values, which caused the drop in per-share book value in 1993.

Common Stock Quarterly Price Record

Here are the high and low prices of Cardinal Health, Inc., common stock during the fiscal years ending March 31, 1992, and 1993:

	1st Quarter	2nd Quarter	3rd Quarter	4th Quarter
1992				
Low	$27.60	$30.60	$23.00	$26.25
High	33.20	38.00	38.50	34.00
1993				
Low	24.75	27.00	25.25	24.50
High	30.00	32.25	30.25	29.75

In every quarterly period, a patient investor could purchase shares of Cardinal at prices well below the high of the prior quarter, particularly in the third and fourth quarters of 1992, as well as in the third and fourth quarters of 1993. Note: Because the company's fiscal year ends on March 31, share prices for the final nine months of calendar year 1993 are not shown in this chart.

CREATING A PORTFOLIO FOR AGGRESSIVE GROWTH

To eliminate the risk from having all your money in one stock, hold at least ten stocks in your aggressive growth portfolio. Seek stocks of companies that have solid records of earnings growth and that are expected to continue to increase their earnings at above-average rates. Invest in companies whose share earnings have compounded at a minimum 10 percent annual rate in recent years and can be expected to continue that performance.

For most aggressive investors building a portfolio of stocks for growth, dividend income is a secondary consideration. In many cases, it is in the best interest of shareholders for companies to reinvest their earnings back into the business to help finance future growth. Many rapidly expanding companies pay little or no dividends. Because the share-price movement of such companies can be quite volatile, you should carefully consider the amount of risk you are able to tolerate. Diversifying your assets into the shares of a number of companies helps to reduce your risk exposure.

Following is a group of other companies that fit the criteria many investors look for in establishing a portfolio of aggressive growth stocks with good potential for the future. These stocks trade on the NYSE, the AMEX or OTC.

Company	Exchange and Symbol	Earnings Growth in Past 5 Years	Beta	Yield	12/31/93 Price
ADC Telecommunications	OTC/ADCT	82%	0.95	Nil	35⅝
Airgas, Inc.	NYSE/ARG	275	1.20	Nil	21¾
Andrew Corp.	OTC/ANDW	101	1.00	Nil	38½.
Applied Materials	OTC/AMAT	57	1.65	Nil	38¾
Brinker International	NYSE/EAT	158	1.35	Nil	46
Computer Associates	NYSE/CA	159	1.55	0.4	40
Forest Labs	AMEX/FRX	139	1.25	Nil	47⅝
Green Tree	NYSE/GNT	311	1.65	0.8	48
HealthCare COMPARE	OTC/HCCC	816	1.55	Nil	24⅝
Omnicare, Inc.	NYSE/OCR	372	1.15	0.6	32
Oracle Systems	OTC/ORCL	74	1.50	Nil	28¾

What the Companies Do

ADC Telecommunications, Inc., designs, manufactures and markets a wide variety of communications products for telephone companies and large private networks. The Cable Management division, which produces jacks, plugs, cross-connects, etc., accounts for some 54 percent of total sales. Transmission products contribute about 19 percent of sales; networking about 27 percent. More than half of sales are to telecommunications companies. Private companies account for 26 percent of sales; international sales, 16 percent; and the government, about 6 percent. (The company has about 2,300 employees and 1,600 shareholders.)

Airgas, Inc., is the largest independent distributor of industrial, medical, and specialty gases in the United States. The company also is involved in the manufacture of carbon products and nitrous oxide, and calcium carbide. Distribution comprises about 93 percent of revenues. The company has a network of more than 300 distributors in 36 states and Canada. (The company has about 2,800 employees and 4,100 shareholders.)

Andrew Corporation is a major worldwide supplier of electronic communications products and systems. The Commercial Products division makes microwave, cellular and satellite station antennas, towers and coaxial cable. This division accounts for more than

70 percent of company sales. The Government Products division provides radar and navigational systems for defense and other markets and accounts for 15 percent of sales. Network Products designs and develops image processors, interfaces and converters for communication, with 13 percent of sales. Foreign sales make up 38 percent of the total. The company invests about 5 percent of sales in research and development. (The company has about 3,000 employees and 1,050 shareholders.)

Applied Materials, Inc., is a major producer of wafer fabrication equipment for semiconductor makers. Product areas include chemical and physical vapor deposition, used to layer conducting or insulating films on silicon wafers; epitaxy, used to form a pure silicon layer on which circuits are constructed; etch, used to inscribe circuits on wafers; and ion implantation, used to alter conductivity of wafer regions. Foreign sales account for more than 60 percent of the total. The company invests about 13 percent of sales in research and development. (The company has about 4,500 employees and 990 shareholders.)

Brinker International operates company-owned and franchised restaurants. Chili's Grill & Bar restaurants feature a limited menu of broadly appealing food and a full-service bar in a casual atmosphere. The company also operates Grady's American Grill, a casual, upscale dinner house; and Romano's Macaroni Grill, an upscale Italian theme restaurant. There are about 200 company-owned and 58 franchised Chili's, 17 Grady's and 13 Macaroni Grills. (The company has about 28,000 employees and 1,245 shareholders.)

Computer Associates International, Inc., produces software that enables computers to run more efficiently. The company develops, markets and services more than 300 software products for IBM-compatible mainframes, minicomputers, and microcomputers. The company acquired Software International Corporation and Integrated Software Systems Corporation in 1986, UCCEL Corporation in 1987, Applied Data Research in 1988 and Cullinet Software, Inc., in 1989. (The company has 7,200 employees and 10,000 shareholders.)

Forest Laboratories, Inc., manufactures ethical and nonprescription drugs used mainly for treating pain and cardiovascular and respiratory disorders. Important products include Aerobid inhalent for asthma, Flumadine flu medicine, Levothroid thyroid hormone replacement and Tessalon cough suppressant. The company also manufactures generic drugs based on controlled-release dosage technology. Business in the

United Kingdom accounts for about 11 percent of sales and 8 percent of profits. (The company has about 1,170 employees and 3,450 shareholders.)

Green Tree Financial Corporation purchases, pools, sells and services conditional sales contracts for purchasers of manufactured housing. FHA- and VA-backed mortgages, which account for about 40 percent of the total, are converted into certificates guaranteed by the Government National Mortgage Association (GNMA). The company also provides home-improvement financing, contract-related insurance, and motorcycle financing. The company operates 42 regular service centers and conducts business in 48 states. (The company has about 1,200 employees and 360 shareholders.)

HealthCare COMPARE Corporation is an independent provider of medical cost management services and provides comprehensive managed-care programs. The company acquired AFFORDABLE Health Care Concepts in 1988 and merged with Occupational-Urgent Care Health Systems, Inc., in 1992. (The company has about 1,400 employees and 1,200 shareholders.)

Omnicare, Inc., provides pharmacy management services and drug therapy to nursing homes via its Sequoia Pharmacy Services Group. The company has more than 70,000 beds under contract in nine states. (The company has about 1,100 employees and 1,250 shareholders.)

Because the company sold a number of subsidiary companies in 1989, 1990 and 1992, total sales have shown a decline over the past five years. Sales increased sharply in 1993.

Oracle Systems Corporation is the world's largest producer of database management systems (DBMS), software that permits users to create, retrieve and manipulate data in computer-based files. The company's main products support ORACLE, a related DBMS, which lets people manipulate and retrieve data by requesting it, using an industry-standard, command language, SQL. License fees contribute 60 percent of total revenues, with training and services accounting for the other 40 percent. Foreign sales are about 62 percent of the total, contributing 34 percent of profits. The company invests about 9.5 percent of sales in research and development. (The company has about 9,250 employees and 2,500 shareholders.)

SUMMARY

All investments involve risk. Aggressive investing generally means more risk. The important thing to remember is that the return you expect should correlate to the risk you take. If you take on a higher degree of risk, expect a higher return on your money. To properly manage your investment portfolio, decide in advance the degree of risk you are prepared to accept.

If your investment objective is capital appreciation, you probably are more interested in the "total return" on your investment, rather than just the income you receive or price appreciation. For a portfolio of aggressive growth stocks, review the historical record of different categories of stocks. For instance, you may be more likely to find success by investing in a group of medium- or small-capitalization stocks than by investing in giant, established companies.

CHAPTER 14

Investing in Foreign Companies

The U.S. market now accounts for about only a third of the world's total stock market value. So if you restrict yourself to that market, you ignore the growth potential of the other two-thirds, located mainly in Europe and Asia. An individual investor easily can buy shares in many companies headquartered outside the United States without dealing directly with foreign exchanges.

Investors seeking foreign-domiciled company investments can buy *American depositary receipts* (ADRs) in U.S. markets, instead of buying shares in overseas markets. ADRs are traded on the NYSE, the AMEX and the OTC market. They also are called *American depositary shares*.

ADRs, invented in 1927 by J. P. Morgan, are receipts for the shares of foreign-based corporations, and they are held in American bank vaults. Three American banks—the Bank of New York, Citibank and J. P. Morgan—are the major depository institutions for ADRs. They provide custody of the foreign shares, change dividends into dollars and help distribute company reports.

The owner of an ADR in the United States is entitled to the same dividends and capital gains accruing to a shareholder who purchases shares on an exchange in the home country of the company. Each ADR represents a specified number of common shares of the company it represents. Quoted prices reflect the latest currency exchange rates, for

ADRs are denominated in U.S. dollars. Prices of ADRs are reported in the stock listings of *The New York Times, The Wall Street Journal* and other newspapers, as well as in electronic databases.

Foreign corporations with ADRs normally are well-established and financially stable companies with worldwide operations. In many cases, you will be familiar with them because their products and services are offered in the United States. Altogether, some 1,000 ADRs are traded on American exchanges, with 10 to 15 new ADRs added each month. More than 250 trade on the NYSE and the AMEX, with the largest number listed on the AMEX. For a complete list of ADRs and how they work, see *The McGraw-Hill Handbook of American Depository Receipts,* McGraw-Hill, Monterey Ave., Blue Ridge Summit, PA 17294; 800-233-1128.

ADRS WITH POTENTIAL FOR GROWTH

In selecting shares of foreign corporations, evaluate ADRs the same way you would shares of U.S. companies. Consider such issues as your personal investment objective, the relative safety of the company and whether the timing is right in terms of the particular industry and company. If you own mutual funds, a simple way to see what the pros are buying is to check your mutual fund report and see what its largest international holdings are.

One industry that appears to give investors in ADRs potential for long-term capital appreciation in the 1990s is *telecommunications*. A telecommunications company that exhibits the relative safety and timeliness that prudent investors look for is highlighted in this chapter.

★ *Recommended Company*

Hong Kong Telecommunications, Ltd.
U.S. address:
777 Third Avenue
New York, NY 10017
212-593-4813

Chairman: Lord Young
Where ADRs trade: NYSE
Symbol: HKT

Number of shareholders: 25,439
Number of employees: 15,888

Hong Kong Telecommunications, Ltd., was formed in 1987 when Hong Kong Telephone Company and a subsidiary of Cable & Wireless Company merged. In December of 1988, a global offering of 877.5 million shares took place. Of these, slightly more than 6 million ADRs were sold in the United States at $17.50 per ADR. They then were listed on the NYSE. Each ADR represents 30 common shares.

What the Company Does
With total revenues in excess of $3 billion, Hong Kong Telecommunications has exclusive franchises for local telecommunications services in Hong Kong through 1995 and international services through 2006. International calls represent about 63 percent of revenues; local calls and other telecommunications account for 27 percent and equipment sales and other services, the other 10 percent.

Overview
The company has continued to post double-digit profit gains. Because of its dynamic economy and strategic location, Hong Kong's telephone usage is high. The territory has more lines, both conventional and cellular, per capita than the United States. Over the most recent five-year period, Hong Kong Telecommunications's earnings grew at more than 20 percent annual compound rate. Analysts project similar results for the near future.

Buying Hong Kong Telecommunications ADRs is a way to participate in the China market. The economic statistics for China are impressive; the economy grew at more than 10 percent yearly in the early 1990s. The company's business with China jumped more than 34 percent in fiscal 1992 and accounted for 30 percent of its international revenues and most of its profits.

Hong Kong Telecommunications completed the world's first 100 percent digital system. Measured in lines per employee, productivity has steadily improved as the company automated its system. Digital central office switches increase the company's reliability and allow revenue-enhancing services to be added at little additional cost.

The company has been forced to cut the price of its overseas calls, it main revenue source, because of changes in Hong Kong's telecommunicating rate structure. Higher volume is expected to make up for the reductions.

FIGURE 14.1 Selected Financial Data for Hong Kong
Telecommunications ADRs

	Revenues (Millions)	Net Profit (Millions)	Net Profit Margin	Per ADR Earnings	Dividends
1988	$1,516	$425	28.0%	$1.15	$ .87
1989	1,812	509	28.1	1.37	1.08
1990	2,085	678	32.5	1.82	1.27
1991	2,355	694	29.5	1.87	1.46
1992	2,775	841	30.3	2.26	1.67
1993	3,113	929	29.9	2.49	1.95

Figure 14.1 presents selected financial data for Hong Kong Telecommunications for the years 1988 to 1993.

Profit Opportunities in Hong Kong Telecommunications ADRs
Since their initial listing on the NYSE in December of 1988, the Hong Kong Telecommunications ADRs have consistently moved upward from the 1988 low of 18¼ to a high of 67⅞ in 1993. Buying opportunities have been available each year as the ADRs backed off from new highs reached over the intervening years.

Common Stock Quarterly Price Record
Following are the high and low prices of Hong Kong Telecommunications ADRs during the fiscal years ending March 31, 1992, and 1993:

	1st Quarter	2nd Quarter	3rd Quarter	4th Quarter
1992				
Low	23¾	25	28⅞	30
High	26¼	28¾	32¾	34
1993				
Low	32⅛	31⅛	30⅝	36
High	40⅜	35⅜	38¾	40½

The market price of the Hong Kong Telecommunications ADRs moved up steadily during the 1992 fiscal year, with few opportunities to buy at prices lower than had already been attained, except in the fourth quarter. The 1993 fiscal year saw a more normal pattern, as investors had the chance to buy ADRs at much lower prices than in the prior quarters, especially in the second and third quarters.

Hong Kong Telecommunications ADRs remain an interesting investment choice for investors seeking representation in foreign-based companies. The shares have shown positive earnings and price momentum, although recent price levels seem to fully anticipate discount projected earnings growth for the next two to three years, limiting long-term capital appreciation.

OTHER FOREIGN TELECOMMUNICATIONS COMPANIES

ADRs are traded for a number of other foreign companies in the telecommunications industry. Some of the better known companies are listed as follows, with their countries of domicile and the exchanges on which they trade.

Company	Home Country	Exchange Where ADRs Trade
Alcatel Alsthom	France	NYSE
British Telecommunications PLC	England	NYSE
Cable & Wireless PLC	England	NYSE
Ericsson Telephone AB	Sweden	OTC
Reuters Holdings PLC	England	OTC
Telecom Corporation of New Zealand, Ltd.	New Zealand	NYSE
Telefonica de Espana, S.A.	Spain	NYSE
Compania de Telefonos de Chile, S.A.	Chile	NYSE
Telefonos de Mexico, S.A.	Mexico	NYSE
Vodafone Group PLC	England	NYSE

THE ADR UNIVERSE

If you are interested in an in-depth exploration of foreign equities that are available in ADRs, take a three-month trial subscription to *Morningstar American Depositary Receipts* 800-876-5005 for $35. This publication lets you compare 700 foreign equities using single-page profiles complete with written analyses and detailed statistics. All financial data are calculated in U.S. dollars. The biweekly service covers foreign companies in more than 30 countries, including Japan, Canada and countries in Western Europe and emerging markets.

SUMMARY

Today, two-thirds of the world's total stock market value is represented by companies located in foreign countries, mainly Europe and Asia. To participate in the potential international economic growth, do not overlook this huge arena. You can avoid dealing directly with foreign exchanges by purchasing ADRs in U.S. markets. These ADRs entitle you to the same dividends and capital gains accruing to a shareholder who buys shares on an exchange in the home country of the company.

CHAPTER 15

Buying Stocks with Low PE Ratios

Price-earnings (PE) ratios are a favorite measure for many value stock investors who are looking for stocks that they believe the market has undervalued.

As we saw in Chapter 3, we find a stock's PE ratio by dividing the price by its earnings per share. The PE ratio may use either the reported earnings from the latest year (called the *trailing PE*) or an analyst's forecast of next year's earnings (called a *forward PE*). For example, a stock selling for $50 a share that earned $2.50 the past year has a trailing PE of 20. If the same stock has projected earnings of $5 next year, it will have a forward PE of 10. Some observers use a combination of these two standards, such as actual earnings for the past six months and anticipated earnings for the next six months. Daily newspapers list the trailing PE along with a stock's price and trading activity.

Also known as the *multiple,* the PE ratio gives investors an idea of how much they are paying for a company's earning power. The higher the PE, the more investors are paying, and so the more earnings growth they are anticipating. Stocks with PEs over 20 generally are young, fast-growing companies. They tend to be more risky to purchase than low PE stocks, because it is easier for a company to fail to achieve high-growth expectations than low-growth predictions. Low PE stocks usually are found in low-growth or mature industries, in stock groups that have fallen out of favor or in old, established blue-chip companies with long records of earnings stability and regular dividends. Often, low PE stocks have higher yields than high PE stocks, which typically pay no dividends at all.

According to the *Value Line Investment Survey* on April 1, 1994, the median estimated PE ratio of all stocks with earnings (in their universe of 1,700 companies) was 16.5. Interestingly, the median PE ratio of all stocks at the market high on September 4, 1987, was 16.9. At the market low, occurring on December 23, 1974, the median PE ratio was 4.8. *Value Line* uses the trailing six-months earnings and the expected prospective six-months earnings in computing its PE ratios. The relatively high multiple in place on April 1, 1994, would be expected to decline. The decline can result from a drop in stock prices, an increase in company earnings or a combination of the two.

This chapter focuses on companies with earnings multiples under ten that analysts believe have good potential for continued growth and have better-than-average financial strength. My recommended stock is Raymond James Financial, Inc., a Florida-based financial services holding company. Additional information is provided on other low-PE ratio companies with good earnings potential and financial stability.

★ *Recommended Company*

Raymond James Financial, Inc.
880 Carillon Parkway
St. Petersburg, FL 33716
813-573-3800

Chairman and CEO: Thomas A. James
Number of shareholders: 6,000
Number of employees: 3,800
Where the stock trades: NYSE
Symbol: RJF

What the Company Does
Raymond James Financial, Inc., is a diversified holding company that provides financial services throughout the United States and Europe to individuals, corporations, government bodies and employee benefit plans through its wholly owned investment firms of Raymond James & Associates, Investment Management & Research and Robert Thomas Securities. In addition to traditional broker-dealer financial services, the firm's investment advisory affiliates—Eagle Asset Man-

agement, Heritage Asset Management, Focus Investment Advisors, Awad & Associates, Raymond James Trust Company, RJ Leasing, RJ Credit Partners, RJ Properties and Raymond James Realty Advisors—professionally manage in excess of $8.5 billion in client assets.

Incorporated in 1974, the company had its initial public offering on July 1, 1983. The initial share price was $3.29 each, after adjustment for two stock dividends and three stock splits. The stock has been listed on the NYSE since 1986.

Comments

In its 1993 fiscal year, consistent with a record performance by the securities industry, Raymond James Financial attained new records in revenues and net income. Raymond James had its fifth consecutive year of record results. During the five-year period, the company's revenues and net income grew at compound rates of 22 percent and 53 percent, respectively, while their after-tax rate of return on average equity was 24 percent. Revenues in 1993 increased 25 percent to $451 million and net income was $49 million, a 20 percent improvement over the prior year.

Taking advantage of the favorable operating climate, Raymond James Financial recently nearly doubled the size of its headquarters, added two new members to its family of mutual funds and equipped its sales associates with the faster personal computers available for office use. Analysts estimate that per-share net profit can improve from $2.28 in 1993 to $2.50 in fiscal 1994 and $3.00 in 1995.

The company's very successful core business has permitted diversification into new ventures. In one such move, Raymond James made a leveraged purchase of a $42 million Boeing 757 aircraft using $8 million in cash and leased it to Delta Airlines. The plane offers the benefit of a tax shelter through depreciation, making superior returns possible over its seven-year tax life. Also, earnings volatility should be somewhat lower by acquiring a source of income outside the stock market.

Analysts believe Raymond James stock offers good potential for appreciation in the next several years. The company has strong earnings momentum, although Wall Street recently has been less bullish on the shares of brokerage firms. However, the stock should be a good investment for long-term investors seeking capital growth. Over the five-year period through 1993, the stock has been trading at an average PE ratio of between six and seven.

FIGURE 15.1   Results of a $10,000 Investment in Raymond James
Financial, Inc., Common Stock Made in 1984 with
Dividends Reinvested

	Average Share Price	Annual Dividends	Value of Shares Owned	Total # Shares Owned
1984	2	Nil	$10,000	5,000
1985	2⅜	$ 100	11,975	5,042
1986	4¼	201	21,624	5,089
1987	5⅛	254	26,332	5,138
1988	3¼	256	16,955	5,217
1989	4⅜	313	23,135	5,288
1990	5½	370	29,452	5,355
1991	9½	535	51,404	5,411
1992	14¾	865	80,667	5,469
1993	16⅞	1,148	93,436	5,537

Results of a $10,000 Investment

Raymond James Financial, Inc., share prices have moved generally upward since its low in 1984, growing from an average price of 2 in 1984 to 16⅞ in 1993. Those prices have been adjusted to account for three-for-two stock splits in 1991, 1992 and 1993, as well as 10 percent stock dividends in 1985 and 1987. The company has paid cash dividends to stockholders each year since 1985.

Figure 15.1 shows the ten-year results of a $10,000 investment in Raymond James Financial common stock from 1984 to 1993. It is assumed that the stock was purchased at the average of the high and low prices in 1984 and that dividends have been applied to the purchase of additional shares. The company typically has paid out around 10 percent of net profits in dividends to stockholders. A $10,000 investment would have purchased 5,000 shares in 1984 (adjusted). Brokerage commissions are not considered.

The December 31, 1993, closing price of Raymond James Financial, Inc., on the NYSE was 16⅝. The value of the original 1984 $10,000 investment on that date, with dividends reinvested in additional shares, was $92,052.

Historical Financial Data

Raymond James Financial has produced a solid record of growth in both revenues and earnings since its IPO in 1983. Total revenues have risen from $70.6 million in 1983 to more than $451.7 million in 1993.

FIGURE 15.2   Per-Share Financial Results of Raymond James Financial, Inc., from 1984 to 1993

	Earnings Per Share	Book Value	Sales	Average Price Per Share	Average PE Ratio
1984	$ .12	$1.88	$ 4.21	2	16.6
1985	.29	2.16	5.45	2⅜	8.2
1986	.38	2.84	7.69	4¼	11.2
1987	.45	3.13	8.25	5⅛	11.4
1988	.28	3.22	9.18	3¼	11.6
1989	.59	3.80	12.02	4⅜	7.4
1990	.84	4.68	12.42	5½	6.5
1991	1.25	5.85	13.71	9½	7.6
1992	1.89	7.58	17.01	14¾	7.8
1993	2.28	9.64	21.62	16⅞	7.4

Net profits grew from $5.1 million in 1983 to $49.3 million in 1993. There were some setbacks along the way. Both sales and earnings dropped in 1984 from the prior year, and earnings also dropped in 1988 from the previous year.

Shareholders have seen earnings per share move up from a low of $.12 in 1984 to $2.28 in 1993. (See Figure 15.2.) Over the same period, book value has gone up from $1.88 per share in 1984 to $9.64 per share in 1993.

Over the past ten years, the PE ratio has fluctuated between a low of 6.5 times earnings to as high as 16.6 times earnings, a reflection of changing investor confidence about the future earnings growth of the company. Except for a dip in 1988, earnings per share have shown steady growth.

Common Stock Quarterly Price Record

Following are the high and low prices of Raymond James Financial, Inc., common stock during the 1992 and 1993 fiscal years, adjusted for three-for-two stock splits in 1992 and 1993:

	1st Quarter	2nd Quarter	3rd Quarter	4th Quarter
1992				
High	14¼	19⅝	18⅜	14⅜
Low	9¾	13½	11⅜	11⅜
1993				
High	15⅝	18⅞	16⅞	19⅜
Low	11½	14⅞	15⅛	15

This chart illustrates that patience can pay off in buying shares of stock. In every quarter during 1992 and 1993, it was possible to buy shares at a price below the high price of the previous quarter. In most cases, the opportunities for lower prices were dramatic.

CREATING A PORTFOLIO OF STOCKS WITH LOW PE RATIOS

If you decide to build a portfolio of stocks with low PE ratios, reduce risk by owning at least ten stocks. Seek out the stocks of companies with PEs under ten that have solid records of earnings growth and are expected to continue to increase their earnings in the future.

Following is a list of companies with PE multiples of less than ten that analysts believe have potential for future earnings growth and are above average in financial strength. Per-share information has been adjusted for any stock splits and stock dividends. These stocks trade on the NYSE or on the AMEX.

Company	Exchange and Symbol	Approximate PE Ratio	April 5, 1994 Price	Yield
Alex. Brown	NYSE/AB	4	24¾	2.4%
Bankers Trust NY	NYSE/BT	6	69½	5.2
Bear Stearns	NYSE/BSC	5	19⅝	3.1
Chrysler Corporation	NYSE/C	8	54½	1.5
Citicorp	NYSE/CCI	8	38¼	Nil
Conseco, Inc.	NYSE/CNC	5	53½	.9
Edwards (A. G.)	NYSE/AGE	7	17½	3.2
Holly Corporation	AMEX/HOC	8	27½	1.5
Legg Mason	NYSE/LM	7	21⅛	1.9
Lincoln National Corp.	NYSE	9	39	4.2
Merrill Lynch & Co.	NYSE/MER	6	37¼	2.1

Telephonos de Mexico ADR	NYSE/TMX	9	57¾	2.6
Travelers, Inc.	NYSE/TRV	9	35⅜	1.4

What the Companies Do

Alex. Brown, Inc., is a financial services holding company. Its primary subsidiary is Alex. Brown & Sons, Inc., a major investment banking and securities brokerage firm. The company engages in retail and institutional brokerage, investment banking services to municipal and corporate clients, real estate advisory services, market making and trading of securities, and research services. Alex. Brown has 21 offices in 12 states and the District of Columbia, plus representative offices in London and Geneva. (The company has 1,880 employees and 1,200 shareholders.)

Its IPO in 1986 was $23 per share. A three-for-two stock split occurred in 1987.

Per-Share Financial Summary

	1986	1993
Revenues	$17.89	$40.90
Earnings	1.59	5.61
Dividends	.07	.55
Average Stock Price	16	25⅛

Bankers Trust New York Corporation owns Bankers Trust, the eighth largest banking company in the United States based on assets. Bankers Trust concentrates on wholesale banking, having sold its retail business in the early 1980s. International operations account for more than 50 percent of pretax income. Its employees cost about 24 percent of gross income. (The company has about 12,600 employees and more than 25,000 common shareholders.)

Bankers Trust NY has total assets in excess of $94 billion, more than double its assets of $45 billion in 1984. There were two-for-one stock splits in 1981 and 1985.

Per-Share Financial Summary

	1984	1993
Earnings	4.24	12.40
Dividends	1.26	3.24
Average Stock Price	24	74⅝

The Bear Stearns Companies, Inc., is a holding company whose main subsidiary is Bear, Stearns & Company, Inc., an investment banking, securities trading and brokerage firm. Bear Stearns is one of the largest U.S. dealers in fixed-income securities. It is designated a "primary dealer" by the Federal Reserve Bank of New York. The company also is engaged in specialist and security clearance activities. Employee costs are about 34 percent of total revenues. The firm has offices in New York, six regional offices in the United States and seven offices in Europe and the Far East. (The company has about 6,300 employees and 3,000 shareholders.)

The Bear Stearns Companies, Inc., had its initial public stock offering in October of 1985 at $8 per share adjusted for a 3-for-2 stock split in 1986.

Per-Share Financial Summary

	1985	1993
Revenues	$16.18	$23.71
Earnings	.90	2.86
Dividends	.11	.53
Average Stock Price	8⅛	19½

Chrysler Corporation is the third largest automobile and truck manufacturer in the United States. Principal divisions produce Plymouth, Dodge and Chrysler cars and Dodge trucks. The company also produces automotive parts and accessories, and defense-related products, primarily for the U.S. Government. Chrysler imports and sells Mitsubishi cars. It acquired American Motors Corporation in 1987. (The company has about 128,000 employees and 202,000 shareholders.)

Per-Share Financial Summary

	1984	1993
Revenues	$71.61	$122.80
Earnings	5.22	6.67
Dividends	.38	.60
Average Stock Price	12¼	45⅛

Citicorp, the largest banking company in the United States, owns Citibank, N.A. The company has more than 3,500 locations in 32 states, the District of Columbia and 92 foreign countries. Total assets in 1993 totaled more than $216 billion. (The company has about 81,000 employees and 64,000 shareholders.)

Per-Share Financial Summary

	1984	1993
Earnings	$3.23	3.53
Dividends	1.03	Nil
Average Stock Price	17	30¼

Conseco, Inc., is mainly engaged in the acquisition and operation of life insurance companies. The company concentrates on investment-oriented, long-term savings products. Single premium deferred annuities account for more than 71 percent of premiums collected, with flexible premium deferred annuities producing 10 percent, single premium immediate annuities contribute 6 percent, universal life 3 percent and other products 10 percent. (The company has about 1,100 employees and 950 shareholders.)

The company had its initial public offering of stock in November of 1985 at $1.75 per share (adjusted for splits in 1991 and 1992).

Per-Share Financial Summary

	1985	1993
Earnings	$.13	$6.64
Dividends	Nil	.19
Average Stock Price	1⅞	60⅛

A. G. Edwards, Inc., is a holding company whose principal broker-dealer subsidiary was founded as a partnership in 1887, was incorporated in 1967 and went public in 1971. It is a member of all leading securities and commodities exchanges. Commissions account for about 55 percent of revenues. The company has more than one million clients, and has 475 offices in 48 states and the District of Columbia. (The company has about 9,500 employees and 14,000 shareholders.)

Stock splits occurred in 1981, 1983, 1986, 1991, 1992 and 1994.

Per-Share Financial Summary

	1984	1993
Revenues	$5.86	$21.16
Earnings	.50	2.57
Dividends	.21	.46
Average Stock Price	6⅛	21¾

Holly Corporation is a refiner and marketer of petroleum products. The chief markets for its 60,000-barrel-per-day refinery are Arizona, New Mexico and Texas. Major products are gasoline, 54 percent of sales; jet fuel, 10 percent; diesel fuel, 24 percent; asphalt, 8 percent; and other products, 4 percent. (The company has about 500 employees and 2,100 shareholders.)

Stock splits occurred in 1985 and 1988.

Per-Share Financial Summary

	1984	1993
Revenues	$53.43	$76.41
Earnings	.21	2.42
Dividends	.12	.30
Average Stock Price	5	27⅞

Legg Mason, Inc., is a financial services holding company. Its main subsidiary is Legg Mason Wood Walker, a regional securities broker-dealer and investment banking firm. The company acquired Western Asset Management Company, Warren W. York & Company and Howard Weil Financial Corporation in 1986. It later acquired Latimer and Buck in 1990 and Dorman and Wilson in 1991. (The company has 2,440 employees and 1,350 shareholders.)

There were stock splits in 1986 and 1993 and a stock dividend in 1985.

Per-Share Financial Summary

	1984	1993
Revenues	$10.17	$33.88
Earnings	.41	2.98
Dividends	.12	.32
Average Stock Price	6⅝	22⅜

Lincoln National Corporation is a holding company with operations in individual and group life/health insurance, property/casualty insurance, reinsurance and pension management. Individual life and annuity accounts for 26 percent of business; health, 35 percent; and property/casualty, 39 percent. (The company has about 15,700 employees and 14,850 shareholders.)

The stock was split in 1983 and 1993.

Per-Share Financial Summary

	1984	1993
Revenues	$27.97	$37.33
Earnings	1.86	4.06
Dividends	.86	1.55
Average Stock Price	16⅞	41½

Merrill Lynch & Company, Inc., a holding company, controls one
of the largest securities brokers, with more than 12,000 account executives. It has about 510 offices in 49 states and 27 countries. (The
company has about 40,000 employees and 12,000 shareholders.)
The stock was split in 1983 and 1993.

Per-Share Financial Summary

	1984	1993
Revenues	$31.43	$81.32
Earnings	.52	6.14
Dividends	.40	.70
Average Stock Price	14⅝	39⅝

Telefonos de Mexico, S. A. (ADR) (Telmex) provides all domestic
and international fixed-link and cellular mobile telephone services in
Mexico. Telmex is Mexico's third largest company and the largest that
is publicly traded. It has 6.7 million telephone lines in service, of which
52 percent are digital. The stock is represented by ADRs, which were
listed for trading on the NYSE in May of 1991. (The company has
about 49,000 employees.)

Per-Share Financial Summary

	1991	1993
Revenues	$10.00	$14.90
Earnings	3.52	5.60
Dividends	.17	.96
Average ADR Price	30⅛	56⅛

The Travelers, Inc., is a diversified financial services company with
interests in consumer finance, insurance services and investment services. Operating units include Smith Barney Shearson, American Capital Management, Commercial Credit and Primerica Financial Services.
(The company has about 16,000 full-time employees and 33,000
shareholders.)

Stock of the present company began trading on the NYSE in 1987.
There were two stock splits in 1993.

Per-Share Financial Summary

	1987	1993
Revenues	$ 5.26	$20.78
Earnings	1.00	3.74
Dividends	.12	.45
Average Stock Price	12⅞	36¾

SUMMARY

Value investors often use PE ratios as a favorite measure in seeking out stocks that they believe the market has undervalued. They look for stocks with below-average PEs. The PE ratio of a stock is found by dividing the price by its earnings per share. The PE ratio may either use the reported earnings from the latest year (called the trailing PE) or use an analyst's forecast of next year's earnings (called a forward PE). Daily newspapers list the trailing PE along with a stock's price and trading activity. Low PE stocks generally are found in low-growth or mature industries, in stock groups that have fallen out of favor or in old, established blue-chip companies with long records of earnings stability and regular dividends. Often, low PE stocks have higher yields than high PE stocks, which typically pay no dividends at all.

CHAPTER 16

Opportunities in Closed-End Funds

By far the biggest risk a long-term investor faces is *company risk,* the variation in a stock's return resulting from the unique characteristics of that stock and the industry in which it operates. In fact, company risk accounts for about 70 percent of the total risk that stock investors face. See Chapter 9 for more on risk.

As we have discussed, by maintaining a diversified portfolio of stocks, you eliminate 70 percent of the total risk inherent in stock market investing. The other 30 percent is accounted for by movements in the overall stock market that have an effect on your investment.

A simple and cost-effective way to diversify is to invest in closed-end funds. Closed-end funds are sponsored by investment companies, which, unlike open-end funds, do not stand ready to issue and redeem shares on a continuous basis. Instead, closed-end funds have a fixed capitalization represented by shares that are publicly traded, often on major stock exchanges. One interesting and potentially profitable aspect of closed-end funds is that they often are available for purchase at a *discount* from their net asset value (NAV).

By the end of 1993, about 500 closed-end funds were operating, and an additional 38 funds had been offered through Fall 1994. In contrast, only 56 closed-end funds traded on U.S. stock exchanges in 1983. For investors, an important consideration is when to buy. In an initial closed-end fund offering, the price typically reflects a 7 percent sales fee. You usually can save money by waiting a few months to buy a new fund until the sales promotion has died down and the price no longer is supported by the broker-dealers who marketed the issue. In most cases, the market price then will drop to the fund's NAV or lower.

Like open-end mutual funds, *closed-end* funds operate by pooling the money of shareholders and investing it in a diversified securities portfolio having a specified investment objective. The funds provide professional management, economies of scale and the liquidity available with public trading on a major exchange. While the NAV of closed-end funds is calculated the same way as for open-end funds, the price an investor pays or receives for shares traded on an exchange may be above or below the NAV. This is because the price of shares is determined on an auction market basis, the same as for all other traded shares of stock. Thus, the investor in a closed-end fund has an additional tier of risk, and possible profit, that the open-end fund investor does not have. The value per share responds not only to the fluctuation in value of the underlying securities in the fund's portfolio but also to supply-and-demand factors that influence the fund's share price as it trades on an exchange.

Closed-end funds hold two main attractions for investors, versus open-end mutual funds:

1. Management of a closed-end fund is not concerned with continuous buying and selling of securities in its portfolio to accommodate new investors and redemptions, as is the responsibility of an open-end fund, and which may conflict with ideal market timing. Thus, a well-managed closed-end fund often can buy and sell on more favorable terms.
2. Shares of closed-end funds frequently are available for purchase at a discount from NAV.

The resulting benefit of these two factors is that annual earnings of closed-end funds sometimes exceed the earnings of open-end funds with similar portfolios.

Shares of closed-end funds are purchased and sold through securities broker-dealers. Commissions, which vary from broker to broker, are payable both when shares are purchased and again when they are sold. Typically, shares are traded in 100-share lots, but "odd lots" of fewer than 100 shares also may be transacted.

The price, or *market value,* of closed-end shares is determined by supply-and-demand factors affecting the market. Shares may trade at a premium or at a discount relative to the NAV of the fund. Factors at work in determining share price include the composition of the portfolio, the yield, the general market and the year-end tax selling. Some funds have buyback programs designed to support the market price, reduce the number of shares outstanding and increase earnings per share. When shares are first issued, they tend to sell at a premium for a time, then fall back when brokers stop aggressively promoting them and turn their attention to other products.

In addition to daily transactions of closed-end funds contained in the financial sections of major newspapers, *Barron's National Business and Financial Weekly* publishes a special section each week with a complete listing of closed-end funds. Closed-end funds selling at a premium or a discount to NAV also are listed separately each Monday in *The New York Times* and *The Wall Street Journal.*

TYPES OF CLOSED-END FUNDS

Like open-end mutual funds, closed-end funds are classified according to their stated objectives. Of 538 closed-end funds tracked by *Morningstar Closed-End Funds* late in 1994, 71 percent were classified as taxable and municipal bond funds. *Morningstar* divides closed-end funds into the following classifications.*

Equity Funds

Domestic equity funds seek capital appreciation by investing primarily in U.S. stocks. This group includes growth stock funds, small-company funds and special-sector funds (financial, health, precious metals, utilities, natural resources, etc.). Their investment policies may be conservative, calling for growth-and-income characteristics, or they may be very aggressive, utilizing short-selling and leveraging techniques.

Europe stock funds seek capital appreciation by investing primarily in European stocks.

---

*Source: *Morningstar Closed-End Funds* (Morningstar, Inc., 225 W. Wacker Dr., Chicago, IL 60606; 312-696-6000).

Latin America stock funds seek capital appreciation by investing primarily in Latin American stocks.

Pacific stock funds seek capital appreciation by investing primarily in stocks of the Pacific Rim and Australia.

World stock funds seek capital appreciation by investing primarily in stocks listed in markets around the globe, including the United States.

Hybrid Funds

Income funds invest in both equity and debt securities primarily for the purpose of realizing income. Generally, funds in this group will not invest more than 50 percent of their assets in bonds.

Convertible bond funds invest primarily in bonds and preferred stocks that can be converted into common stocks.

Fixed-Income (Taxable) Funds

Corporate bond funds seek income by investing in fixed-income securities, primarily corporate bonds of various credit quality ratings.

Corporate high-yield bond funds seek income generally by investing at least 80 percent of their assets in bonds rated below BBB.

Government bond funds seek income by investing in mortgage-backed securities, U.S. Treasury securities and/or the securities of government agencies.

International bond funds seek current income. Capital appreciation is sometimes a secondary objective. These funds invest primarily in non-U.S.-currency-denominated bonds, and they frequently are offerings of foreign governments.

Multisector bond funds seek income by investing in a variety of fixed-income securities, including corporate bonds, government bonds and international bonds. Equity securities sometimes are included in the portfolios.

Municipal Bond (Tax-Free) Funds

National municipal bond funds seek income by investing in U.S. tax-free bonds and are not restricted to an individual state.

Single-state municipal bond funds seek income by investing in the tax-free bonds of an individual state.

Dual-Purpose Funds

A special form of closed-end fund is the *dual-purpose fund.* This type of fund contains two classes of stock: (1) Common shareholders receive all capital gains realized on the sale of securities in the fund's portfolio; (2) Preferred shareholders receive all the dividend and interest income from the portfolio. Dual-purpose funds have a specific expiration date, when preferred shares are redeemed at a predetermined price and common shareholders claim the remaining assets. They then vote to either liquidate or continue the fund on an open-end basis. Dual-purpose funds are listed separately under their own heading by *Barron's* in its weekly closed-end funds report.

BUYING CLOSED-END FUNDS AT A DISCOUNT

Because the market price of closed-end fund shares is determined by supply-and-demand factors, the shares may trade at a discount or premium relative to the NAV of the fund. Occasionally, the variance can be substantial. Figure 16.1 shows the funds that traded with the widest discounts and highest premiums on January 31, 1994.

Particular funds usually have specific reasons why they trade at steep discounts from their NAVs. For example, Engex Fund has an uncertain future after having indicated an intent to terminate its status as a closed-end fund. In addition, the fund has been reducing the number of holdings in its portfolio. On September 30, 1993, it held only 13 stocks, with one security accounting for more than 32 percent of the fund's value.

Substantial annual returns enjoyed by funds in the World Pacific/Asia objective may account for their popularity with investors and the resulting high premiums for the shares. The Taiwan Fund, for example, gained more than 36 percent (NAV returns) in 1993, while the Indonesia Fund was up an astounding 80 percent. Good results get the attention of investors, who then optimistically bid up the price in hopes of still more gains. Volatility has a price, though; what goes up quickly can react sharply when sour news comes along.

FIGURE 16.1 Closed-End Funds with the Widest Discounts as
of 1/31/94

Fund	Discount	Objective
Engex Fund	−23.6%	Domestic equity
Convertible Holdings Capital Shares	−20.2	Convertible
Baker, Fentress & Company	−19.1	Domestic equity
America's All Season Fund	−17.8	World stock
Quest for Value Dual Purpose Fund Capital Shares	−17.0	Domestic equity
Gemini II Capital Shares	−16.3	Domestic equity
Counsellors Tandem Securities Fund	−15.9	Domestic equity
Inefficient Market Fund	−15.2	Domestic equity
NAIC Growth Fund	−14.9	Domestic equity
Tri–Continental Corporation	−14.4	Domestic equity

Closed–End Funds with the Highest Premiums

India Growth Fund	+32.5%	World Pacific/Asia
Taiwan Fund	+32.0	World Pacific/Asia
Indonesia Fund	+32.0	World Pacific/Asia
Korea Fund	+28.8	World Pacific/Asia
Japan Equity Fund	+28.6	World Pacific/Asia
China Fund	+28.4	World Pacific/Asia
Templeton Emerging Markets Fund	+28.0	World stock
Singapore Fund	+27.3	World Pacific/Asia
Korea Equity Fund	+26.0	World Pacific/Asia
Van Kampen Merritt Intermediate–Term High-Income Trust Fund	+24.6	Corporate high-yield bonds

Source: *Morningstar Closed-End Funds* (Morningstar, Inc., 225 W. Wacker Dr., Chicago, IL 60606; 312-696-6000).

The inclination of closed-end funds to sell at premiums, and, even more often, at discounts has yielded many profit opportunities to astute investors, while baffling those who subscribe to the theory of an efficient market. Many wonder how the market's valuation of a closed-end fund can differ, sometimes substantially, from its underlying asset value, which unlike most investments, can be so clearly determined. Investors' constant attempts to properly value assets and their profit potential that drives the market. So it is strange that even when investors are handed quite precise valuations in the form of NAVs, they often value closed-end funds differently.

HOW THE PREMIUM/DISCOUNT PHENOMENON AFFECTS INVESTMENT PROFITS

Adroit selection and timing of closed-end fund purchases and sales occasionally can result in spectacular profits. An example is the *Latin American Discovery Fund,* which is traded on the NYSE. Its initial public offering was on June 16, 1992.

The Latin American Discovery Fund seeks long-term capital appreciation by investing at least 80 percent of its assets in Latin American equity securities, including ADRs. The fund invests at least 55 percent of its assets in Argentine, Brazilian, Chilean and Mexican stocks.

The NAV of the fund's shares rose more than 53 percent in 1993, from $15.23 per share to $23.31 per share on December 31. But the shares were selling in the market at $13.25 per share at the beginning of 1993, a discount from NAV of 13 percent. By the end of 1993, investors had bid up the price of Latin American Discovery Fund shares on the NYSE to $27.13, a premium of 16.4 percent. If you had bought shares of the fund in the beginning of 1993 and sold them on December 31, you would have realized a profit of 104.7 percent (not counting transaction costs). Ownership of shares in an open-end mutual fund with the same increase in NAV would have limited your profit to 53 percent.

Of course, the effect of discounts and premiums can work against an investor as well. This can be illustrated by a 1993 investment made in the *Bergstrom Capital Fund,* which trades on the AMEX. The NAV total return of this fund was −3.8 percent in 1993. The NAV dropped from $102.68 per share in the beginning of January to $95.07 per share on December 31. An income distribution of $1.10 per share was paid during the year and a capital gains distribution of $ .90 a share. But in the beginning of the year, the shares were trading at $132.12 a share, a premium of 28.7 percent over the NAV. At the end of the year, the shares, with a market price of $94.50 each, were selling at a discount from the NAV of −.6 percent. Thus, an investor in shares of Bergstrom Capital would have had a 25.6 percent loss for the year. If this fund were an open-end mutual fund, in which case the investor would have

FIGURE 16.2 Market Returns by Investment Objective Through
January 31, 1994

	5 Years	10 Years
Equity Funds		
Europe Stock	11.95%	–
Latin America Stock	47.50	38.27%
Pacific Stock	23.52	–
World Stock	15.52	5.70
Domestic Equity	15.46	11.95
Hybrid Funds		
Income	12.62	–
Convertible	16.34	10.71
Fixed-Income Funds		
Corporate Bond	11.67	12.31
High-Yield Corporate Bond	9.68	–
Government Bond	10.14	–
International Bond	8.96	–
Multisector Bond	11.09	–
Municipal Bond – National	8.89	–
Municipal Bond – Single State	9.94	–
Indexes		
S&P 500 Index	13.69	15.38
Morgan Stanley Europe	8.91	–
Morgan Stanley Latin America	49.30	–
Morgan Stanley Pacific	–1.74	17.61
Lehman Brothers Aggregate Bond	11.23	11.76
First Boston High-Yield Bond	13.33	–
Salomon Brothers World Government Bond	10.22	–
Lehman Brothers Municipal Bond Index	10.05	10.90
U.S. Treasury Bills	5.39	6.24
Consumer Price Index	3.78	3.65

Source: *Morningstar Closed-End Funds,* Morningstar, Inc.

been able to buy and sell shares at NAV, he or she would have suffered
a loss of just 6.3 percent.

PERFORMANCE RESULTS OF
CLOSED-END FUNDS

Because closed-end funds provide the means to diversify easily and
inexpensively, it makes sense to take a look at average long-term

performance records of various investment categories and compare them against alternative investments. Figure 16.2 shows annualized total returns of each investment objective, as well as those of certain market indexes and T-bills, for the five- and ten-year periods ending January 31, 1994. Ten-year returns are omitted in cases where the information was not available.

HIGHLY REGARDED CLOSED-END FUNDS

Figure 16.3 is a number of closed-end funds that are highly regarded by investment analysts in terms of both performance and how much risk the funds take to achieve that performance. Funds are included that have been in operation for at least five years and are listed by investment objective. Average total returns (change in value plus capital and income distributions) are shown based on both NAV and market price of the funds' shares. At different times, certain funds may trade at a premium or discount. For instance, the Asia Pacific Fund traded at a discount for most of 1987 through 1991, then at a premium during most of 1992 and 1993. Many high-performing funds have been established in the past five years but are not included in this list. Except where otherwise noted following category headings, five-year returns are for the period ending December 31, 1993.

SUMMARY

By far the biggest risk long-term investors face is company risk, the variation in a stock's return resulting from the unique characteristics of that stock and the industry in which it operates. Company risk accounts for about 70 percent of the total risk that stock investors face. The solution to company risk is diversification. A simple and cost-effective way to diversify is to invest in closed-end funds, which, unlike open-end funds, do not stand ready to issue and redeem shares on a continuous basis. Instead, closed-end funds have a fixed capitalization represented by shares that are publicly traded, often on major stock exchanges. An interesting and potentially profitable aspect of closed-end funds is that they often are available for purchase at a discount from their NAV.

FIGURE 16.3   Highly Regarded Closed-End Funds Regarding
Performance and Risk

Five-Year Average Annual Total Return

	NAV	Market Value
Equity Funds		
Europe		
Germany Fund	11.89%	13.43%
Swiss Helvetia Fund	14.65	19.68
Latin America		
Mexico Fund	49.11	62.13
Pacific/Asia		
Asia Pacific Fund	34.49	49.00
Malaysia Fund	29.37	34.77
Scudder New Asia Fund	23.31	33.40
World		
Templeton Emerging Markets Fund	38.94	49.44
Domestic		
Adams Express Company	15.59	15.29
Bergstrom Capital	19.39	20.45
Central Securities Fund	17.69	21.79
First Financial Fund	26.19	29.18
Liberty All-Star Equity Fund	16.67	21.46
Quest for Value Dual Purpose Fund—Capital Shares	22.06	27.12
Royce Value Trust	15.03	16.99
Income		
Gemini II Income Shares	13.81	11.97
Hampton Utilities Trust—Preferred Shares	9.01	10.70
Quest for Value Dual Purpose Fund—Income Shares	11.22	16.07
Convertible (January 31, 1994)		
Bancroft Convertible Fund	12.87	14.20
Castle Convertible Fund	14.13	15.74
Ellsworth Convertible Growth and Income Fund	12.87	13.94
Lincoln National Convertible Securities Fund	20.11	23.90
Putnam High Income Convertible and Bond Fund	16.11	16.27
TCW Convertible Securities Fund	14.35	17.08

FIGURE 16.3   Highly Regarded Closed-End Funds Regarding
Performance and Risk (Continued)

	NAV	Market Value
Bonds		
Corporate Bonds (October 29, 1993)		
Circle Income Shares	9.65	7.92
1838 Bond-Debenture Trading Fund	12.79	14.32
John Hancock Income Securities Trust	11.92	12.43
John Hancock Investors Trust	11.67	13.93
Montgomery Street Income Securities	12.47	12.71
Pacific American Income Shares	12.05	12.42
Transamerica Income Shares	13.08	10.98
USLife Income Fund	12.44	14.53
Government Bonds (October 29, 1993)		
American Government Income Fund	15.81	15.11
American Government Income Portfolio	16.08	16.86
Multisector Bonds (November 30, 1993)		
ACM Government Income Fund	13.96	13.89
ACM Government Opportunity Fund	13.94	13.51
ACM Government Securities Fund	14.02	14.30
ACM Managed Income	17.47	16.84
Oppenheimer Multi-Sector Income Trust	10.89	10.37
Putnam Master Income Trust	12.16	11.54
National Municipal Bonds (September 30, 1993)		
Dreyfus Strategic Municipals	9.24	10.23
MFS Municipal Income Trust	7.75	7.42
Municipal High Income Fund	8.59	6.73
Nuveen Premium Income Municipal Fund	10.83	10.17
Single-State Municipal Bonds (November 30, 1993)		
Nuveen New York Municipal Value Fund	9.38	10.07

PART THREE

The Wide World of Stocks

CHAPTER 17

The World of Publicly Traded Stocks

Through a quarterly updated program, members of the American Association of Individual Investors (AAII) can screen and analyze more than 7,000 stocks. Even this does not include the shares of all companies that are publicly traded in the United States!

The most important markets for trading activity in the United States are the NYSE, the AMEX and the OTC.

Almost all the largest, most established companies, plus many smaller growth companies, are traded on the NYSE. With more than 2,800 issues listed, the NYSE operates with a specialist system of trading: Buyers and sellers are brought together by a specialist on the floor of the exchange. The NYSE's requirements for being listed on the exchange are the most stringent of all the places where stocks are traded in the United States. Two of the most important requirements are: (1) A corporation must have a minimum aggregate market value of $16 million, and (2) annual net income must exceed $2.5 million before federal income taxes.

The shares of more than 1,000 medium and smaller-sized companies are traded on the AMEX. The AMEX uses the same specialist trading system as the NYSE. Requirements for listing on the AMEX are less stringent than on the NYSE, though the exchange requires that a company have a reliably profitable business.

For the most part, shares of smaller, emerging-growth companies without long histories of earnings and dividends trade on the over-the-counter market. Trading on the OTC is done under a system of competing market makers who communicate by telephone and computer terminal. While a broker acts as an intermediary between a buyer and seller, a dealer acts as a principal in a securities transaction. Most brokerage firms act as both brokers and principals. The National Association of Security Dealers Automated Quotation System (Nasdaq), owned by the National Association of Securities Dealers (NASD), is a computerized system that provides brokers and dealers with price quotations for securities traded OTC, as well as for many NYSE listed securities. Nasdaq quotes are published in the financial pages of most newspapers. The largest and most actively traded stocks, numbering more than 3,200 issues, are included in the Nasdaq National Market List. The stocks of more than 1,500 smaller companies are carried in the Nasdaq Small Cap Issues list.

For ease in studying and reporting on stocks, many analysts and investment services divide them into industry groups. There is no universally accepted industry grouping standard. For example, *Forbes* magazine breaks the world of publicly traded stocks into the following 21 industry sectors:

Aerospace and defense	Entertainment and information
Business services and supplies	Financial services
Capital goods	Food distributors
Chemicals	Food, drink and tobacco
Computers and	Forest products and packaging
communications	Health
Construction	Insurance
Consumer durables	Metals
Consumer nondurables	Retailing
Electric utilities	Transport
Energy	Travel

The *Value Line Investment Survey*, taking a more detailed approach, analyzes 97 industry sectors. For example, while *Value Line* also looks at aerospace and defense as one industry, it separates financial services into banks, Canadian banks, Midwest banks, financial services, domestic investment companies, foreign investment companies, income investment companies and securities brokerage.

Part Three reveals several industry sectors that are either timely or might be interesting to readers seeking shares of companies that have capital-gain and/or income opportunities. You will find an overview of each industry group, followed by one company recommended for potential investors to investigate. You will find helpful information, such as where the stock trades, its symbol and the company's corporate address, which is useful if you would like to see the latest annual report. Most companies will be happy to send you a copy, even though you are not a shareholder. Just direct your request to Shareholder Relations at the company's address.

You also will find a short description of the company and its business. Tables also are included for each recommended company that illustrate how you would have fared if you had bought $10,000 of the company's stock at its average trading price in 1984. You will see what your investment would have been worth after ten years at the average share price in 1993. If the company paid dividends during the period, the assumption is made that all dividends were applied to purchase additional shares. In some cases, where the company's stock began trading after 1984, the data begins in the year trading began.

Other information provided includes selected per-share financial results over the years of review and, where the information was available, the high and low quarterly stock price record for the two most recent years.

Abbreviated information is presented on a number of other companies in each industry group that analysts consider to have above-average potential for earnings growth over the next several years.

When data for a particular item in a listing does not apply, it is designated as N/A, meaning "not applicable."

CHAPTER 18

Banks

Record earnings were turned in by the bank industry in 1992 and 1993. Many banks will have to push harder to keep the momentum going in 1994 and beyond, although analysts expect profits to continue to grow.

Long-term challenges facing the group include the difficulty in increasing net interest income and fee income resulting from growing competition with nonbank financial service providers. Analysts report that most banks are unable to reduce their already low consumer deposit rates any further and, until the yields on loans and investments start rising, probably will experience more pressure on their lending margins. Plus, already intense competition in various businesses that contribute fee income, such as credit-card lending, trust services and mortgage banking, is expected to increase. On the other hand, credit quality should continue to improve, and banks' provisions from earnings to their loan loss reserves ought to decline further. And many banks will continue to trim operating costs.

The Senate Banking Committee recently cleared a bill allowing banks to operate nationwide branch networks, and Congress seems likely to approve the bill in 1994. Big banks generally have supported the move to interstate banking, while small banks, fearing competition from larger banks, mostly have opposed the movement. But opposition usually has been waning.

Consolidation activity is expected to increase. But many recent bank mergers have taken place at relatively high multiples of book value. Acquiring banks will have to carefully consider the strategic advantages of building market share against the amount of initial earnings dilution that results from any given deal.

Investment Outlook

Aside from the takeover speculation that affected some banks, investor pessimism regarding the industry's ability to stand up to growing competition from other financial service providers and the somewhat smaller earnings gains likely to be achieved in the next few years caused a slippage in the prices of many bank stocks in early 1994. But most banks should report respectable earnings growth in 1994, and some have announced substantial dividend increases. Investors should focus on banks with winning strategies and those experiencing good revenue growth.

★ Recommended Stock

State Street Boston Corporation
225 Franklin Street
Boston, MA 02101
617-786-3000

Chairman and president: Marshall N. Carter
Number of shareholders: 4,400
Number of employees: 9,300
Where the stock trades: OTC: Nasdaq
Symbol: STBK

What the Company Does

State Street Boston Corporation has 13 domestic offices and 13 offices overseas. It is the third largest U.S. manager of tax-exempt assets and the largest manager of international index assets, with assets under management totaling $142 billion at the end of 1993. Combining securities processing and custody with sophisticated multicurrency accounting capabilities, State Street Boston provides a broad array of record-keeping, reporting and banking services to collective investment funds, corporate pension plans, public retirement funds, union pension funds, banks, insurance companies, endowments and foundations. These services account for about 40 percent of gross income.

The bank had $1.6 trillion in assets under its custody as of December 31, 1993.

Reason for Recommendation

State Street Boston Corporation is benefiting from a booming mutual fund industry and the globalization of investments. Fiduciary compensation, including a significant contribution from institutional money management fees, helped the bank post a 13 percent common stock earnings gain in 1993. State Street's unique structure and technological focus enables it to process an increasing number of trades while simultaneously dealing with the complexities of cross-border investing. As total assets under custody climb toward $1.6 trillion, the bank's role in the expanding institutional trust field (of which mutual funds servicing is only one part) has become evident.

The price of the stock in early 1994 was well below its 1993 high, based on news of pricing pressure in its mature custody business. Note that State Street is a processing company, not a typical bank. Its loan portfolio accounts for only about 14 percent of assets versus a more standard bank's ratio of 50 percent to 65 percent. The result to net profits is a smoothed-out earnings stream. State Street has made major capital investments in 1992 and 1993 (with about 10 percent of gross revenues invested in 1993), which have somewhat hidden the firm's earnings potential, and possibly limited its stock valuation.

Analysts believe that because of the formidable barriers to entry by competitors, State Street's preeminent position should be recognized, and its stock's market multiple will widen in the near future. Based on the earnings projections of some analysts of 15 percent annual gains over the next several years, the stock should offer good capital-gains potential during that period.

Investment Results

State Street Boston Corporation's steady earnings growth over the years has been a boon to stockholders. An investment made at the average price at which the shares traded in 1984 (adjusted for splits) would have bought 2,105 shares. With annual dividends used to purchase additional shares, the initial $10,000 would have grown to a value of $98,242 in 1993 (based on the average share price in that year). Figure 18.1 shows the results of a $10,000 investment in State Street Boston Corporation stock from 1984 to 1993. Brokerage commissions are not considered. All numbers are adjusted for two-for-one stock splits in 1985, 1986 and 1992.

FIGURE 18.1   Results of a $10,000 Investment in State Street Boston
Corporation Common Stock with Dividends Reinvested
from 1984 to 1993

	Average Share Price	Annual Dividends	Shares Bought from Dividends	Total # Shares Owned	Value of Shares Owned
1984	4¾	$ 273	57	2,162	$10,269
1985	8⅛	324	39	2,201	17,883
1986	12	396	33	2,234	26,808
1987	13¼	491	37	2,271	30,090
1988	11¾	590	50	2,321	27,272
1989	16⅝	696	41	2,362	39,268
1990	16¼	803	49	2,411	39,178
1991	23¾	940	39	2,450	58,187
1992	37⅛	1,102	29	2,479	92,032
1993	39⅛	1,289	32	2,511	98,242

The December 31, 1993, closing price of State Street Boston Corporation common shares traded on the Nasdaq Exchange was $37½. The market value of $94,162 on that date was more than nine times the original $10,000 invested in 1984.

Figure 18.2 shows selected per-share data of State Street Boston Corporation during the period from 1984 to 1993. The data has been adjusted for stock splits.

Earnings per share increased over the prior year in every year from 1984 to 1993. Book value per share also increased each year during that period. The average PE ratio (average annual price per share divided by earnings per share) gradually increased during the period from as low as 7.9 times earnings to about 17 times earnings in 1992 and 1993, reflecting a rise in investors' expectations for continued future earnings growth for the company. Remember that a high PE ratio often indicates that a stock is vulnerable to adverse news.

Common Stock Quarterly Price Record

The high and low prices of State Street Boston Corporation common stock during the 1992 and 1993 fiscal years, adjusted for a two-for-one stock split in 1992, were:

FIGURE 18.2   Selected Per-Share Data of State Street Boston
Corporation from 1984 to 1993

	Earnings Per Share	Book Value	Average Price Per Share	Percentage of Profits Paid in Dividends	Average PE Ratio
1984	$ .60	$ 4.05	4¾	18%	7.9
1985	.73	4.74	8⅛	18	11.1
1986	.92	5.59	12	18	13.0
1987	1.06	6.45	13¼	19	12.5
1988	1.20	7.22	11¾	20	9.8
1989	1.38	8.28	16⅝	21	12.0
1990	1.55	9.51	16¼	21	10.5
1991	1.81	10.97	23¾	20	13.1
1992	2.07	12.70	37⅛	21	17.9
1993	2.33	14.56	39⅛	22	16.8

	1st Quarter	2nd Quarter	3rd Quarter	4th Quarter
1992				
High	33⅛	38¾	39	44⅞
Low	29¼	30¾	33⅝	35⅜
1993				
High	49⅛	45¾	35¾	39¾
Low	41	29¼	31¾	35⅜

Note: State Street's fiscal years end December 31.

Excluding the 4th quarter of 1993, it was possible during each quarterly period to buy shares at a price substantially below the high price of the prior quarter. Careful buying of shares can have a long-term positive impact on your total investment return.

CREATING A PORTFOLIO OF STOCKS IN THE SPECIALTY BANK INDUSTRY

Following are a number of banks that are considered by analysts to be favorably positioned for capital appreciation.

Company	1993 Earnings Per Share	12/31/93 Share Price	Dividend Yield	PE Ratio*
Bankers Trust New York Corp.	12.40	79⅛	4.6%	6.4
Morgan (J. P.) & Company, Inc.	8.48	69⅜	4.2	8.2
NationsBank	4.95	49	3.8	9.9
SouthTrust Corporation	1.94	19	3.7	9.8
SunTrust Banks, Inc.	3.77	45	2.8	11.9
Synovus Financial Corporation	1.11	18⅝	2.6	16.8

*December 31, 1993, share price divided by 1993 earnings per share.

What the Companies Do

Bankers Trust New York Corporation (BT–NYSE) owns Bankers Trust, the eighth largest bank in the United States based on assets. The company sold its retail business in the early 1980s and now concentrates on wholesale banking. International operations account for more than 50 percent of pretax income. Total assets were $92 billion at the end of 1993. (The company has about 12,600 employees and 25,600 common shareholders.)

There was a two-for-one stock split in 1985.

Per-Share Financial Summary	1984	1993
Earnings	$4.24	$12.40
Dividends	1.26	3.24
Average Stock Price	24	74⅝

J. P. Morgan & Company, Inc. (JPM–NYSE) owns Morgan Guaranty Trust Company of New York, which was the fourth largest U.S. bank on the basis of assets at the end of 1992. The company mainly serves large corporations. It has one of the largest trust departments in the United States and branches in many foreign countries. International operations account for more than 50 percent of revenues and more than 75 percent of pretax earnings. Assets totaled $133 billion at the end of 1993. (The company has about 15,000 employees and 28,000 shareholders.)

There were two-for-one stock splits in 1985 and 1987.

Per-Share Financial Summary

	1984	1993
Earnings	$2.94	$8.48
Dividends	1.03	2.48
Average Stock Price	17⅛	69⅜

NationsBank (NB–NYSE) was formed by the merger of NCNB Corporation with C&S/Sovran on December 31, 1991. The company has more than 1,900 offices in Florida, Georgia, Kentucky, Maryland, North Carolina, South Carolina, Tennessee, Texas, Virginia and Washington, D.C. It has a leading share of bank deposits in five of those states. Assets totaled $157 billion at the end of 1993. (The company has about 57,400 employees and 89,400 shareholders.)

The stock was split two-for-one in 1986.

Per-Share Financial Summary

	1984	1993
Earnings	$2.04	$4.95
Dividends	.59	1.64
Average Stock Price	14⅞	51¼

SouthTrust Corporation (SOTR–OTC) is the largest bank holding company in Alabama and the 44th largest in the United States based on assets at the end of 1992. SouthTrust owns 25 banks with 174 offices in Alabama, Florida, Georgia, South Carolina and North Carolina. Assets totaled $14.7 billion at the end of 1993. (The company has about 6,300 employees and 8,500 shareholders.)

There was a five-for-three stock split in 1985, a three-for-two split in 1991 and a three-for-two split in 1993.

Per-Share Financial Summary

	1984	1993
Earnings	$.76	$1.94
Dividends	.23	.60
Average Stock Price	4⅞	19⅜

SunTrust Banks, Inc. (STI–NYSE), the third largest bank holding company in the Southeast, was created by the merger of Trust Company of Georgia and Sun Banks on July 1, 1985. Assets totaled more than $40 billion at the end of 1993. The company has a nearly uninterrupted stretch of annual earnings gains since the late 1980s.

There was a 10 percent stock dividend in 1985 and a two-for-one split in 1986.

Per-Share Financial Summary

	1984	*1993*
Earnings	$1.29	$3.77
Dividends	.55	1.16
Average Stock Price	11⅞	45½

Synovus Financial Corporation (SNV–NYSE) is a holding company that owns 31 banks in Georgia, Alabama and Florida. The company owns Synovus Securities, a full-service broker, and 80.7 percent of Total Systems Services, a bank-card data processor. A recently formed subsidiary issues the AT&T Universal Card. Assets totaled $5.6 billion at the end of 1993. (The company has about 4,500 employees and 13,400 shareholders.)

There was a two-for-one stock split in 1984 and three-for-two splits in 1985, 1986, 1988 and 1993.

Per-Share Financial Summary

	1984	*1993*
Earnings	$.33	$1.11
Dividends	.10	.36
Average Stock Price	3¾	17¾

SUMMARY

While the bank industry turned in record earnings in 1992 and 1993, many banks will have to push harder to keep the momentum going in 1994 and beyond, although analysts expect profits to continue to grow. Long-term challenges facing the group include the difficulty in increasing net interest income and fee income resulting from growing competition with nonbank financial service providers. Most banks should report respectable earnings growth in the near-term, and some have announced substantial dividend increases. Investors should focus on banks with winning strategies and those experiencing good revenue growth.

CHAPTER 19

Casino Gaming

Casino gaming, in various forms and with various restrictions, is growing and spreading rapidly in new jurisdictions across the United States.

Las Vegas, the epicenter of world gaming, is being transformed to a family-oriented resort city. In late 1993, the city absorbed the openings of three major new casino resorts: Mirage's Treasure Island, Circus Circus's Luxor and the huge M-G-M Grand resort—biggest of them all, with no ill effects to the established competitors. The newer properties all feature nongambling attractions such as theme park–style fantasy rides. The city operates on the idea that "supply creates demand," and that has worked out so far. Still, some analysts believe that Las Vegas is approaching a saturation point. Only time will tell if demand continues to grow there at an acceptable pace in coming years.

A federal law granting Native Americans the right to own and operate casinos on reservations has encouraged new operations. Established gaming companies are grabbing pieces of the action through joint ventures and management contracts. The Foxwoods casino on a Connecticut reservation has been very successful. Other Native Americans want to open a casino in upstate New York. In most cases, the Native Americans are inviting experienced gaming companies in to build and manage their proposed facilities. A joint venture has been signed by Caesars World to build and run a Native American reservation casino in Palm Springs, California.

The fastest-growing area for the gaming industry has been the Mississippi River region. Floating riverboat or dockside casinos have been authorized by most states along the river and currently are operating in Illinois, Tennessee, Mississippi and Louisiana. More are scheduled to open in Indiana and Missouri. The properties tend to be relatively small in size; boats are cheap to build and open—$50 million to $80 million—compared to as much as ten times that amount for a major casino resort. But they can generate high returns for the amount of their investment. Promus Companies already has opened four Harrah's casino boats and plans to open at least three more in 1994. Other riverboat or dockside casinos have been opened by Jackpot Enterprises and Bally Manufacturing. Both established casino operators and new firms have become involved.

Slumping business recovered nicely in 1993 in the Atlantic City, New Jersey, casino industry. That city is threatened by competition from new gaming markets, especially from Native American reservations or other legalized gaming in the East. A relaxation of some constricting regulations has permitted Atlantic City casino operators to make their products more attractive. Casinos in that city now are open around the clock and offer poker and horse race simulcasting and betting.

Investment Outlook

Gaming equipment makers are clear beneficiaries of the new boom in the industry, with International Game Technology, my recommended stock, having seen its sales and earnings soar as a result of the new markets. Investors in gaming industry stocks should move cautiously because these issues tend to have high PE ratios and usually are quite risky.

★ *Recommended Stock*

International Game Technology
520 South Rock Boulevard
Reno, NV 89502
702-688-0100

Number of shareholders: 1,400
Number of employees: 2,150
Where the stock trades: NYSE
Symbol: IGT

What the Company Does

International Game Technology (IGT) is an industry leader in the design, manufacture and marketing of gaming machines and proprietary software systems for computerized wide-area gaming-machine networks. IGT is the only gaming-machine manufacturer licensed to do business in every regulated gaming jurisdiction in the world.

The company's two major divisions are IGT-North America and IGT-International. IGT-North America maintains manufacturing facilities in Reno, Nevada, and Winnipeg, Manitoba, Canada. It sells to and services the traditional gaming markets of Nevada and Atlantic City, as well as the emerging casino-style markets of western mining towns, riverboats and Native American reservations. IGT-North America is also the world's leading supplier of proprietary gaming software systems, including wide-area progressive systems for casinos and central computer systems for monitoring government-sponsored video gaming terminal networks.

IGT-International is responsible for the manufacturing and sales of IGT equipment for all gaming jurisdictions outside of North America, including Australia, Asia, Europe, Latin America and Africa. Headquartered in Reno, Nevada, this division has a manufacturing facility in Sydney, Australia, and sales and distribution facilities in Hoofddorp, The Netherlands; Wellington, New Zealand; and other locations.

Reason for Recommendation

International Game Technology is in the midst of an explosion in demand for its gaming machines from new markets. Its mainstay markets in Nevada and Atlantic City have remained strong. IGT's unit sales increased 50 percent in its 1993 fiscal year (ended September 30) over the prior year, having sold about 69,000 machines. This was more than double the number sold in fiscal 1991. During the two-year period, sales to new markets, such as Native American reservation casinos and riverboat casinos, rose more than 400 percent and now account for about two-thirds of IGT's total sales.

IGT's manufacturing business is mainly the assembly of components. Creation of software systems is the company's greatest area of value-added in its products. Because costs of this activity are relatively fixed, the company benefits from the economies of scale. The dramatic increases in unit production and sales have helped widen IGT's operating margins in recent years.

Further expansion is anticipated. The company has entered into an agreement to buy land in Reno for a new corporate and North American headquarters, operations facility and research-and-development center. Part of these facilities should be completed in 1995. IGT's international company also has bought a new manufacturing and office complex in Australia and is considering additional assembly facilities.

While the market seems fearful of a gambling glut and share prices have backed off from their highs, such a glut poses less of a problem to IGT than to the casino operators. As the market leader and the only company licensed to sell in all jurisdictions, analysts believe that IGT should continue to make sales and earnings gains in the foreseeable future.

Investment Results

After slumbering for many years, the stock of IGT started moving rapidly in 1991. Patient investors were suddenly rewarded when the market recognized that rapidly increasing sales and earnings from 1988 on was not a fluke. An investment of $10,000 in 1984 would have bought 10,000 shares at the average market price in that year. Figure 19.1 shows the year-by-year results of a $10,000 investment in IGT stock from 1984 to 1993. Brokerage commissions are not considered. All numbers are adjusted for two-for-one stock splits in 1990, 1991, 1992 and 1993.

The December 31, 1993, closing price of IGT common shares traded on the NYSE was $29½. The market value of $295,531 on that date was more than 29 times the original $10,000 invested in 1984.

Figure 19.2 shows selected per-share data of IGT during the period from 1984 to 1993. The data have been adjusted for stock splits.

Earnings per share were very erratic in the early years, until finally beginning regular growth in 1988. Book value per share also began to move up steadily in 1988. By 1991, the public caught on to what was happening and the share price began its upward move. PE multiples in 1985 to 1987 were essentially meaningless as the company reported little or no earnings. But when investors saw the growth potential, the PE ratio reflected substantial future growth of earnings potential, peaking at more than 51 times earnings in 1993 when the stock sold as

FIGURE 19.1   Results of a $10,000 Investment in International Game Technology Common Stock with Dividends Reinvested from 1984 to 1993

	Average Share Price	Annual Dividends	Shares Bought from Dividends	Total # Shares Owned	Value of Shares Owned
1984	1	Nil	0	10,000	$ 10,000
1985	⅞	Nil	0	10,000	8,250
1986	⅝	Nil	0	10,000	6,250
1987	¾	Nil	0	10,000	7,500
1988	1⅛	Nil	0	10,000	11,250
1989	1⅝	Nil	0	10,000	16,250
1990	1¾	Nil	0	10,000	17,500
1991	6⅞	Nil	0	10,000	68,750
1992	18⅝	Nil	0	10,000	186,250
1993	32⅝	$600	18	10,018	326,837

high as $41⅜. By early 1994, the shares were being traded at about $27 a share, bringing the PE multiple down to around 33 times earnings.

Common Stock Quarterly Price Record

The high and low prices of IGT common stock during the 1992 and 1993 fiscal years, adjusted for two-for-one stock splits in 1992 and 1993, were:

	1st Quarter	2nd Quarter	3rd Quarter	4th Quarter
1992				
High	12	17⅜	17⅛	22⅛
Low	6¼	10⅞	11¼	12⅞
1993				
High	26⅜	33	39¾	41⅜
Low	17⅞	23¾	28½	32⅛

Note: IGT's fiscal years end September 30.

In every quarter during 1992 and 1993, investors could buy shares at a price substantially below the high price of the prior quarter. Careful buying of shares can have a long-term positive impact on your total investment return.

FIGURE 19.2   Selected Per-Share Data of International Game
Technology from 1984 to 1993

	Earnings Per Share	Book Value	Average Price Per Share	Percentage of Profits Paid in Dividends	Average PE Ratio
1984	$ .09	$ .50	1	0%	11.1
1985	.01	.51	⅞	0	82.5
1986	d .06	.46	⅝	0	N/A
1987	.01	.38	¾	0	75.0
1988	.08	.58	1⅛	0	14.1
1989	.11	.70	1⅝	0	14.8
1990	.17	.82	1¾	0	10.3
1991	.26	1.10	6⅞	0	26.4
1992	.52	1.83	18⅝	0	35.8
1993	.80	3.03	32⅝	7	40.9

d = deficit

CREATING A PORTFOLIO OF STOCKS IN THE CASINO GAMING INDUSTRY

Brief information follows on a number of companies that are considered by some analysts to be favorably positioned for capital appreciation.

Company	1993 Earnings Per Share	12/31/93 Share Price	Dividend Yield	PE Ratio*
Caesars World, Inc.	$3.40	53⅜	Nil	15.7
Circus Circus Enterprises	1.35 E	36¾	Nil	27.2
Jackpot Enterprises, Inc.	.80	13⅝	2.7%	17.0
Mirage Resorts, Inc.	1.45 E	23⅞	Nil	16.5
Promus Companies, Inc.	.89	45¾	Nil	51.4

*December 31, 1993, share price divided by 1993 earnings per share.

WHAT THE COMPANIES DO

Caesars World, Inc. (CAW–NYSE), owns and operates casino-hotels. Its major properties are Caesars Palace in Las Vegas, with 1,500 rooms; Caesars Tahoe in Stateline, Nevada, with 440 rooms; and Caesars Atlantic City, with 641 rooms. The company also owns four nongaming resorts in the Pocono Mountains in Pennsylvania and markets private-label merchandise. Sales totaled $983 million in 1993. (The company has about 9,700 employees and 9,800 shareholders.)

Per-Share Financial Summary

	1984	1993
Revenues	$21.03	$39.95
Earnings	.66	3.40
Dividends	Nil	Nil
Average Stock Price	10⅞	45⅝

Circus Circus Enterprises, Inc. (CIR–NYSE) owns and runs six Nevada casino-hotels, including Excalibur and Luxor in Las Vegas, and Circus Circus in Las Vegas and Reno, and two in Laughlin. The company has 536,000 square feet of casino space, the largest amount in the United States, and 12,700 hotel rooms. Circus Circus is opening additional gaming facilities outside Nevada. Its lodging occupancy rates are close to 100 percent. (The company has about 13,600 employees and 2,300 shareholders.)

There were two-for-one stock splits in 1987 and 1991, and a three-for-two split in 1993.

Per-Share Financial Summary

	1984	1993
Revenues	$2.44	$11.45 E
Earnings	.28	1.35 E
Dividends	Nil	Nil
Average Stock Price	2⅝	38¾

Jackpot Enterprises, Inc. (J–NYSE), owns, operates and services gambling machines located primarily in chain stores in Nevada. It also owns The Nugget stand-alone slot casinos in Reno. In 1993, the company had 4,811 machines at 490 locations under exclusive subleases. Sales totaled $83 million in 1993. (The company has about 800 employees and 2,000 shareholders.)

There was a 10 percent stock dividend in 1993.

Per-Share Financial Summary

	1984	1993
Revenues	$1.10	$9.05
Earnings	.06	.80
Dividends	Nil	.29
Average Stock Price	3½	19⅞

Mirage Resorts, Inc. (MIR–NYSE), owns and operates the Mirage and Treasure Island casino-hotels on the Las Vegas Strip, the Golden Nugget casino-hotel in downtown Las Vegas and the Nevada Club casino in Laughlin, Nevada. The company owns land in Atlantic City. Mirage Resorts had total sales of $953 million in 1993. (The company has about 11,300 employees and 12,000 shareholders.)

Stock split five-for-two in 1993.

Per-Share Financial Summary

	1984	1993
Revenues	$4.47	$10.75
Earnings	.09	.58
Dividends	Nil	Nil
Average Stock Price	4¾	19⅛

Promus Companies, Inc. (PRI–NYSE), owns and operates Harrah's casino-hotels in Las Vegas, Reno, Lake Tahoe (two properties) and Laughlin. The company also has a casino-hotel in Atlantic City and a casino-riverboat in Joliet, Illinois. In addition, Promus owns the Embassy Suites, Hampton Inn and Homewood Suites hotel brands with a total of more than 68,000 rooms at 454 properties. Of these, 104 are company owned and managed; 350 are licensed. The casino segment of the business generates about 80 percent of revenues and 81 percent of operating profits. Revenues totaled more than $1.2 billion in 1993. (The company has about 23,000 employees and 16,800 shareholders.)

Promus Companies, Inc., was incorporated in 1989 as an indirect subsidiary of Holiday Corporation. In February of 1990, one share of Promus common stock was spun off to stockholders of each Holiday Corporation share in a restructuring associated with the acquisition of the Holiday Inn, Inc., business by Bass Public Limited Company. Promus stock began trading on the NYSE in February of 1990.

The stock was split two-for-one and three-for-two in 1993.

Per-Share Financial Summary

	1990	1993
Revenues	$12.56	$12.25
Earnings	.30	.89
Dividends	Nil	Nil
Average Stock Price	6⅞	36¼

SUMMARY

Casino gaming, in various forms and with various restrictions, is growing and spreading rapidly in new jurisdictions across the United States. Las Vegas is being transformed to a family-oriented resort city. A federal law granting Native Americans the right to own and operate casinos on reservations has encouraged established gaming companies to grab pieces of the action through joint ventures and management contracts. The fastest-growing area for the gaming industry has been the Mississippi River region. Floating riverboat or dockside casinos have been authorized by most states along the river. Gaming-equipment makers are clear beneficiaries of the new boom in the industry, but investors in any gaming-industry stocks should move cautiously because these issues tend to have high PE ratios and usually are quite risky.

CHAPTER 20

Computers

The economic situation seems favorable for the computer industry, although the depressed economies in much of Europe and Japan likely will hold back demand for the near-term, for about half of the computer group's sales comes from overseas. But by 1995, many of the overseas economies again will be on the rise, which should spur demand for computer products. Also, as countries in the former Soviet bloc recover from the shock of adapting to open markets, they, too—along with China—should become an increasingly important market for computers.

The ever-increasing power of smaller computers has remained the driving force in this industry. First came the minicomputer, pioneered by Digital Equipment Corporation, then microprocessor-based personal computers, which captured business from larger machines. That trend created pricing pressure, which drove down the price, and profit margins, for makers of all size machines. As the capabilities of the smaller computers increased, users began to off-load applications from mainframes and minicomputers to networks of personal computers and servers, which put further pressure on mainframe manufacturers.

Makers of the big machines cut their prices sharply and to preserve, or restore, profitability slimmed down their cost structures. Mainframe manufacturers such as Unisys, Amdahl and IBM are working to move their products to a less-expensive technology that will let them compete more effectively with smaller, microprocessor-based equipment.

Pricing pressures also are creating a shakeout in the personal computer market. IBM's premium prices once provided room for smaller, more flexible competitors to stake out for themselves big pieces of the market. But these days are past, and now all manufacturers are forced to engage in steep price cuts. This has led buyers to turn to name brands, which now are available at a very small premium to the low-cost clones. Several companies already have been forced out of business, and further consolidation is likely. Analysts expect competition to remain intense, but look for the profitability of computer manufacturers to improve over the next few years.

Investment Outlook

Investors interested in the computer industry can find a suitable selection of stocks that have good price appreciation potential in the rest of the decade. Selectivity is important, however, as is diversification, because earnings predictability is difficult in this industry and stock prices tend to be volatile.

★ Recommended Stock

Cisco Systems, Inc.
1525 O'Brien Drive
Menlo Park, CA 94025
415-326-1941
800-553-NETS

Chairman: D. T. Valentine
Number of shareholders: 2,370
Number of employees: 1,450
Where the stock trades: OTC: Nasdaq
Symbol: CSCO

What the Company Does
Cisco Systems is the leading supplier of the fast-growing field of internetwork technology. The company's line of high-performance multiprotocol routers, bridges, communications servers and network management products holds more than a 50 percent share of the

internetworking market, worldwide. Cisco takes an active role in defining, developing, implementing and educating users about new industry standards. The company participates actively in developing industry standards and works with strategic technology and marketing partners to provide internetworking solutions of performance, functionality and reliability. Foreign business accounts for about 36 percent of sales.

Cisco was founded in 1984 by computer scientists from Stanford University to commercialize the technology used in developing a campuswide network to integrate local networks of various computer systems. Its first multiprotocol routers were shipped in March of 1986. Shares were offered initially to the public on February 16, 1990, at $1.13 per share, adjusted for stock splits.

Reason for Recommendation

By 1994, Cisco Systems, Inc., had become the acknowledged leader in internetwork technology, with more than a 50 percent share of the market worldwide. The company also operates as a strategic partner with many large customers, who have built some of the most extensive internetworks in the world. The company works closely with those customers to address their unique requirements and to provide global customer support directly and through international distribution channels.

Sales and earnings have nearly doubled in each of the past three years. In the 1993 fiscal year, ended July 25, sales were $649 million, up from $339 million in 1992 and $183 million in 1991. Net earnings kept pace, rising from $43 million in 1991 to $172 million in 1993. In early 1994, the company reported its 16th consecutive quarter of growth in revenue and profitability since it went public in February of 1990. Analysts continue to be confounded, with Cisco Systems turning in stronger earnings figures than predicted.

Demand for internetworking products continues to grow, spurred by mounting computerization. Computer networks have been multiplying at a faster rate than hardware units as a result of business needs to communicate and share data. Cisco dominates the internetworking market with systems that use different communication protocols.

An agreement with IBM enables Cisco Systems to include IBM's advanced peer-to-peer network software in Cisco products. Another agreement provides access to a synchronous transfer mode switching technology controlled by AT&T. Other agreements with Xerox and

FIGURE 20.1   Results of a $10,000 Investment in Cisco Systems, Inc.
Common Stock in 1990

	Average Share Price*	Annual Dividends	Value of Shares Owned
1990	2	$0	$ 10,000
1991	5½	0	27,500
1992	14⅛	0	70,625
1993	26	0	130,000

*Adjusted for stock splits.

Ameritech have resulted in those companies being resellers of Cisco
products. Cisco Systems also is allied in various technologies with
leading European firms such as France Telecom, Alcatel and Thomson.

Investment Results
Since Cisco's initial public offering of stock in 1990, shareholders
have done exceedingly well. Rapidly increasing earnings have driven
the stock price from a split-adjusted average of $2 per share in 1990
to an average of $26 in 1993.

Figure 20.1 shows the results of a $10,000 investment in Cisco
Systems, Inc., common stock from 1990 to 1993. It is assumed that the
stock was purchased at the average of the high and low prices in 1990.
There were two-for-one stock splits in March of 1991, 1992, 1993 and
1994. No cash dividends have been paid. Brokerage commissions are
not considered.

The December 31, 1993, closing price of Cisco Systems, Inc., on
the Nasdaq National Market was 32¼. The value of the original
$10,000 investment on that date was $161,250.

Historical Financial Data
Cisco Systems, Inc., has had a phenomenal record of growth. From
total sales of $1.5 million in 1987, three years before its public offering,
sales rocketed to $69 million in 1990 and then to $649 million in 1993.
Earnings were $100,000 in 1987, $13.9 million in 1990 and $172
million in 1993. Figure 20.2 sets forth important per-share data for the
company during the period from 1987 to 1993. All yearly numbers
relate to the company's end-of-July fiscal years and are adjusted for
stock splits.

FIGURE 20.2   Per-Share Financial Results of Cisco Systems, Inc. From 1987 to 1993

	Earnings Per Share	Book Value	Average Price Per Share	Percentage of Profits Paid in Dividends	Average PE Ratio
1987	$.00	$ .00	$ .02	N/A	N/A
1988	.01	.02	.03	N/A	N/A
1989	.02	.04	.13	N/A	N/A
1990	.06	.32	.32	2	33.3
1991	.17	.56	.80	5½	32.4
1992	.33	1.02	1.41	14⅛	42.8
1993	.66	1.92	2.62	26	39.4

The PE multiple has remained high during the first four years of public trading for Cisco Systems shares, reflecting strong investor expectations of future earnings growth. Potential investors, keep in mind that a high PE ratio also generally indicates vulnerability to any bad news that may appear and may lead to a price correction. Such a correction occurred in 1994, when the stock slid from its early 1994 high of 40¾ to 29 by mid-April.

Common Stock Quarterly Price Record

Following are the high and low prices of Cisco Systems, Inc., common stock during the fiscal years ending July 26, 1992, and July 25, 1993, adjusted for stock splits:

	1st Quarter	*2nd Quarter*	*3rd Quarter*	*4th Quarter*
1992				
Low	$ 4.75	$5.65	$ 9.06	$ 8.53
High	5.75	9.37	10.68	12.93
1993				
Low	$11.25	$14.62	$20.22	$20.18
High	14.78	23.12	23.93	28.12

The rapidly rising price of Cisco stock made it difficult in most quarters for investors to benefit from significant price drops to acquire shares. Except for the fourth quarter of 1992 and the past two quarters of 1993, there were few price corrections to take advantage of.

CREATING A PORTFOLIO OF STOCKS IN THE COMPUTER INDUSTRY

The competitive computer industry includes many companies, some waxing and some waning. Following is information on a small number of firms that analysts believe have good potential for earnings growth over the next several years. Many other companies in this fast-growing industry are worth a close look.

Company	1993 Earnings Per Share	12/31/93 Share Price	Dividend Yield	PE Ratio*
AST Research, Inc.	$1.32	22¾	Nil	17.2
American Power Conversion	.53	23¾	Nil	44.8
Cabletron Systems, Inc.	4.20	112½	Nil	26.8
Compaq Computer Corporation	5.44	73⅞	Nil	13.6
EMC Corporation	.60	16½	Nil	27.5
Silicon Graphics, Inc.	.60	24¾	Nil	41.3
SynOptics Communications	1.35	27⅞	Nil	20.6
3Com Corporation	1.22	47	Nil	38.5

*December 31, 1993, share price divided by 1993 earnings per share.

What the Companies Do

AST Research, Inc. (ASTA–OTC), manufactures and sells high-performance, IBM-compatible desktop, notebook and pen-based computers, and network servers. The company sells computers under these brand names: Premmia, featuring high-performance upgradable microprocessor architecture; and Bravo, emphasizing full functionality at affordable prices. Foreign business accounts for about 41 percent of sales. Sales totaled $1.4 billion in 1993. (The company has about 4,500 employees and 1,200 shareholders.)

Per-Share Financial Summary

	1984	1993
Revenues	$4.77	$44.72
Earnings	.35	1.32
Dividends	Nil	Nil
Average Stock Price	4⅛	19⅛

The company's stock was split two-for-one in 1991.

American Power Conversion Corporation (APCC–OTC) makes a line of *uninterruptible power supply* (UPS) products designed for use with personal computers, workstations and other electronic devices. UPSs are used to maintain incoming power within an acceptable range and provide backup power during outages. The company sells its products mainly through computer distributors. Its prices range from $29.99 to $5,199. Sales totaled $250 million in 1993. (The company has about 800 employees and 2,000 shareholders.)

Per-Share Financial Summary

	1988	1993
Revenues	$.21	$2.75
Earnings	.04	.53
Dividends	Nil	Nil
Average Stock Price	¼	17⅝

The company's stock initially was offered to the public in July of 1988 at $ .25 per share on a split-adjusted basis. The stock was split five-for-four in 1989, three-for-one in 1990, and two-for-one in 1991, 1992 and 1993.

Cabletron Systems, Inc. (CS–NYSE), develops, manufactures and markets products that interconnect *local area networks* (LANs) and provides design, consulting, installation and support for LAN systems. Products include electronic network interconnection equipment, high-speed Ethernet adapter cards for personal computers, network management software and LAN transmission media. Foreign business accounts for about 30 percent of the total. Sales totaled $600 million in 1993. (The company has about 2,300 employees and 1,000 shareholders.)

Per-Share Financial Summary

	1989	1993
Revenues	$3.99	$21.00
Earnings	.87	4.20
Dividends	Nil	Nil
Average Share Price	13⅛	96¾

The company's initial public offering was in May of 1989 at $15.50 per share.

Compaq Computer Corporation (CPQ–NYSE) produces laptop and desktop personal computers that are IBM-compatible. The company is a leader in the market for portable computers and has a leading share of the IBM-compatible desktop market. Compaq sells its products through mail order and about 10,600 outlets throughout the world. Foreign business accounts for about 55 percent of the total. Sales totaled $6.9 billion in 1993. (The company has about 10,000 employees and 8,100 shareholders.)

Per-Share Financial Summary

	1984	1993
Revenues	$6.28	$85.25
Earnings	.24	5.44
Dividends	Nil	Nil
Average Stock Price	4⅝	58¾

The company's stock was split two-for-one in 1990.

EMC Corporation (EMC–NYSE) designs, manufactures, markets and supports high-performance storage products and provides related services for selected mainframe and midrange computer systems primarily manufactured by IBM and Unisys. The company's product lines include Symmetrix, Harmonix and Champion. Sales totaled $765 million in 1993. (The company has about 2,000 employees.)

Per-Share Financial Summary

	1986	1993
Revenues	$.51	$4.18
Earnings	.14	.60
Dividends	Nil	Nil
Average Stock Price	1¾	12¼

The company's stock was split three-for-two in 1987 and 1992, and two-for-one in 1993 and 1994.

Silicon Graphics, Inc. (SGI–NYSE), is the leading maker of visual computing systems for technical, scientific and corporate applications. The company offers a full-size range, from desktop Indy at under $5,000 to Onyx supercomputers and Challenge Servers at $800,000. All systems are operable from the same software and within networks. Overseas business accounts for nearly half of the total. Sales totaled nearly $1.1 billion in 1993. (The company has about 3,800 employees and 3,500 shareholders.)

Per-Share Financial Summary

	1986	1993
Revenues	$.98	$8.29
Earnings	.02	.60
Dividends	Nil	Nil
Average Stock Price	3¼	18¼

The company's stock was initially offered to the public on November 5, 1986, at $2.81 per share, adjusted for two-for-one splits in 1992 and 1993.

SynOptics Communications (SNPX–OTC) is the leading supplier of LAN integration and management systems. LattisNet, the company's main product family, is an integrated system that provides network connectivity, network management and internetworking solutions. International business accounts for about 30 percent of the total. Sales totaled $704 million in 1993. (The company has about 1,250 employees and 1,000 shareholders.)

Per-Share Financial Summary

	1988	1993
Revenues	$.92	$11.11
Earnings	.15	1.35
Dividends	Nil	Nil
Average Stock Price	2½	31½

The company's IPO was initially offered at $2.25 per share in August of 1988, adjusted for a two-for-one stock split in 1990 and a three-for-one split in 1993.

3Com Corporation (COMS–OTC) designs, manufactures, markets and services networking products to worldwide customers. The company's products support a wide range of networking solutions and protocols based on industry standard and open systems. Product lines include network adapters, internetworking products, wiring hubs, network management and communication servers and protocols. Sales totaled $617 million in 1993. (The company has about 2,000 employees and 1,250 shareholders.)

Per-Share Financial Summary

	1984	1993
Revenues	$1.23	$20.01
Earnings	.16	1.22
Dividends	Nil	Nil
Average Stock Price	7¾	34⅛

The company's IPO occurred in March of 1984 at $6 per share.

SUMMARY

The economic situation looks favorable for the computer industry, although the depressed economies in much of Europe and Japan will likely be a drag on demand in the near-term, for about half of the computer group's sales comes from overseas. The ever-increasing power of smaller computers has remained the driving force in this industry. Pricing pressures are creating a shakeout in both the mainframe and personal-computer markets. Analysts expect competition to remain intense, but they look for the profitability of computer makers to improve over the next few years. For investors interested in this group, careful selection is important, because earnings predictability is difficult in this industry and stock prices tend to be volatile.

CHAPTER 21

Computer Software and Services

The dynamic and fast-growing computer software and services industry was largely untouched by the 1990–1991 recession. Industry sales and earnings continued to grow throughout 1991 and the slow recovery in the following year. The main reason is that these companies' products and services can cut costs for businesses, so purchases in tough economic times make sense. Some offerings, such as electronic data exchange services, give business a competitive edge, just what companies look for when revenues are off. As the economic upswing takes on more muscle in the middle of the decade, individuals and companies should be more willing to purchase software.

Analysts expect to see continued good demand in traditional areas such as personal productivity applications, including word processors, spreadsheets and database management programs. The market is far from saturated, and new users will provide growth in these areas. The rapid drop in the price of personal computers has put the power to buy those machines in more hands. The industry also should see growth from current users of products who are upgrading to the enhanced versions of applications that these companies constantly roll out. The upgrading extends to computer purchasers who are taking advantage of falling prices to load up with extras, such as additional internal memory, larger hard disks and CD-ROM drives. This makes it possible for them to buy more sophisticated software and to run multimedia applications, such as Microsoft's Encarta CD-ROM–based encyclopedia.

The home market also seems ready to offer good growth opportunities for the software and services industry. Microsoft is mounting a major campaign in this area. The company also is attempting to expand the reach of its software beyond personal computers to take in other office machines. Its Windows at Work product, for example, is intended to run on equipment such as fax machines and printers to make the equipment easier to use.

The service providers in this industry also should be able to find new areas of growth. Many companies concentrate on what they do best, and contract out for ancillary services, such as payroll processing, which will provide continuing opportunities for companies such as Automatic Data Processing. Another example is the need to increase efficiency in processing medical claims to reduce the rate of growth of medical care costs. This also is likely to bring additional business to many of these companies.

Emerging markets provide another fertile field for growth. Oracle, for instance, is working with other companies to develop the facilities to provide media services, such as movies and news, on demand.

Investment Outlook

In general, this industry should continue to turn in excellent performances. A number of stocks in the group may significantly outperform the market averages in the near future. Conservative investors should remember, though, that many of the equities in the computer software and services industry are more volatile than average and earnings often are difficult to predict.

★ Recommended Stock

Microsoft Corporation
One Microsoft Way
Redmond, WA 98052-6399
206-882-8080

Chairman and CEO: William H. Gates
Number of shareholders: 27,775
Number of employees: 14,400

Where the stock trades: OTC: Nasdaq
Symbol: MSFT

What the Company Does

Microsoft Corporation is the largest independent maker of personal computer (PC) software. Systems software and languages accounted for 34 percent of sales in 1993. These products include MS-DOS, by far the most widely used operating system for IBM PCs and IBM-compatible computers; Windows; and LAN Manager. About 58 percent of sales come from applications software, including word processing, spreadsheet, database management and other business programs. The other 8 percent of sales come from Microsoft Mouse, other hardware and books. The company invests approximately 12.5 percent of sales in research and development. Foreign sales account for about 48 percent of total sales and 37 percent of pretax profits.

Reason for Recommendation

In early 1994, Microsoft revenues and earnings continued to advance sharply. Demand was strong, particularly for the Office package of products, which also was being readied for the international market. Furthermore, initial orders indicated strong demand for an upgraded version of Excel.

Chicago, Microsoft's next major revision of its operating system and user interface, is scheduled for release in 1995. Analysts expect the product to be a big seller, given the huge user base (a source of upgrade sales) and the likelihood that many personal computer manufacturers will bundle the product with their machines.

Microsoft is changing the way revenues are recognized, deferring revenues for new products and booking them over the life of a product. This will lower revenue growth in 1995, but in the long run it will be a plus, because it will smooth out fluctuations.

Microsoft's prospects are very bright, based on its broad array of products. The company will likely continue to enjoy success as it moves to broaden its reach into new markets, such as multimedia products. The stock looks attractive for investors seeking capital appreciation.

Investment Results

Since its initial public offering in 1986, stockholders have been generously rewarded. One hundred percent stock dividends were distributed in 1987 and 1990, plus three-for-two splits were made in

FIGURE 21.1   Results of a $10,000 Investment in Microsoft Corporation
Common Stock from 1986 to 1993

	Average Share Price	Annual Dividends	Shares Bought from Dividends	Total # Shares Owned	Value of Shares Owned
1986	4	Nil	0	2,500	$ 10,000
1987	11⅛	Nil	0	2,500	27,812
1988	12⅞	Nil	0	2,500	32,187
1989	15	Nil	0	2,500	37,500
1990	27¼	Nil	0	2,500	68,125
1991	53½	Nil	0	2,500	133,750
1992	80¼	Nil	0	2,500	200,625
1993	84¼	Nil	0	2,500	210,625

1991 and 1992. A $10,000 investment made at the average price at which the shares traded in 1986 would have grown to a value of $210,625 in 1993 (based on the average share price in that year). The company did not pay any cash dividends from 1986 to 1993. Figure 21.1 shows the year-by-year results of a $10,000 investment in Microsoft stock from 1986 to 1993. Brokerage commissions are not considered.

The December 31, 1993, closing price of Microsoft Corporation common shares traded on the Nasdaq was $80⅝. The market value of $201,625 on that date was more than 20 times the original $10,000 invested in 1986.

Figure 21.2 shows selected per-share data of Microsoft Corporation during the period from 1986 to 1993. The data has been adjusted for stock splits.

In each of the eight years from 1986 to 1993, earnings per share increased from the year earlier. Book value per share also increased each year during that period. The average PE ratio ranged from the low 20s to the mid-30s during the period, reflecting investors' optimism about the potential for continued future earnings growth for the company. Microsoft has chosen to retain all its after-tax earnings to fuel the company's future growth.

FIGURE 21.2 Selected Per-Share Data of Microsoft Corporation from 1986 to 1993

	Earnings Per Share	Book Value	Average Price Per Share	Percentage of Profits Paid in Dividends	Average PE Ratio
1986	.17	.61	4	0	23.5
1987	.31	1.01	11⅛	0	35.9
1988	.49	1.56	12⅞	0	26.3
1989	.67	2.29	15	0	22.4
1990	1.04	3.59	27¼	0	26.2
1991	1.65	5.17	53½	0	32.4
1992	2.41	8.06	80¼	0	33.3
1993	3.15	11.50	84¼	0	26.7

Common Stock Quarterly Price Record

The high and low prices of Microsoft Corporation common stock during 1992 and 1993, adjusted for a three-for-one stock split in 1992, were:

	1st Quarter	2nd Quarter	3rd Quarter	4th Quarter
1992				
High	$60	$74⅝	$88⅞	$86⅛
Low	40⅜	57½	73	65¾
1993				
High	$82	$95	$94¼	$98
Low	65½	75¾	76¾	79¾

As the previous chart shows, a patient investor does not need to pay top price for common shares. In nearly every quarter during 1992 and 1993, you could have bought shares substantially below the high price of the previous quarter. The exception was only a slight drop in the third quarter of 1992. But even in that case, the stock dropped significantly in the fourth quarter. Careful buying of shares can have a long-term impact on your total investment return.

CREATING A PORTFOLIO OF STOCKS IN THE COMPUTER SOFTWARE AND SERVICES INDUSTRY

The computer software and services industry consists of a large number of companies ranging from very small privately owned businesses to large publicly held corporations. Total revenues for the industry in 1993 were about $35 billion. Seven companies accounted for about 62 percent of the business: Automatic Data Processing, Inc. ($2.2 billion); Computer Associates International, Inc. ($2.1 billion); Computer Sciences Corporation ($2.5 billion); Electronic Data Systems Corporation ($8.5 billion); Microsoft Corporation ($3.7 billion); Novell, Incorporated ($1.1 billion); and Oracle Systems Corporation ($1.5 billion).

The following information is presented on other companies in the computer software and services industry that are highly regarded by analysts. These firms have been selected for their potential for growth. Some of these stocks tend to be volatile, and it often is difficult for analysts to predict earnings of the companies. So conservative investors may want to look elsewhere. Following each company's name at the start of the description is its ticker symbol and the exchange where the stock is traded.

Company	1993 Earnings Per Share	12/31/93 Share Price	Dividend Yield	PE Ratio*
Acclaim Entertainment	$ .63	21¼	0.0%	33.7
Adobe Systems	1.18	22¼	0.7	18.9
Automatic Data Processing, Inc.	2.08	55¼	1.1	26.6
Computer Associates	2.20	40	0.4	18.2
Computer Sciences Corp.	1.75	33⅛	0.0	19.0
General Motors "E"	1.51	29¼	1.5	19.4
Lotus Development Corp.	1.69	55	0.0	32.5
Oracle Systems Corp.	.54	28¾	0.0	53.2
Parametric Technology	.75	38¾	0.0	51.7
Sybase, Inc.	.86	42	0.0	48.8

*December 31, 1993 share price ÷ 1993 earnings per share.

What the Companies Do

Acclaim Entertainment, Inc. (AKLM–OTC), publishes interactive entertainment software under the following labels: Acclaim, LJN, Flying Edge and Arena. The software is made for use with the hardware platforms manufactured by Nintendo and Sega. The company launched Acclaim Distribution in June of 1993. Acclaim supervises the development of titles by independent designers and licenses property rights such as The Simpson, Terminator II, Incredible Crash Dummies, Marvel Comics and Mortal Kombat. Eighty-one percent of 1992 net revenues came from Nintendo as a licenser and/or manufacturer of software. (The company has about 193 employees and 860 shareholders.)

Sales grew from less than $40 million in 1988, the year Acclaim went public, to more than $325 million in 1993. Sales in 1993 were up 62 percent from 1992.

Adobe Systems, Inc. (ADBE–OTC), develops and supports computer software products and technologies that enable users to create, display, print and communicate all forms of electronic documents. The company's PostScript page-description language accounted for about 47 percent of 1993 revenues. The balance of revenues came from applications software, which includes Illustrator, a graphics illustration program; Photoshop, an image enhancement tool; Acrobat, document-processing software; and typeface software. The company spends more than 20 percent of its revenues on research and development. (The company has about 900 employees and 1,050 shareholders.)

Adobe sales have risen from $16 million in 1986, the year it went public, to more than $300 million in 1993. During the same period, per-share earnings increased from $ .10 to $1.18. The stock has gone from an average price of 2½ in 1986 to an average of 26¼ in 1993, after adjusting for stock splits in 1987, 1988 and 1993.

Automatic Data Processing, Inc. (AUD–NYSE), is the nation's largest payroll and tax-filing processor with 275,000 accounts, which accounted for 59 percent of its 1993 revenues. Financial services provides front-office quotation workstations and back-office record-keeping, order-entry and proxy services for brokerage firms; and contributes 23 percent of the company's revenues. The company also provides specialized services for auto and truck dealerships, including accounting, inventory, leasing and parts ordering. (The company has about 20,500 employees and 18,600 shareholders.)

The company has shown steady growth. Sales have grown from $753 million in 1983 to more than $2.2 billion in 1993. Profits have kept pace, rising from $ .47 per share in 1983 to $2.08 in 1993. The stock's market price has risen from an average of 9⅝ per share in 1983 to 51⅞ in 1993.

Computer Associates International, Inc. (CA–NYSE), makes software that enables computers to run more efficiently. It develops, markets and services more than 300 software products for IBM-compatible, DG and DEC mainframes, minicomputers and microcomputers. The company acquired Software International Corporation and Integrated Software Systems Corporation in 1986, UCCEL Corporation in 1987, Applied Data Research in 1988 and Cullinet Software, Inc., in 1989. (The company has about 7,200 employees and 10,000 shareholders.)

The company went public in 1980. In 1983, its annual sales were about $85 million, growing to more than $2 billion in 1993. Earnings per share rose from $ .11 in 1983 to more than $2.00 in 1993. The yearly average price per share of the stock rose from 3¼ in 1983 to 32¼ in 1993.

Computer Sciences Corporation (CSC–NYSE) designs, engineers, installs, integrates and operates computer-based systems and communication systems. The company's services include data processing, credit reporting, claims processing, tax processing and data communications. Automated systems also are provided for health-care organizations. The systems group accounts for about 50 percent of revenues, with 20 percent coming from commercial services and consulting and 30 percent from industry services. (The company has about 26,500 employees and 8,400 shareholders.)

Computer Sciences Corporation has had steady growth since the early 1980s. Revenues have risen from $712 million in 1983 to more than $2.5 billion in 1993. Earnings per share have gone from $ .44 in 1983 to $1.75 in 1993. Shareholders saw the price of their shares rise from an average of 6½ in 1983 to an average of 28⅜ in 1993. The shares were split three-for-one in January 1994.

Electronic Data Systems Corporation (EDS), represented by General Motors Series "E" common stock (GME–NYSE), is a wholly owned subsidiary of General Motors and is a leader in the design, operation and integration of large data-processing and communications systems. About 41 percent of total revenues come from work the company does for General Motors, including benefits administration, dealer networks, engineering and manufacturing technologies, and comprehensive business information systems. EDS does similar work for finance and insurance institutions, which accounts for about 18 percent of its revenues. Another 34 percent of revenues are derived from government agencies and other international, commercial and communications customers. (The company has about 71,000 employees and 393,000 shareholders.)

EDS became a wholly owned subsidiary of General Motors in 1984 when GM purchased all of its common stock. Sales have increased from $774 million in 1984 to $8.5 billion in 1993. Profits per share have grown from $ .32 in 1984 to $1.51 in 1993. The average yearly share price of EDS has gone from 5¼ in 1984 to 31 in 1993.

Lotus Development Corporation (LOTS–OTC) is one of the largest independent makers of personal computer software. The most popular personal computer application in the world, 1-2-3, combines spreadsheet, database and graphing functions into a single program. Lotus also sells Ami Pro, a word-processing application; Freeland Graphics, a presentation graphics package; Notes, a work-group product; and cc:Mail, an electronic-mail application. Foreign sales account for about 45 percent of total sales. Lotus invests about 13 percent of sales into research and development. (The company has about 4,400 employees and 30,000 shareholders.)

Lotus Development Corporation went public in 1983, at which time its sales totaled $53 million. In 1993, total sales were more than $1.1 billion. Earnings per share rose from $ .33 in 1983 to $1.69 in 1993. The average price of a common share was 8⅛ in 1983, rising to an average of 38⅞ in 1993.

Oracle Systems Corporation (ORCL–OTC) is the world's largest maker of database management systems (DBMS), a software that allows users to create, retrieve and manipulate data in computer-based files. The company's main products support ORACLE, a relational DBMS, which allows people to manipulate and retrieve data by requesting it using an industry-standard command language, SQL. Licensing fees account for about 60 percent of revenues, with the balance coming from training and services. Foreign sales provide about 62 percent of sales and 40 percent of profits. The company invests about 9.5 percent of sales in research and development. (Oracle Systems has about 9,200 employees and 2,500 shareholders.)

Oracle had its IPO in 1986. Annual sales have grown from $55 million in 1986 to more than $1.5 billion in 1993. Earnings per share were $ .03 in 1986, rising to $ .54 in 1993. The average price of the stock rose from 1¼ in 1986 to 25½ in 1993. Per-share earnings and market price have been adjusted to account for stock splits in 1987, 1989 and 1993.

Parametric Technology Corporation (PMTC–OTC) develops, markets and supports a group of fully integrated software products for the automation of the mechanical design process. The company's Pro/Engineer product line is a parametric, feature-based solid modeling technology that is hardware-independent and operates on a wide variety of workstations. The company invests about 7 percent of sales in research and development. Foreign sales account for about 37 percent of total revenues. (The company has about 900 employees and 670 shareholders.)

Parametric Technology went public in December of 1989. After adjusting for stock splits in 1991, 1992 and 1993, the average yearly share price has gone from 2¾ in 1989 to 33⅝ in 1993. Sales have grown from $11 million in 1989 to $163 million in 1993. Per-share earnings in the same years have increased from $ .04 to $ .75.

Sybase, Incorporated (SYBS–OTC) provides relational database management systems (RDBMS) for use in network-based client-server computing environments. The company's products include database server products, development tools and connectivity products. In addition, the company provides consulting and professional services as well as technical support. Licensing fees account for about 72 percent of the company's total revenues. Foreign sales account for about 23 percent of the total. Sybase invests about 16 percent of sales in research and development. (The company has about 2,500 employees and 1,080 shareholders.)

Sybase, Inc., had its initial public offering in 1991. Sales have grown from $159 million in that year to $426 million in 1993. Per-share earnings have gone up from $ .19 to $ .86 in the same years. The average annual price of the stock has gone from 9⅛ in 1991 to 33⅛ in 1993, after adjustment for a two-for-one stock split in 1993.

SUMMARY

The computer software and services industry survived the recession in the early 1990s with few ill effects. The industry should prosper as the recovery strengthens and growth should continue in its traditional areas, such as productivity-enhancing applications. Analysts expect the industry will move ahead aggressively into new endeavors such as the emerging effort to provide media services—for example, movies on demand. A number of stocks in this industry should enjoy above-average market performance in the next few years. However, conservative investors should be aware that many of the equities in this growth industry are more volatile than average, and predicting earnings for companies in this industry is difficult.

CHAPTER 22

Financial Services

The financial services industry includes a diverse group of companies that include consumer finance companies, thrift institutions, brokerage and commodity firms, and leasing and finance operations. Just as many large corporations do, this industry often overlaps with others. Loews Corporation, for example, is included in the financial services industry, yet it produces and sells cigarettes through its wholly owned subsidiary Lorillard, Inc. At the same time, Loews owns an 83 percent interest in CNA Financial Corporation, a multiple-line insurance company; it owns 97 percent of Bulova Corporation, maker of watches; and it has a 25 percent interest in CBS, Inc.

Recent years have seen a renewed enthusiasm for financial matters. This has been reflected in the growth of services such as tax preparation, real estate services, nontraditional life insurance, and annuities and other asset-accumulation products. Financial services appears to be a growth industry over the long term.

As the stock market climbed to new highs, brokerage industry profits surged. Records were broken in nearly all areas of the business, from municipal underwritings and initial public offerings, to commission revenue, trading volume and mutual fund fees. And mutual fund companies themselves participated in the prosperity, with total fund assets soaring to new records as the market kept going up and new money flowed into the funds.

Financial services companies generally reinvest their earnings to finance further growth, so investors seeking dividend yield should probably look elsewhere.

★ Recommended Stock

T. Rowe Price Associates, Inc.
100 East Pratt Street
Baltimore, MD 21202
410-547-2000

President and CEO: George J. Collins
Number of shareholders: 1,839
Number of employees: 1,538
Where the stock trades: OTC: Nasdaq
Symbol: TROW

What the Company Does
The company provides investment advisory and administrative services to the T. Rowe Price family of no-load mutual funds, to investment products it sponsors and to private accounts of other institutional and individual investors. At the end of 1993, the firm had more than $54 billion of assets under its management, with $34.7 billion of that amount in the mutual funds it manages. Stocks accounted for 51 percent of total assets, up from 42 percent in 1992. Net cash flow into the funds totaled $3.9 billion, of which $3.7 billion went into equities. Appreciation accounted for $4.6 billion of the rise in mutual fund assets during 1993. The company introduced 11 new mutual funds in 1993 and expects to offer an equal number again in 1994.

History
T. Rowe Price was founded by Thomas Rowe Price in 1937. It was incorporated in Maryland in 1947. Its first mutual fund, the Growth Stock Fund, was offered in 1950. The New Horizons Fund was offered in 1960 and the New Era Fund in 1969. By the end of 1993, 55 funds were under management. An IPO of 3,784,700 shares of common stock was made in 1986 at $6 per share (adjusted for two subsequent two-for-one stock splits).

FIGURE 22.1   Results of a $10,000 Investment in T. Rowe Price
Common Stock from 1986 to 1993

	Average Share Price	Annual Dividends	Shares Bought from Dividends	Total # Shares Owned	Value of Shares Owned
1986	8⅝	$ 57	6	1,162	$10,022
1987	8⅝	127	14	1,176	10,143
1988	6⅞	188	27	1,203	8,270
1989	11⅝	288	24	1,227	14,263
1990	11½	368	32	1,259	14,478
1991	16⅛	415	25	1,284	20,704
1992	20⅝	449	21	1,305	26,915
1993	26⅝	574	21	1,326	35,304

Reason for Recommendation

T. Rowe Price has continued to benefit from a confident stock market with steadily rising prices and an influx of new money into its funds. Total assets under management at the end of 1993 exceeded $54 billion, up from less than $42 billion at the end of 1992. Management fees have increased along with asset growth, spurring profits, which have increased steadily since 1990. The international funds have been showing particularly strong inflows of cash. Analysts expect that earnings will continue to rise for the balance of this decade, assuming moderate gains in stock prices.

Part of the optimism for the future of T. Rowe Price results from increasingly popular company-sponsored defined contribution plans. Many companies are using them as the primary vehicle to fund employee retirement benefits. With some 55 mutual funds it manages, Price is well positioned to provide plan participants with a wide variety of investment alternatives, together with all the required record-keeping services. This part of the business should continue to grow rapidly as companies move away from costly defined-benefit-type pension plans.

T. Rowe Price has built a solid position in some of the fastest growing sectors of the financial services industry. It has the financial and management resources to sustain the growth that lies ahead.

FIGURE 22.2   Per-Share Financial Results of T. Rowe Price From
1986 to 1993

	Earnings Per Share	Book Value	Average Price Per Share	Percentage of Profits Paid in Dividends	Average PE Ratio
1986	$ .50	$1.44	8⅝	7%	16.4
1987	.62	2.01	8⅝	15	14.3
1988	.77	2.76	6⅞	18	9.7
1989	1.00	3.52	11⅝	20	11.6
1990	.85	3.90	11½	35	14.4
1991	1.02	4.60	16⅛	30	14.6
1992	1.19	5.35	20⅝	29	16.9
1993	1.59	6.70	26⅝	26	16.2

Investment Results

Over the past eight years, T. Rowe Price has never had a year in which its sales did not exceed that of the previous year. Earnings per share have kept pace. Only in 1990 did per-share earnings fail to move forward. The company has typically paid a little less than 30 percent of its profits in dividends in the past few years. If you had invested $10,000 in T. Rowe Price shares in 1986, the year of its initial public offering (at the average price the stock traded at during the year), with dividends reinvested each year in additional shares, you would have owned 1,326 shares with a value of $38,454 at the end of 1993. Brokerage commissions have not been considered. Figure 22.1 illustrates the $10,000 investment in T. Rowe Price common stock from 1986 to 1993.

The December 31, 1993, closing price of T. Rowe Price common stock shares traded in the OTC market was $29. As mentioned previously, the original $10,000 investment had multiplied by more than 3.5 times in seven years to a market value of $38,454. The $574 dividend paid in 1993 represented a yield of 5.7 percent on the original $10,000 investment.

Two interesting aspects of the investment in T. Rowe Price can be seen in Figure 22.2. First, while the stock price did not pursue a continual upward move, the average yearly price dipped in 1988 and 1990; a patient investor benefited in those years because dividends bought more shares at lower prices than at higher prices. Second, the company increased its dividend payout every year.

Except for 1990, the profits of T. Rowe Price increased each year. Book value per share increased every year since the stock's initial public offering in 1986. The average PE ratio held quite steady at about 14 to 16 times earnings over the eight-year period. The gradual rise in the price of common stock shares has treated shareholders nicely.

Common Stock Quarterly Price Record
Following are the high and low prices of T. Rowe Price common stock during 1992 and 1993, adjusted for a two-for-one stock split in November 1993:

	1st Quarter	2nd Quarter	3rd Quarter	4th Quarter
1992				
High	$24.88	$18.88	$21.38	$23.38
Low	18.25	16.38	17.75	18.25
1993				
High	$25.50	$24.13	$31.63	$32.88
Low	21.25	20.25	22.63	27.00

As this chart shows, a patient investor did not have to pay top price for common shares. In every quarter during 1992 and 1993, you could have bought shares at least 15 percent below the high price of the previous quarter. Buying shares carefully can have a long-term impact on your total investment return.

CREATING A PORTFOLIO OF FINANCIAL SERVICES STOCKS

The financial services group is made up of consumer finance companies, securities brokerage firms and firms engaged in such services as tax preparation, real estate services, nontraditional life insurance, and annuities and other asset-accumulation products. The industry seems to be growing. Dividend yields generally are not generous among companies in this group, but earnings should grow nicely over the next several years.

Following are a number of other highly regarded companies in the financial services industry. These firms have been selected for their financial stability and potential for growth. As always, it makes sense to diversify your stock portfolio among at least ten stocks.

Company	Annual Dividend	12/31/93 Price	Dividend Yield	PE Ratio*
ADVANTA Corp. "A"	.20	33¼	0.6%	15.3
Alliance Capital Management	1.09	27⅜	4.0	14.9
Block (H & R), Inc.	1.12	40¾	2.7	27.2
CUC International	Nil	36	0.0	41.7
First Financial Management	.10	56¾	0.2	28.2
Franklin Resources	.32	45⅞	0.7	18.8
Green Tree Financial Corporation	.37	48	0.8	12.7
Travelers, Inc.	1.60	31⅛	5.1	9.7

*Ratio of December 31, 1993, share price to 1993 earnings per share.

What the Companies Do

ADVANTA Corporation (ADVNA–OTC) is a direct marketer of consumer financial services. The company's business includes gold and standard credit-card issuance and servicing, the origination of home-equity loans through ADVANTA Mortgage, equipment-leasing services through ADVANTA Leasing, credit insurance and deposit products. At the end of 1993, the company had $6.1 billion of total assets under management. (The company has about 1,300 employees and 625 common shareholders.)

The company was founded in 1951 as Teachers Service Organization. It went public in 1985 with an IPO priced at $2.42 per share (adjusted for stock splits in 1992 and 1993).

Per-Share Financial Summary

	1985	1993
Interest Income	$3.02	$3.81
Earnings	.24	1.95
Dividends	Nil	.16
Average Stock Price	3¼	32⅞

Alliance Capital Management, L.P. (AC–NYSE) was formed in 1987 with the initial purpose of providing investment management services to institutional investors. The *master limited partnership* (MLP) is one of the largest investment advisers in the United States, now providing investment management services directly to institutional clients and through broker-dealers to individual clients. Assets under management exceed $63 billion. (The company has about 850 employees and 1,260 unit-holders.)

As an MLP, the company distributes more than 90 percent of its "cash flow" to unit-holders. Units began public trading in 1988.

Per-Share Financial Summary

	1988	1993
Revenues	$2.37	$6.92
Earnings	.22	1.48
Distributions	.47	1.42
Average Unit Price	5¼	22⅜

The units were split two-for-one in 1993.

H & R Block, Incorporated (HRB–NYSE), operates and franchises a network of 9,511 company-owned and franchised offices worldwide. Tax-preparation services account for 48 percent of operating revenues and 65 percent of profits; temporary personnel services contribute 30 percent of revenues and 7 percent of profits. The company acquired CompuServe in 1980, Access Technology in 1988, MicroSolutions in 1990 and Meca Software in 1993. (The company has about 3,600 permanent employees and 33,450 shareholders.)

Per-Share Financial Summary

	1984	1993
Revenues	$5.11	$11.67
Earnings	.56	1.78
Dividends	.29	1.09
Average Stock Price	5½	37¼

The shares were split two-for-one in 1985, 1987 and 1991.

CUC International (CU–NYSE) is a consumer services company. It provides its more than 27 million members with access to a variety of services, including home shopping, travel, insurance, auto, dining, checking-account enhancements and extended warranties. The Comp-U-Card Division sells its services to credit-card customers of financial institutions, oil companies and major retailers. Other services are marketed to community banks, thrift institutions and credit unions. (The company has about 3,200 employees and 1,000 shareholders.)

Per-Share Financial Summary

	1984	1993
Revenues	$ .81	$7.85
Earnings	.06	.77
Dividends	Nil	Nil
Average Stock Price	2½	28¼

The shares were split three-for-two in 1985, 1986, 1991, 1992 and 1993.

First Financial Management Corporation (FFM–NYSE) markets information-processing services. Its Merchant Credit Card Group provides credit-card authorizations and financial clearing. The Data Imaging Group serves 4,000 customers with computer output micrographics and electronic printing. The company acquired NaBanco, Endata and First Data Management in 1987; The Computer Store and MicroBilt in 1989. (The company has about 12,600 employees and 1,770 shareholders.)

Per-Share Financial Summary

	1984	1993
Revenues	$3.43	$27.89
Earnings	.25	2.10
Dividends	Nil	.10
Average Stock Price	4⅜	47¼

The shares were split three-for-two in 1985, 1987 and 1992. There was a 5 percent stock dividend in 1989.

Franklin Resources, Inc. (BEN–NYSE), is a financial services holding company. Through subsidiaries, it is engaged in investment management, stock-transfer services and the distribution of 71 mutual funds in the Franklin Group. The company acquired Templeton, Galbraith & Hansberger Ltd. in 1992. By the end of 1993, net assets under management exceeded $108 billion. The company also sells tax-sheltered investments and closed-end funds, provides trust services and sponsors oil and gas products. (The company has about 3,500 employees and 1,600 shareholders.)

Per-Share Financial Summary

	1984	1993
Revenues	$ .47	$ 7.98
Earnings	.08	2.12
Dividends	.01	.28
Average Stock Price	⅛	41⅞

The shares were split two-for-one in 1985 and 1986, three-for-two in 1986, five-for-four in 1987, three-for-two in 1989 and two-for-one in 1992.

Green Tree Financial Corporation (GNT–NYSE) purchases, pools, sells and services conditional sales contracts for purchasers of manufactured housing. FHA- and VA-backed loans, which account for about 40 percent of the total, are converted into certificates guaranteed by the Government National Mortgage Association (GNMA). The company also provides home-improvement financing, contract-related insurance and motorcycle financing. Green Tree operates in 48 states through 42 regional service centers. (The company has about 1,200 employees and 360 shareholders.)

Per-Share Financial Summary

	1984	1993
Revenues	$2.09	$10.94
Earnings	.56	3.62
Dividends	Nil	.34
Average Stock Price	4¼	42⅞

The shares were split two-for-one in 1986 and 1993.

The Travelers, Inc. (TIC–NYSE), is a diversified financial services company. Its three main business segments are consumer finance, insurance services (life, accident and health, and property/casualty) and securities brokerage and asset management. The company's operating units include Smith Barney Shearson, American Capital Management, Commercial Credit and Primerica Financial Services. Revenues totaled $6.8 billion in 1993. Public trading in Travelers stock began in 1987. (The company has about 16,000 employees and 33,000 shareholders.)

Per-Share Financial Summary

	1987	1993
Revenues	$5.26	$20.78
Earnings	1.00	3.60
Dividends	.12	.45
Average Stock Price	12⅞	36⅞

The shares were split three-for-two and four-for-three in 1993.

SUMMARY

In recent years, there has been renewed interest in financial matters. The financial services industry, often overlapping with other industries, is comprised of a diverse group of companies that include consumer finance companies, thrift institutions, brokerage and commodity firms, and leasing and finance operations. As the stock market climbed to new highs, brokerage industry profits surged. Records were broken in nearly all areas of the business, from municipal underwritings and initial public offerings to commission revenue, trading volume and mutual fund fees. And mutual fund companies themselves participated in the prosperity, with total fund assets soaring to new records as the market kept going up and new money flowed into the funds. The future looks bright for financial services companies. Dividend yields generally are low in this industry.

CHAPTER 23

Food Processing

The food-processing industry is made up of a wide variety of companies, both in size and in terms of operations and product offerings. Food-processing industry earnings have been up in most years, and analysts generally look for a continuation of the trend. Even with the higher profits, PE ratios of companies in the group are lower than might be expected given the group's remarkable record of consistent earnings growth. Net income has been up in every year since 1982. Of course, not all companies have reported steady growth; some have had quite inconsistent records.

Brand names of the leading companies have been one key to the success of the industry. Consumers have consistently reached first for those brands that they have come to know, such as Sara Lee, Betty Crocker, Kellogg's or Special K, even if they carry a premium price. Often that translates into premium profits for the food company.

In recent years, though, private-label products, those sold under a brand name owned by the retailer and at a lower price, have been gathering more market share, partly because in a sluggish economy people have wanted to save money. But it is also because the quality of private-label products has improved. Strong private-label sales have taken hold in frozen vegetables, refrigerated juices, milk, ice cream and canned fruit. Consumer resistance to private labels has been evident in soft drinks, chips and snacks, coffee and ready-to-eat cereal.

No one knows how large private-label sales will get, but analysts expect growth to continue.

Many food companies are taking advantage of attractive opportunities in foreign markets, as economic and demographic conditions are causing demand to increase. Perhaps the single most positive factor is a rising standard of living, with an accompanying increase in disposable income. A more stable political climate and a rising population in many countries also are favorable. Companies with significant foreign operations generally have seen sales and earnings overseas rise more rapidly than at home. That trend is likely to continue.

Investment Outlook

Conservative investors may find some good opportunities in the food-processing group, particularly on a long-term basis. Many of the big companies are financially stable and have had many years of consistent growth in earnings and dividends. PE ratios for the group are relatively low. And some companies with international diversification could be attractive because foreign markets are expected to grow faster over the next several years than those at home.

★ *Recommended Stock*

Wm. Wrigley Jr. Company
410 North Michigan Avenue
Chicago, IL 60611
312-644-2121

President and CEO: William Wrigley
Number of shareholders: 15,450
Number of employees: 6,700
Where the stock trades: NYSE
Symbol: WWY

What the Company Does
Wm. Wrigley Jr. Company is the world's largest manufacturer and seller of chewing gum, specialty gums and gum base. Its principal chewing gum brands are Doublemint, Spearmint, Juicy Fruit, Big Red, Extra, Orbit and Freedent. A subsidiary, Amurol Products, makes novelty gums, including Bubble Tape, Big League Chew and Hubba

Bubba bubble gum. Foreign sales accounted for 46 percent of the total in 1993.

Reason for Recommendation

Years ago, when asked his philosophy on advertising, the founder of the Wrigley Company replied, "Tell 'em quick, and tell 'em often." He continued, "You must have a good product in the first place, something people want. Explain to folks plainly and sincerely what you have to sell, do it in as few words as possible—and keep everlastingly coming after them." Mr. Wrigley had an unshakable faith in the quality of his products and the power of advertising.

A consistent combination of quality products, effective advertising and reasonable pricing has resulted in nine consecutive years of record sales and earnings. In the highly competitive U.S. market, Wrigley brands' growth in 1993 was the best in 25 years. The company feels that because the ability to attract new consumers to its products is as important as market growth, it has restrained price increases.

The company began building additional manufacturing capacity in 1994 to meet future demand. With three new plants in the works and a major addition scheduled for the company's facility in Biesheim, France, 1994 was expected to be a record-breaking year for capital expenditures.

Wrigley continues to make steady bottom-line progress, with increased shipments worldwide and selective price increases. And the company's predominant domestic market share continues its growth, despite increased advertising and new product introductions by rival gum makers. Part of the reason has been Wrigley's conscious decision to keep the price of a single five-stick pack of each of its major brands—Doublemint, Spearmint, Juicy Fruit and Big Red—at 25 cents since 1988, while competitors were raising their prices.

Foreign sales are booming, with strong growth in Poland, Central Europe and Russia. Wrigley has talked with Polish officials about building a chewing gum plant in Poznan, with construction likely in 1994. The company's plant in China is helping expansion in that country, and India will be getting a new factory. Wrigley's 25 cents per pack worldwide is aimed toward the top 10 percent to 20 percent of the emerging markets, with sales rising for the rest of the population along with per-capita income.

FIGURE 23.1   Results of a $10,000 Investment in Wm. Wrigley Jr.
Company Common Stock with Dividends Reinvested
from 1984 to 1993

	Average Share Price	Annual Dividends	Shares Bought from Dividends	Total # Shares Owned	Value of Shares Owned
1984	2⅞	$ 556	193	3,671	$ 10,554
1985	4¼	624	146	3,817	16,222
1986	6⅝	801	121	3,938	26,089
1987	9⅛	1,102	120	4,048	36,938
1988	12¼	1,461	119	4,167	51,045
1989	14⅞	1,875	126	4,293	63,858
1990	17¼	2,189	126	4,419	76,227
1991	21¾	2,430	111	4,530	98,527
1992	31	2,854	92	4,622	143,282
1993	37¾	3,466	91	4,713	177,915

Investment Results

The Wm. Wrigley Jr. Company has enjoyed consistent success in
its goal to keep sales and earnings moving upward. Investors have been
rewarded by the market's reaction to the company's solid growth. An
investment of $10,000 in 1984 would have bought 3,478 shares at the
average market price in that year (adjusted for stock splits). Figure 23.1
shows the year-by-year results of a $10,000 investment in Wrigley
stock from 1984 to 1993. Brokerage commissions are not considered.
Numbers have been adjusted for a three-for-one split in 1986, a
two-for-one split in 1988 and a three-for-one split in 1992.

The December 31, 1993, closing price of Wm. Wrigley Jr. Company
common shares traded on the NYSE was $44⅛. The market value of
$207,961 on that date was more than 20 times the original $10,000
invested in 1984.

Figure 23.2 shows selected per-share data of Wm. Wrigley Jr.
Company during the period from 1984 to 1993. The data has been
adjusted for stock splits.

Earnings per share rose steadily every year from 1984 to 1993, as
did book value per share. The company has followed a policy of paying
out each year approximately one-half of its earnings in dividends.
Earnings multiples have moved steadily higher as the investment

FIGURE 23.2   Selected Per-Share Data of Wm. Wrigley Jr. Company
from 1984 to 1993

	Earnings Per Share	Book Value	Average Price Per Share	Percentage of Profits Paid in Dividends	Average PE Ratio
1984	$ .31	$1.81	2⅞	56%	9.3
1985	.34	2.04	4¼	50	12.5
1986	.43	2.31	6⅝	50	15.4
1987	.56	2.39	9⅛	50	16.3
1988	.73	2.59	12¼	50	16.8
1989	.90	2.91	14⅞	50	16.5
1990	1.00	3.42	17¼	49	17.3
1991	1.09	3.94	21¾	50	20.0
1992	1.27	4.27	31	49	24.4
1993	1.50	4.94	37¾	50	25.2

community bid up the share price. At 25 times earnings the stock price
appears vulnerable to any bad news that may come along.

Common Stock Quarterly Price Record

Following are the high and low prices of the Wm. Wrigley Jr.
Company common stock during the 1992 and 1993 fiscal years,
adjusted for a three-for-one stock split in 1992:

	1st Quarter	2nd Quarter	3rd Quarter	4th Quarter
1992				
High	$28¹⁷⁄₂₄	$25⁷⁄₂₄	$37⅞	$39⅞
Low	22⅙	22⅛	25¼	31⅝
1993				
High	$34⅞	$36¼	$45½	$46⅛
Low	29½	30⅛	31⅜	41¼

Note: Wrigley's fiscal year ends December 31.

Except for the second quarter of 1992, it was possible in each quarter
to buy shares at a price substantially below the high price of the prior
quarter. Buying shares carefully can have a long-term positive impact
on your total investment return.

CREATING A PORTFOLIO OF STOCKS IN THE FOOD-PROCESSING INDUSTRY

Brief information is presented on a number of companies in the food-processing industry that some analysts consider to be favorably positioned for capital appreciation.

Company	1993 Earnings Per Share	12/31/93 Share Price	Dividend Yield	PE Ratio*
Campbell Soup Company	$2.21	41	3.0%	18.6
ConAgra, Inc.	1.58	26⅜	2.8	16.7
General Mills, Inc.	3.45	60¾	3.2	17.6
Hershey Foods Corporation	2.86	49	2.6	17.1
Kellogg Company	2.92	56¾	2.7	19.4
Sara Lee Corporation	1.40	25	3.0	17.9

*December 31, 1993 share price divided by 1993 earnings per share.

What the Companies Do

Campbell Soup Company (CPB–NYSE) is a leading manufacturer of canned soups, spaghetti, fruit and vegetable juices, frozen foods, salad dressings, bakery products, pickles and olives. The company's brand names include Campbell's, Franco-American, V8, Swanson, Pepperidge Farm, Vlasic, Mrs. Paul's, Prego, Godiva, Le Menu, Great Starts, Open Pit, Casera, Marie's and Healthy Request. Foreign operations account for about 28 percent of sales. Sales totaled $6.5 billion in 1993. (The company has about 46,900 employees and 43,000 shareholders.)

Per-Share Financial Summary

	1984	1993
Revenues	$14.17	$26.17
Earnings	.74	2.21
Dividends	.29	.92
Average Stock Price	7⅞	40⅜

Campbell Soup stock was split two-for-one in 1985, 1987 and 1991.

ConAgra, Inc. (CAG–NYSE), is the nation's second largest food processor. Its first segment, Agri-Products, includes agricultural chemicals, formula feed and fertilizer. The Trading & Processing segment includes flour, by-products and feed ingredients. The Prepared Foods segment includes Banquet, Armour Classics, Chun King, Patio and Healthy Choice frozen foods. This segment also sells Armour and Swift-Eckrich processed meats. Sales totaled $21.5 billion in 1993. (The company has about 84,000 employees and 28,700 shareholders.)

The company's common stock was split three-for-two in 1984, two-for-one in 1987, three-for-two in 1990 and three-for-two in 1992.

Per-Share Financial Summary

	1984	1993
Revenues	$22.15	$94.46
Earnings	.46	1.58
Dividends	.16	.60
Average Stock Price	5¼	28¼

General Mills, Inc. (GIS–NYSE), processes and markets consumer foods. Major brands include Big G cereals, Betty Crocker desserts, Gold Medal flour, Gorton's seafood and Yoplait yogurt. These operations contribute about 66 percent of sales and 81 percent of profits. The company also operates more than 1,000 restaurants in the United States, Canada and Japan, which account for the other 34 percent of sales and 19 percent of profits. Restaurants include Red Lobster, The Olive Garden and China Coast. Sales totaled $8.1 billion in 1993. (The company has about 121,000 employees and 33,800 shareholders.)

The stock split two-for-one in 1986 and 1990.

Per-Share Financial Summary

	1984	1993
Revenues	$30.93	$50.69
Earnings	1.24	3.45
Dividends	.51	1.68
Average Stock Price	12¾	65½

Hershey Foods Corporation (HSY–NYSE) is the largest public U.S. producer of chocolate and confectionery products. Its major brands are Hershey's, Reese's, Kit Kat, Bar None, Mr. Goodbar and Y & S. The company also makes pasta. Brand names include San Giorgio, American Beauty, Delmonico, Skinner and Ronzoni. Sales totaled $3.5 billion in 1993. (The company has about 13,700 employees and 31,000 shareholders.)

The stock was split three-for-one in 1986.

Per-Share Financial Summary

	1984	1993
Revenues	$20.13	$39.80
Earnings	1.16	2.86
Dividends	.41	1.14
Average Stock Price	11⅝	49¾

Kellogg Company (K–NYSE) is the world's largest manufacturer of ready-to-eat cereals. It holds about 37 percent of the U.S. market and 52 percent of the non-U.S. market. The company also produces frozen foods, dessert items and other convenience foods. Brand names include Kellogg's, Frosted Flakes, Rice Krispies, Frosted Mini-Wheats, Special K, Froot Loops!, Nutri-Grain, Apple Jacks, All-Bran, Pop-Tarts, Eggo and Mrs. Smith's. Foreign operations contribute about 43 percent of sales and 34 percent of profits. Sales totaled $6.3 billion in 1993. (The company about 16,600 employees and 23,000 shareholders.)

The company's common stock was split two-for-one in 1985 and 1991.

Per-Share Financial Summary

	1984	1993
Revenues	$10.57	$26.70
Earnings	.75	2.92
Dividends	.43	1.32
Average Stock Price	8¾	57⅝

Sara Lee Corporation (SLE–NYSE) is a diversified international consumer packaged goods producer with operations in coffee, specialty meats, frozen baked goods and food-service distribution. Food group brands include Douwe Egberts, Hillshire Farms, Jimmy Dean, Ball Park, Kahn's, Mr. Turkey and Sara Lee. Consumer Products group brands include Hanes, L'eggs, Kiwi, Aris, Bali, Champion, Isotoner, Playtex, Coach and Dim. Foreign operations account for about 35 percent of sales. Sales totaled $14.6 billion in 1993. (The company has about 138,000 employees and 88,000 shareholders.)

The stock was split two-for-one in 1986, 1989 and 1992.

Per-Share Financial Summary

	1984	1993
Revenues	$15.84	$30.04
Earnings	.41	1.40
Dividends	.16	.56
Average Stock Price	3¾	26

SUMMARY

The food-processing industry varies widely in terms of operations and product offerings. Industry earnings have been up in most years, and analysts generally look for a continuation of the trend. Even with the higher profits, PE ratios of companies in the group are lower than might be expected given the group's remarkable record of consistent earnings growth. Conservative investors may find some good opportunities in the food-processing group, particularly on a long-term basis.

CHAPTER 24

Grocery Stores

In the 1980s, consumers tended to satisfy their food needs at the store closest to home, valuing convenience over price savings. This enabled grocers to increase prices at a rate of 2 percent or more each year without losing customer traffic. But the recent recession caused some shifts in food retailing.

By 1990, shoppers had become willing to travel out of their way in search for bargains. Low-priced competition, such as that from warehouse club stores, emerged to meet this demand. As a result, grocers have been stripped of much of the aggressive pricing power they once enjoyed. Rather than increasing prices, the average supermarket actually *lowered* prices by about 1 percent in 1992 and 1993. That means that grocers no longer can count on a sales gain from price increases. They are forced to work much harder to maintain the kind of earnings growth that investors had come to expect. Grocers have been restructuring their business to uncover and eliminate unnecessary costs from their operations.

Grocery stores have been engaged in a strategy that calls for an increase in the allocation of capital to information systems that link product inflows and outflows at the store level with computers located at warehouses and suppliers' facilities. More inventory then can be supplied on a just-in-time basis, eliminating significant inventory storage and handling expenses. Some of these expense savings are passed on to consumers in an effort to protect or gain market share.

The New Supercenters

Supercenters will likely be the main source of future competition for grocery stores. These units combine a supermarket and general merchandise outlet under the same roof. Wal-Mart and K mart are the two leading entrants in this field. They feature low prices, using food products as loss leaders, to attract shoppers into buying their bigger-ticket and higher-margin general merchandise products.

The two main strengths of the Supercenters are price and the ability to expand. By itself, Wal-Mart has ten times the market capitalization of the largest grocery company. With that clout, it is able to saturate a geographic area with new stores much more quickly than any competitors previously faced by grocers. A major weakness of Supercenters is their size. Averaging 170,000 square feet per unit, they have four times the selling space of the typical grocery store. That limits the availability of viable sites for new stores.

A problem faced by the Supercenters is poor execution. For instance, the quality of their perishables has not always been acceptable. The result is that only the most price-conscious shopper continues to patronize this area consistently. While these execution problems are mainly the result of inexperience, and will likely be corrected, a substantial number of customers may form permanently negative impressions of the formats.

Investment Outlook

The grocery business is an open book to its operators. There are few operating innovations that are not available from the grocers trade association. Ideas are readily shared. This limits the returns that any one grocery company can gain from successfully implementing a new idea. Generally, success comes not from innovations, but from doing a good job in executing operations on a daily basis. Such measures as return on assets or capital, or for heavily leveraged firms, operating income returns on capital, provide a good barometer of how a company is executing its operations.

Generally, investors can expect better results from grocery chains with large stores. Formats in the 40,000- to 60,000-square-foot range are not so susceptible to competition as smaller stores. Smaller locations often feature superior product mixes and operating efficiency, but lack the one-stop shopping convenience and product variety that many shoppers want.

Although the recession seems to be over, the mostly negative changes it left on the grocery store industry probably will remain during the economic recovery. But there are investment opportunities for capital appreciation in the group.

★ *Recommended Stock*

Albertson's, Inc.
250 Parkcenter Boulevard
Boise, ID 83726
208-385-6200

Chairman and CEO: Gary Michael
Number of shareholders: 14,700
Number of employees: 75,000 (about 40 percent are unionized)
Where the stock trades: NYSE
Symbol: ABS

What the Company Does
Albertson's is the fourth largest retail food-drug chain in the United States. The company operates 676 retail grocery stores in 19 Western, Midwestern and Southern states. Store formats include about 235 combination food stores and drugstores, averaging 58,000 square feet; 270 superstores, averaging 42,000 square feet; 105 conventional supermarkets, averaging 27,000 square feet; and 45 warehouse stores, averaging 40,000 square feet. The company sources 68 percent of its merchandise from 11 company-owned distribution centers it operates.

Reason for Recommendation
Analysts expect Albertson's revenues to grow by more than 10 percent each year for the next several years. The company will continue to add about 10 percent to its selling space per year. While much of this space will be allocated to lower-volume service departments, such as bakeries, Albertson's average sales per square foot should remain strong. This is because the effect of the new service department space will likely be offset by price increases, which will be easier to

pass along in an economic recovery. The company also looks for enhanced promotional efficiency and more refined marketing data.

Albertson's strategy has been to rely more on consistently low pricing than on promotional gimmicks to attract customers. As a result, any new competitor in one of Albertson's market areas will face a tough time if it expects to beat Albertson's stores on price. Customers who like one-stop shopping are drawn to Albertson's large stores, which contain many specialty departments.

The company has a five-year plan to set the direction for its growth, with a $2.6 billion capital-expansion program. It expects to continue building combination food stores–drugstores in new and existing markets, remodel stores on a regular ten-year cycle, enhance its distribution capabilities and increase the use of computer technology. The company's goal is for each supermarket to be the best in its neighborhood and for the company to be the best in its industry.

Albertson's looks like a good vehicle for a growth-minded investor. It is a well-run grocery-store chain and maintains a high return on capital.

Investment Results

Albertson's, Inc., has increased its sales in each of the past 15 years, growing from less than $2 billion in 1977 to more than $11 billion in 1993. Profits have grown apace, from $23.4 million in 1977 to more than $340 million in 1993. Shareholders have benefited handsomely. The common stock has grown from an average price of 3¼ in 1984 to an average price of 26½ in 1993, closing the year at 26¾. There were two-for-one stock splits in 1983, 1987 and 1993. Dividends, paid at the rate of $ .09 per share in 1984, grew to $ .36 per share in 1993. The company typically pays out a little less than 30 percent of profits in dividends to common shareholders. Figure 24.1 shows the results of a $10,000 investment in Albertson's, Inc. common stock from 1984 to 1993.

The December 31, 1993, closing price of Albertson's, Inc., common stock shares traded on the NYSE was $26¾. On the last day of trading in 1993, an original $10,000 investment had a market value of $98,787. The value of the $10,000 had multiplied by nearly ten in ten years. With annual dividends reinvested into additional shares each year, the original 3,077 shares purchased in 1984 had grown to 3,693 shares. The $1,311 in dividends paid in 1993 represented a yield of 13.1 percent on the original $10,000 investment.

FIGURE 24.1 Results of a $10,000 Investment in Albertson's, Inc., Common Stock from 1984 to 1993

	Average Share Price	Annual Dividends	Shares Bought from Dividends	Total # Shares Owned	Value of Shares Owned
1984	3¼	$ 277	85	3,162	$10,276
1985	3¾	316	84	3,246	12,172
1986	5	357	71	3,317	16,585
1987	6¾	398	59	3,376	22,788
1988	7⅞	472	60	3,436	26,886
1989	12⅛	687	56	3,492	42,340
1990	15½	838	54	3,546	54,968
1991	21	993	47	3,593	75,453
1992	22½	1,149	51	3,644	81,990
1993	26½	1,311	49	3,693	97,864

In each year from 1984 to 1993, earnings per share increased from the year earlier (see Figure 24.2). Book value per share also increased each year during that period. The average PE ratio gradually rose from about 11 times earnings to 20 to 21 times earnings in the past three years. This indicates growing optimism on the part of investors regarding the company's future earnings potential.

Common Stock Quarterly Price Record

Following are the high and low prices of Albertson's, Inc., common stock during the 1992 and 1993 fiscal years, adjusted for a two-for-one stock split in December 1993:

	1st Quarter	2nd Quarter	3rd Quarter	4th Quarter
1992				
High	$22½	$21¾	$23¾	$26¾
Low	19⅝	18½	19⅝	22⅛
1993				
High	$29	$29¾	29¼	28
Low	23⅜	25¼	24⅛	23⅜

In every quarter during 1992 and 1993, it was possible to buy shares below the high price of the previous quarter. Buying shares carefully

FIGURE 24.2   Per-Share Financial Results of Albertson's, Inc., from 1984 to 1993

	Earnings Per Share	Book Value	Average PE Ratio	Percentage of Profits Paid in Dividends	Average Price Per Share
1984	$ .30	$1.72	10.8	28%	3¼
1985	.32	1.95	11.7	30	3¾
1986	.38	2.22	13.1	28	5
1987	.47	2.51	14.4	26	6¾
1988	.61	2.99	12.8	23	7⅞
1989	.73	3.47	16.6	27	12⅛
1990	.88	4.06	17.6	27	15½
1991	.97	4.54	21.6	29	21
1992	1.05	5.25	21.4	31	22½
1993	1.35	5.30	19.6	27	26½

can have a positive long-term impact on your total investment return. Albertson's fiscal year ended January 30 in 1992 and January 28 in 1993.

CREATING A PORTFOLIO OF GROCERY-STORE INDUSTRY STOCKS

The U.S. grocery-store industry is made up of about 12,700 stores, ranging from small, local operations to huge 170,000-square-foot Supercenters. In 1993, the gross sales of this industry was more than $124 billion, up from $107 billion in 1989. Profits in the grocery business are historically low in relation to sales. In 1993, the average store showed a net profit of 1.46 percent of sales. This was an improvement over 1989, when net profits averaged 1.03 percent. However, earnings in 1993 averaged about 11 percent of total capital and 22 percent of net worth. The average dividend-paying grocery company paid out about 25 percent of profits in dividends to shareholders. Dividend yields range from as low as 0.6 percent by Casey's General Stores to as much as 4 percent on Marsh Supermarkets (B stock).

Following are three other companies in the grocery-store industry that are highly regarded by analysts and have been selected for their financial stability and potential for growth.

	1993 Earnings Per Share	*12/31/93 Share Price*	*Dividend Yield*	*PE Ratio**
Company				
Casey's General Stores	$ .07	12¼	0.6%	17.9
The Kroger Company	1.50	20⅛	0.0	15.4
Safeway, Inc.	1.00	21¼	0.0	22.0

*Ratio of December 31, 1993, share price to 1993 earnings per share.

What the Companies Do

Casey's General Stores (CASY–OTC) operates convenience stores in eight Midwestern states. Most of the stores are located in Iowa and Missouri. The Casey General Store format includes gasoline and a wide selection of food, beverages and nonfood items. Formed in 1968, the company serves the needs of residents in small communities by combining the features of a general store and a convenience outlet. About three-quarters of the company's stores are located in areas with fewer than 5,000 residents. Many of its markets are not served by national chains. The business is seasonal, with gasoline, beverage and ice sales highest in summer and early autumn. In addition to company-owned units, Casey's has nearly 200 franchises. Average retail sales per store is about $1 million. (The company about 2,000 shareholders.)

Per-Share Financial Summary

	1984	1993
Revenues	$13.62	$28.21
Earnings	.23	.73
Dividends	Nil	.07
Average Stock Price	2⅛	9⅝

The stock was split three-for-two in 1985 and two-for-one in 1986 and 1994.

The Kroger Company (KR–NYSE) is the country's largest retail grocery company. It acquired Mini-Mart Convenience stores in 1987. Kroger operates about 1,274 supermarkets in the Midwest, South and West. It has the major market share in all areas where it has a presence. The company also operates about 940 convenience stores. Kroger manufactures and processes 4,000 private-label goods at 37 plants. Kroger's average grocery store size is 38,000 square feet. (The company has about 190,000 employees and 63,000 shareholders.)

Per-Share Financial Summary

	1984	1993
Revenues	$176.58	$207.94
Earnings	1.68	1.50
Dividends	1.00	Nil
Average Stock Price	17¼	18⅛

The stock was split two-for-one in 1986.

Safeway, Incorporated (SWY–NYSE), operates about 1,080 super-markets in Northern California, the Pacific Northwest, the Rocky Mountain region, the Southwest, the Mid-Atlantic region and Western Canada. It holds the number-1 or number-2 market share in each of its market areas. Safeway operates both superstores, with an average of 43,300 square feet, and conventional stores, with an average of 25,800 square feet. The company has a 35 percent equity ownership in Vons Company and a 49 percent interest in Casa Ley, a food retailer in Mexico. (The company has about 105,000 employees.)

Safeway, Inc., is the successor company to Safeway Stores, Inc. The new corporation was formed in a leveraged buyout deal effected by Kohlberg Kravis Robert & Company in 1986. In April of 1990, the company sold 10 million shares of stock to the public at $11.25 per share. An additional 1.5 million shares were issued at the same price in May of 1990 to cover overallotments during the April offering.

Per-Share Financial Summary

	1990	1993
Revenues	$214.61	$151.40 E
Earnings	.83	1.00
Dividends	Nil	Nil
Average Stock Price	13⅝	16⅞

SUMMARY

Some major shifts occurred in the grocery-store industry during the recent recession. Grocers no longer can count on increasing their prices at a rate of 2 percent or more each year without losing customer traffic. Shoppers became willing to travel out of their way searching for bargains. Low-priced competition, such as that from warehouse club stores, emerged to meet this demand. As a result, grocers have been stripped of much of the aggressive pricing power they once enjoyed.

Rather than increasing prices, the average supermarket actually *lowered* prices by about 1 percent in 1992 and 1993. Grocers have been restructuring their businesses to uncover and eliminate unnecessary costs from their operations.

However, despite mostly negative changes that were inflicted on the grocery-store industry, attractive investment opportunities are available in the group.

CHAPTER 25

Health Care

The health-care industry seems well prepared to excel in the era of managed care, where organizations deliver health-care products and services to their members and employer groups. Though pricing will remain under pressure, revenues should benefit from an aging population and advances in medicine.

Except for the rapidly growing health maintenance organizations (HMOs), participants in this group have shifted their focus from an expansion mode to restructuring operations during the past few years. This effort took place because of an overbuilding in some sectors and a change in the demand for services as managed care won greater acceptance. Perhaps the most affected was behavioral medicine, as seen by the recent reduction of excess bed capacity.

After tightening internal cost controls and developing new treatment regimens (often outpatient), many companies are looking for opportunities to improve their competitive positions and increase earnings. Mergers have improved a company's negotiating position with insurers because the provider network is bigger. In this way, mergers and acquisitions offer a chance not only to gain another firm's present business but also to win even more through new contracts.

Construction affords another means of expansion. But this approach is limited to those few areas where capacity is inadequate to meet future needs. The nursing-home and subacute-care field are among those where demand is rising because of an aging population and efforts to curtail costs elsewhere.

A third avenue for expansion is affiliations, particularly useful between companies that operate in different fields and stand to benefit from each other's expertise. Columbia/HCA and Medical Care America created a health-care network that offers insurers one-stop shopping for integrated services. In like manner, Liberty Mutual and PacifiCare will jointly pursue the workers' compensation market in California, based on their respective abilities to manage indemnity and medical risk.

Acquisitions offer opportunities for cutting costs by enabling merged companies to cut redundant support systems and find savings on supply agreements. Over the next several years, analysts expect that studies of a treatment's cost and patients' responses to it will lead to increasingly standardized health care. This will eliminate some procedures, narrow the treatment options available for any given illness and shift the demand for certain drugs, medical supplies and health-care facilities to the most cost-effective combinations. The general trend is toward more outpatient care, either alone or in combination with a brief, intensive course of inpatient therapy.

Investment Outlook

Profit margins in the health-care industry may remain level as economies of scale are realized and less costly treatments are developed. With industry growth, profits should remain on a fairly rapid growth curve for the next few years. But investors interested in this group should focus also on the near-term prospects, given the uncertainties associated with health-care reform.

★ Recommended Stock

U.S. Healthcare, Inc.
980 Jolly Road
P.O. Box 1109
Blue Bell, PA 19422
215-628-4800

Principal Executive Officer: Leonard Abramson
Number of shareholders: 2,600

Number of employees: 2,850
Where the stock trades: OTC: Nasdaq
Symbol: USHC

What the Company Does

U.S. Healthcare, Inc., owns and operates HMOs in Pennsylvania, New Jersey, Delaware, New York, Connecticut, Massachusetts, Maryland, New Hampshire and the District of Columbia. Its HMO members receive medical care from independent primary-care physicians and other providers with whom the HMOs have contractual arrangements. Members also are offered pharmacy, dental, vision, mental health, substance abuse and preventive health care services, including wellness programs. The company had more than 1.5 million enrollees at the end of 1993.

Through non-HMO subsidiaries, the company also provides management services to other health organizations. Corporate Health Administrators provides services to self-insured employers, including claims processing, patient management and access to select network providers. Workers Comp Advantage offers managed-care services to employers and insurance carriers for workers' compensation, nonoccupational disability and automobile injury–related health care. U.S. Quality Algorithms provides quality and outcome measurement and improvement programs and health-care data-analysis systems for providers and purchasers of health care.

Reason for Recommendation

U.S. Healthcare is a national leader in managed health care, highly regarded for its high-quality, consumer-oriented services. The company has grown rapidly over the past decade, while doing an excellent job of containing costs. Its revenues, comprised of premiums, management fees and other income, have risen from $206 million in 1984 to more than $2.6 billion in 1993. Profits during the same period have gone from $10.8 million to $299.7 million.

The company's medical-expense ratio, which measures medical claims as a percentage of premium revenues, hit an all-time low of 68.7 percent in the last quarter of 1993, bringing the full-year ratio down to 72.7 percent from 77.1 percent in 1992. This strong improvement resulted from U.S. Healthcare's stringent underwriting practices, which include favorable per-diem contracts with providers and excellent utilization controls, leading to a tight rein on costs. Analysts following the company believe USHC will continue to keep costs under control and expect the ongoing expense ratio to average about 72 percent.

The company's intense marketing efforts in New York and New England should drive membership growth. Enrollment in these under-penetrated regions grew by 36 percent and 20 percent, respectively, in 1993 and continued increases are expected. Membership growth should increase at a 10 percent rate in the near-term. Analysts believe that this, coupled with the best medical-expense ratios in the HMO industry, should permit earnings to rise at close to 20 percent during this period.

U.S. Healthcare, Inc., a low-cost provider of quality health care with a dominant market position, appears well situated to prosper in a changing health-care environment. Its stock seems to be in a position to outperform the average equity over the next several years. Conservative investors, however, should be aware that the shares can have volatile price movements.

Investment Results

After going through a difficult period of low profits from 1987 to 1989, the company rebounded smartly and shareholders have been amply rewarded. The stock traded at an average price of 2⅛ in 1984, rose to an average of 5⅛ in 1986, then traded at an average of $2 per share in 1988. From that point on, the share price rocketed over the next five years to an average of 32½ in 1993, closing the year at 38⅜. These prices have been adjusted for a three-for-two stock split on March 29, 1994.

Figure 25.1 shows the results of a $10,000 investment in U.S. Health-care, Inc. common stock from 1984 to 1993. It is assumed that the stock was purchased at the average of the high and low prices in 1984. A $10,000 investment in 1984 would have purchased 4,705 shares, adjusted for 2 three-for-two stock splits in 1984, 2 three-for-two splits in 1985 and additional three-for-two splits in 1991, 1992 and 1994. Brokerage commissions to purchase the shares are not considered.

The December 31, 1993, closing price of U.S. Healthcare on the NASDAQ National Market was 38⅜. The value of the original $10,000 investment on that date was $243,642.

Historical Financial Data

U.S. Healthcare, Inc., had early success, then stumbled. Although revenues rose steadily from $205 million in 1984 to $1 billion in 1989, and $2.6 billion in 1993, earnings in the early years were spotty. From

FIGURE 25.1   Results of a $10,000 Investment in U.S. Healthcare, Inc., Common Stock from 1984 to 1993

	Average Share Price	Annual Dividends	Shares Bought from Dividends	Total # Shares Owned	Value of Shares Owned
1984	2⅛	$ 0	0	4,705	$ 9,998
1985	4⅜	47	10	4,715	20,628
1986	5	188	37	4,752	23,760
1987	2¾	237	86	4,838	13,304
1988	1⅞	241	129	4,967	9,313
1989	3⅛	347	111	5,078	15,868
1990	5⅞	507	86	5,164	30,338
1991	13¾	826	60	6,224	85,580
1992	25⅝	1,306	50	6,274	160,771
1993	32½	2,447	75	6,349	206,342

$10.8 million in 1984, net profits grew to $35.8 million in 1986, then fell to $1.1 million in 1987. From that low point, earnings rose rapidly, hitting $299.7 million in 1993. Figure 25.2 sets forth important per-share data for the company during the period from 1984 to 1993. All yearly numbers relate to the company's fiscal years and are adjusted for stock splits.

The PE ratio was high during the early years illustrated, then became in effect meaningless when earnings all but disappeared in 1987. As profits recovered, the PE ratio moved back to more normal levels, remaining in the general range of the overall market.

Common Stock Quarterly Price Record

Following are the high and low prices of U.S. Healthcare common stock during the fiscal years ending December 31, 1992, and 1993, adjusted for stock splits:

	1st Quarter	2nd Quarter	3rd Quarter	4th Quarter
1992				
High	$25¼	$24⅜	$30¼	$33⅜
Low	18	20	22¾	27⅜
1993				
High	$38⅝	$34⅝	$34⅝	$39⅝
Low	26⅜	25⅜	27½	28½

FIGURE 25.2 Per-Share Financial Results of U.S. Healthcare, Inc., from 1984 to 1993

	Earnings Per Share	Book Value	Sales	Average Price Per Share	Average PE Ratio
1984	.07	.34	1.29	2⅛	30.4
1985	.15	.79	2.13	4⅜	29.2
1986	.21	1.13	3.14	5	23.8
1987	.01	.92	4.14	2¾	275.0
1988	.04	.91	4.80	1⅞	46.9
1989	.18	1.05	6.42	3⅛	17.4
1990	.48	1.47	8.39	5⅞	12.2
1991	.93	2.19	10.77	13¾	14.8
1992	1.23	3.13	13.57	25⅝	20.8
1993	1.84	4.75 E	16.35 E	32½	17.7

In every quarterly period during 1992 and 1993, it was possible to purchase shares of U.S. Healthcare stock at prices below the high of the previous quarter. In some cases, the price dropped more than 20 percent, as in the second quarter of 1992 and the second and third quarters of 1993.

CREATING A PORTFOLIO OF STOCKS IN THE HEALTH-CARE INDUSTRY

Following are a small number of stocks that some analysts believe have good potential for capital appreciation. Earnings of these companies are expected to grow faster than the market as a whole over the next several years.

Company	1993 Earnings Per Share	12/31/93 Share Price	Dividend Yield	PE Ratio*
Beverly Enterprises	$ .71	13¼	Nil	18.7
Community Psychiatric Centers	.23	14	Nil	60.9
HealthCare COMPARE Corporation	1.08	24⅝	Nil	22.8

Manor Care, Inc.	1.09	24⅜	0.4%	22.4
Omnicare, Inc.	.91	32	0.6	35.2
PacifiCare Health Systems (A)	2.25	37⅜	Nil	16.6
United Healthcare	1.25	37⅞	0.1	30.3

*December 31, 1993, share price divided by 1993 earnings per share.

What the Companies Do

Beverly Enterprises, Inc. (BEV–NYSE), is the largest operator of nursing homes in the United States. In early 1993, the company operated 838 nursing homes, with a total of 89,305 beds. It also owns 44 retirement and congregate living centers and 21 institutional pharmacies. Nursing homes are located in 34 states and the District of Columbia, with 121 homes in Texas, 81 in California, 75 in Indiana and 63 in Florida. Government medical-assistance programs account for 77 percent of revenues. The occupancy rate in 1992 was 88.4 percent. Revenues totaled $2.8 billion in 1993. (The company has about 93,000 employees and 6,962 shareholders.)

Per-Share Financial Summary

	1984	1993
Revenues	$27.46	$35.20 E
Earnings	.90	.71
Dividends	.15	Nil
Average Stock Price	14⅜	12⅛

The company's stock was split two-for-one in 1986.

Community Psychiatric Centers (CMY–NYSE) owns and operates 47 psychiatric hospitals with a total of 4,228 beds in 17 states, Puerto Rico and England. Of these, 11 hospitals are in California and 9 are in England. A subsidiary, Transitional Hospitals, has 7 long-term critical-care centers, with 551 beds. Revenues totaled $335 million in 1993. (The company has about 7,000 employees and 2,750 shareholders.)

Per-Share Financial Summary

	1984	1993
Revenues	$3.87	$7.79
Earnings	.81	.23
Dividends	.15	.09
Average Stock Price	15⅝	11⅞

There were three-for-two stock splits in 1984 and 1987.

HealthCare COMPARE Corporation (HCCC–OTC) is an independent provider of medical-cost-management services and offers comprehensive managed-care programs. The company acquired AFFORDABLE Health Care Concepts in 1988 and merged with Occupational-Urgent Care Health Systems, Inc., in 1992. Revenues totaled $157 million in 1993. (The company has about 1,400 employees and 1,200 shareholders.)

Per-Share Financial Summary

	1987	1993
Revenues	$.69	$4.40 E
Earnings	.09	1.08
Dividends	Nil	Nil
Average Stock Price	2⅞	21⅛

The company's IPO was in May of 1987 at $2.75 per share, adjusted for two-for-one stock splits in 1990 and 1991.

Manor Care, Inc. (MNR–NYSE), is a leader in the nursing-home and lodging industries. The health-care division, which accounted for 83 percent of 1993 revenues and profits, owns or operates 164 nursing homes containing 22,578 beds in 28 states. In 1993, the nursing-home occupancy rate was 87.7 percent. Medicare and Medicaid account for 41 percent of that division's revenues. The company's lodging division franchises hotels, including Quality, Comfort, Clarion and Rodeway Inns. Revenues totaled $1 billion in 1993. (The company has about 24,000 employees and 3,300 shareholders.)

Per-Share Financial Summary

	1984	1993
Revenues	$6.00	$17.56
Earnings	.39	1.09
Dividends	.06	.09
Average Stock Price	6½	22⅛

The company's stock was split three-for-two in 1984, 1985 and 1992.

Omnicare, Inc. (OCR–NYSE), provides pharmacy-management services and drug therapy to nursing homes through its Sequoia Pharmacy Services Group. At the end of 1992, the company had 70,000 beds under contract in nine states. Sales totaled $159 million in 1993. (The company has about 1,100 employees and 1,250 shareholders.)

Per-Share Financial Summary

	1984	1993
Revenues	$20.79	$16.80 E
Earnings	.26	.91
Dividends	.69	.16
Average Stock Price	18⅞	22¾

PacifiCare Health Systems, Inc. (PHSYA–OTC), owns and operates six primarily group and network HMOs serving the commercial market. The company is the largest provider of Medicare risk contracts. In 1993, it had more than one million members located in five states, with 73 percent in California, 11 percent in Oklahoma, 9 percent in Oregon and Washington and 7 percent in Texas. PacifiCare offers specialty services, including drug-benefit management, a dental plan and a workers' compensation plan. Revenues totaled $2.2 billion in 1993. (The company has about 2,600 employees and 600 shareholders.)

Per-Share Financial Summary

	1985	1993
Revenues	$3.69	$81.49
Earnings	.18	2.25
Dividends	Nil	Nil
Average Stock Price	4¾	41½

The company's stock was initially offered to the public on May 23, 1985, at $4.50 per share and adjusted for two-for-one splits in 1989 and 1992.

United HealthCare Corporation (UNH–NYSE), owns 11 HMOs and manages an additional 10. The company also provides specialty services, including prescription drug-benefit programs, through wholly owned subsidiaries. In 1992, there were more than 1.7 million members in HMOs and 21 million members in specialty services. Revenues totaled $2.5 billion in 1993. (The company has about 4,800 employees and 2,400 shareholders.)

Per-Share Financial Summary

	1984	1993
Revenues	$.49	$16.02
Earnings	.05	1.25
Dividends	Nil	.02
Average Stock Price	1⅛	29⅝

The company's stock was split two-for-one in 1992 and 1994.

SUMMARY

The health-care industry seems well prepared to excel in the era of managed care. Though pricing will remain under pressure, revenues should benefit from an aging population and advances in medicine. Many companies are looking for opportunities to improve their competitive positions and increase earnings. Mergers and acquisitions are proven ways to gain another firm's present business and also to win even more through new contracts. Construction affords another means of expansion and is working well where capacity is inadequate to meet future needs. The nursing-home and subacute-care fields are among those where demand is rising because of an aging population and efforts to curtail costs elsewhere. Acquisitions offer opportunities for cutting costs by enabling merged companies to cut redundant support systems and find savings on supply agreements.

CHAPTER 26

Household Products

Stocks in the household-products industry have traditionally been regarded as *defensive* and have been most sought after by investors when the economy has been doing poorly. Defensive stocks tend to decline less in a market downturn. This is not because they make weapons but because these companies make low-priced products that often are regarded by consumers as necessities that must be purchased whether or not times are good from an economic standpoint. Investors interested in stocks in the household-products group should look for shares of those companies that seem likely to generate more earnings growth than might normally be expected in a so-called defensive sector.

Common stock of companies in this group generally performed sluggishly in 1993. The problem resulted from Wall Street's fears that brand names, which are normally regarded as valuable assets, were becoming less desirable. In some consumer-related industries, such concerns may well be valid. An example is the tobacco sector, where aggressive competition from private-label manufacturers put severe pricing pressure on the well-known brands. But this has not been generally a problem for the household products industry. While cigarette manufacturers have been raising prices faster than the inflation rate for many years in an effort to compensate for declining demand, price competition for household products has been a fact of life for many years. So the private-label manufacturers do not have so much opportunity to offer comparable quality products at significantly lower prices. The major manufacturers have not suffered noticeable losses in market share, nor have they faced pricing pressure that has been disproportionate from what they normally experience.

Just-in-time is the latest method of management for retail inventory. Today, retailers want to hold as few items in stock as possible. Instead of the fear of being out of stock on a regularly carried item, many retailers now would rather deal with stockouts than with excess inventories. The way retailers' strategy works is for manufacturers to deliver goods "just in time" to avoid stockouts.

In the past, manufacturers often enjoyed smooth order patterns for particular items, allowing them to plan their production in terms of labor needs and raw materials purchases. They were able to schedule large production runs, minimizing setup costs. Under the just-in-time demands of retailers, orders are becoming smaller in size and are arriving in less predictable patterns. That makes it much more difficult for manufacturers to plan their own production. In recent years, their profits have suffered as retail inventories shrank to the new, lower norms and as manufacturers adjusted their own operating procedures. As companies learn to accommodate their operations to the new reality, profit margins should improve.

Investment Outlook

Shares of companies in the household-products industry that learn to cope with modern methods of inventory control and that seem likely to generate consistent future earnings growth should do well as the economy continues to generate upward momentum.

★ Recommended Stock

Rubbermaid, Inc.
1147 Akron Road
Wooster, OH 44691
216-264-6464

Chairman and CEO: Wolfgang R. Schmitt
Number of shareholders: 22,500
Number of employees: 12,000

Where the stock trades: NYSE
Symbol: RBD

What the Company Does

Rubbermaid, Inc., makes plastic and rubber products, including kitchenware, laundry and bath accessories, microwave ovenware, patio furniture and ready-to-assemble household furniture, products for home-horticulture, office, food-service, health-care and industrial maintenance.

In 1984, Rubbermaid was first included on the Fortune 500 list and two years later, it was ranked seventh in *Fortune* magazine's annual survey of America's ten most admired corporations, the smallest company to do so. In the *Fortune* 1993 survey, the company was named the "Most Admired Corporation" in America. According to its 1993 annual report, "Rubbermaid's mission is to be the leading world-class marketer of best value, brand-name, primarily plastic products for the consumer, institutional, office products, agricultural, and industrial markets."

Reason for Recommendation

In 1993, Rubbermaid enjoyed its 42nd consecutive year of record sales. Revenues totaled $1.9 billion, up 9 percent from the prior year, with all the sales growth resulting from increases in unit volume. Net earnings for the year were a record $211 million, up 15 percent from 1992. This marked the 56th consecutive year of profitable performance by the company.

Anticipating slower worldwide economic growth in the 1990s, the company has increased its already ambitious new-product program. The introduction of innovative products in 1993 surpassed the 1992 level, as Rubbermaid increased its sales goal for products introduced in the past five years from 30 percent to 33 percent. The objective of entering new markets was accelerated to between 12 and 18 months instead of 18 to 24 months.

Rubbermaid is in a very strong financial position. Growth has been financed through a combination of cash provided from operations and new equity issues, and to a lesser extent through long-term debt financing. Cash provided from operating activities is the primary source of liquidity and amounted to $287 million in 1993. The company's objective is to pay approximately 30 percent of the current year's earnings as dividends and to retain sufficient capital to provide

FIGURE 26.1 Results of a $10,000 Investment in Rubbermaid, Inc.,
Common Stock Made in 1984

	Average Share Price	Annual Dividends	Shares Bought from Dividends	Total # Shares Owned	Value of Shares Owned
1984	4⅞	$205	42	2,093	$10,203
1985	7⅛	230	32	2,125	15,140
1986	11¼	276	24	2,149	24,176
1987	13½	343	25	2,174	29,349
1988	12	413	34	2,208	26,496
1989	15¾	507	32	2,240	35,280
1990	19	604	31	2,271	43,149
1991	28⅜	704	24	2,295	65,120
1992	32⅛	803	25	2,320	74,530
1993	32½	951	29	2,349	76,342

for future investment opportunities to grow sales and earnings at the company's objective annual rate of 15 percent.

Investment Results

Rubbermaid has exhibited steady growth in shares and earnings over many years. Shareholders have benefited from this growth as the share price has gradually moved up.

Figure 26.1 shows the ten-year results of a $10,000 investment in Rubbermaid, Inc., common stock from 1984 to 1993. All numbers have been adjusted for two-for-one stock splits in 1985, 1986 and 1991. It is assumed the stock was purchased at the average of the high and low prices in 1984. A $10,000 investment in 1984 would have purchased 2,051 shares, adjusted for the stock splits. Cash dividends have been applied to purchase additional shares. Brokerage commissions are not considered.

The December 31, 1993, closing price of Rubbermaid, Inc., on the NYSE was 34¾. The value of the original $10,000 investment on that date was $81,627.

Historical Financial Data

Rubbermaid has enjoyed an unbroken string of many years with increasing sales and earnings. Since 1984, sales have grown from $566 million to $1.96 billion in 1993. In the same period, earnings have

FIGURE 26.2   Per-Share Financial Results of Rubbermaid, Inc., from 1984 to 1993

	Earnings Per Share	Book Value	Sales	Average Share Price	Average PE Ratio
1984	$ .34	$1.77	$ 4.19	4⅞	14.3
1985	.40	2.08	4.63	7⅛	17.8
1986	.48	2.45	5.43	11¼	23.4
1987	.58	2.97	6.91	13½	23.3
1988	.68	3.48	8.12	12	17.6
1989	.79	4.06	9.12	15¾	19.9
1990	.90	4.80	9.59	19	21.1
1991	1.02	5.53	10.41	28⅜	27.8
1992	1.15	6.16	11.27	32⅛	27.9
1993	1.32	7.05	12.22	32½	24.6

gone from $46.9 million to $211.4 million. Figure 26.2 sets forth important per-share data for the company during the period from 1984 to 1993. All yearly numbers relate to the company's fiscal years, which end on December 31, and have been adjusted for stock splits.

Rubbermaid has historically sold at a high earnings multiple, reflecting investor expectations of a continuing rise in future earnings. Keep in mind that as a stock's PE ratio climbs, its vulnerability to unfavorable news makes price corrections potentially more severe.

Common Stock Quarterly Price Record

Following are the high and low prices of Rubbermaid, Inc., common stock during the fiscal years ending December 31, 1992, and 1993:

	1st Quarter	2nd Quarter	3rd Quarter	4th Quarter
1992				
High	$37⅜	$34¾	$33⅝	$34⅝
Low	30½	27	28¼	30⅛
1993				
High	$35	$34¾	$34½	$37⅛
Low	29⅝	28⅜	28	32½

Excluding the fourth quarter of 1993, it was possible for the patient investor to buy the stock at a price substantially below the high of the previous quarter. Even in 1993's last quarter, the price dropped more than 5 percent from the previous quarterly high. Timing stock purchases carefully can have an important effect on your long-term investment return.

CREATING A PORTFOLIO OF STOCKS IN THE HOUSEHOLD-PRODUCTS INDUSTRY

Selected issues in this *defensive* industry may have room for continued growth over the next few years. Particularly seek out the shares of financially strong companies with good earnings momentum and the ability to cope with modern methods of inventory control. Following are several strong companies with good earnings prospects.

Company	1993 Earnings Per Share	12/31/93 Share Price	Dividend Yield	PE Ratio*
Colgate-Palmolive Company	$3.38	62⅜	2.6%	18.5
Kimberly-Clark Corporation	3.18	51⅞	3.2	16.3
Lancaster Colony Corporation	3.00	46	1.5	15.3
Newell Company	2.10	40⅜	1.8	19.2
Procter & Gamble Company	2.82	57	2.3	20.2

*December 31, 1993, share price divided by 1993 earnings per share.

What the Companies Do

Colgate-Palmolive Company (CL–NYSE) is the second largest domestic maker of detergents, toiletries and other household products. Its major brands include Fresh Start, Fab, Dynamo, Ajax and Palmolive cleansers; Colgate and Ultra Brite toothpastes; Irish Spring and Palmolive soaps; Palmolive shave cream; Hill's pet food; and Princess House crystal. Foreign operations accounted for 65 percent of 1993 revenues. Sales totaled $7.1 billion in 1993. (The company has about 28,000 employees and 40,000 shareholders.)

Per-Share Financial Summary

	1984	1993
Revenues	$29.57	$47.83
Earnings	.93	3.38
Dividends	.64	1.34
Average Stock Price	11¾	57⅛

The company's stock was split two-for-one in 1991.

Kimberly-Clark Corporation (KMB–NYSE) develops, manufactures and markets Kleenex facial and bathroom tissues and paper towels, Huggies disposable diapers, Kotex feminine napkins and tampons and other consumer products. The company also makes newsprint and groundwood printing papers and paper specialty products for the tobacco, electronics and other industries. In addition, Kimberly-Clark operates aircraft maintenance and commercial airline services. Sales totaled $6.9 billion in 1993. (The company has about 42,000 employees and 25,000 shareholders.)

Per-Share Financial Summary

	1984	1993
Revenues	$19.78	$43.07
Earnings	1.19	3.18
Dividends	.55	1.70
Average Stock Price	11	53¼

The company's stock was split two-for-one in 1984, 1987, and 1992.

Lancaster Colony Corporation (LANC–OTC) makes housewares, as well as industrial and food products. Housewares include table and gift glassware, crystal, lighting components, artificial flowers, ceramics, aluminum cookware and candles. This sector accounts for about 30 percent of sales. Industrial products, including splash guards, car mats and accessories, account for 32 percent of sales. Food products, which include Pfeiffer and Marzetti salad dressings, frozen pies and frozen bread and noodles, account for 38 percent of sales. Sales totaled $630 million in 1993. (The company has about 4,700 employees and 13,500 shareholders.)

Per-Share Financial Summary

	1984	1993
Revenues	$18.96	$27.76
Earnings	.59	2.02
Dividends	.24	.50
Average Stock Price	6⅛	37½

The stock split five-for-four in 1986, three-for-two in 1992 and four-for-three in 1993.

Newell Company (NWL–NYSE) manufactures and markets do-it-yourself hardware, housewares and office products. Its products include aluminum cookware and bakeware, cabinet and window hardware, window furnishings, jar caps and closures, glassware, paint sundries and other consumer goods. Sales totaled $1.6 billion in 1993. (The company has about 3,500 shareholders.)

Per-Share Financial Summary

	1984	1993
Revenues	$8.97	$20.92
Earnings	.41	2.10
Dividends	.13	.69
Average Stock Price	3⅞	36⅞

There were two-for-one stock splits in 1988 and 1989.

Procter & Gamble Company (PG–NYSE) is the country's largest soap and detergent producer. It also makes toiletries, food, paper and industrial products. P&G brands include Always, Bold, Bounce, Bounty, Cascade, Charmin, Cheer, Coast, Comet, Cover Girl, Crest, Crisco, Dawn, Downy, Era, Folgers, Hawaiian Punch, Head & Shoulders, Ivory, Jif, Joy, Luvs, Noxema, Old Spice, Oxydol, Pampers, Prell, Safeguard, Scope, Secret, Tide and Zest. Foreign operations account for about 52 percent of total revenues. Sales totaled $30.4 billion in 1993. (The company has about 103,000 employees and 202,000 shareholders.)

Per-Share Financial Summary

	1984	1993
Revenues	$19.38	$44.64
Earnings	1.29	2.82
Dividends	.60	1.10
Average Stock Price	13¼	52⅛

There were two-for-one stock splits 1989 and 1992.

SUMMARY

Household-products industry shares have traditionally been regarded as *defensive* because these companies make low-priced products that consumers often regard as necessities that must be purchased whether or not times are good from an economic standpoint. Investors interested in stocks in the household-products group should look for shares of those companies that seem likely to generate more earnings growth than might normally be expected in a so-called "defensive sector." Shares of companies in this group that learn to cope with modern methods of inventory control, and seem likely to generate consistent future earnings growth, should do well as the economy generates more upward momentum.

CHAPTER 27

Medical Supplies

New technology has been blamed by many people for fueling the growth of medical costs, while it has been hailed by others for reducing them. Depending on one's perspective, both views are correct, as illustrated by a report from U.S. Healthcare, a major owner and operator of health maintenance organizations (HMOs). That report disclosed how minimally invasive surgery has affected the demand for and cost of cholecystectomy.

In 1988, before the advent of suitable laparoscopic instruments, only 1.35 HMO enrollees per thousand had their gall bladders removed. Four years later, when a minimally invasive approach was possible, the rate rose to 2.15 procedures per thousand enrollees. The increase is related to more people with low-grade gall bladder problems seeking treatment because of the reduced pain and shorter convalescence associated with the new surgical technique. It also stems from the treatment of patients who could not be helped via the old procedure. At the same time, enrollment in the managed-care program grew significantly. This, plus the higher rate of procedures performed, translated into a 60 percent jump in the number of operations paid for by U.S. Healthcare. But because of to shorter hospital stays associated with minimally invasive surgery, the HMOs' total cholecystectomy bill rose only 11.4 percent from 1988 to 1992.

This example shows not only the impact of a new technology on medical costs but also the benefits that it provides to society. Studies are under way to determine which medical procedures produce optimum results at a minimum overall cost. Trials are being conducted by HMOs, the government and universities to form clinical guidelines that will direct the treatment of future patients. According to industry analysts, however, the trials carry some problems. For example, investigations pursued by HMOs for their own use may be poorly designed and come to unfounded, if not completely erroneous, conclusions.

In addition, other studies are being sponsored by drug and medical-device companies to obtain a marketing edge for their products. A movement is afoot to give a government agency the responsibility of deciding if the results actually prove that one product offers superior care or is more cost-effective than another. To promote trials comparing different therapeutic alternatives, the agency also would have the ability to grant a company protection against competition to its product through a mechanism similar to a patent extension.

U.S. sales of medical supplies have been hurt recently because of today's uncertainties and efforts to cut the growth of medical costs. Analysts believe that this is likely to continue in the near future. Business with Europe, having been slowed by reform measures and a weak economy, is expected to pick up. Growth opportunities are offered by other markets, including the Pacific Rim and South America. In the long term, the business environment for the medical-supplies industry should improve as the U.S. marketplace is redefined and the global economy accelerates. Lower prices may affect profit margins and earnings growth will become more volume-driven.

Investment Outlook

New products are the lifeblood of this industry. Their profits can quickly lift a company's net profits. In early 1994, most company share prices already reflected the expected income from new products. The long-term outlook for well-managed medical-supplies companies is bright, given an increasing focus on better health and the new technology coming on stream. But because of the risks created by health-care reform, stocks in this industry should not be expected to resist market downturns. Select cautiously from this group.

★ *Recommended Stock*

Medtronic, Inc.
7000 Central Avenue
Minneapolis, MN 55432-3576
612-574-4000

Chairman: W.R. Wallin
Number of shareholders: 12,275
Number of employees: 9,250
Where the stock trades: NYSE
Symbol: MDT

What the Company Does
Medtronic, Inc., is the world's largest manufacturer of implantable biomedical devices, with sales to more than 80 countries. Founded in 1949, the company created the pacing industry as it is known today with the development of the first wearable external cardiac pacemaker in 1957. Medtronic was incorporated that same year and today has six businesses: bradycardia pacing, tachyarrhythmia management, cardiopulmonary, heart valves, interventional vascular and neurological. International business accounted for 58 percent of sales in the 1993 fiscal year and 70 percent of profits. The company invests about 10 percent of sales in research and development.

Reason for Recommendation
Medtronic, Inc., has improved its position in the pacing market with the launch of a new line of pacemakers overseas. The *Thera* system includes six pacemakers to correct different electrical abnormalities in the heart, a specialized lead that enables one of the units to sense the patient's heart activity, and a portable, menu-driven programmer for setting the pacemaker's operating parameters. The common programming feature is a competitive advantage, because it simplifies the use of the pacemaker. The success of the pacemaker business is critical, for it accounts for about 55 percent of corporate sales and profits.

The new programmer should help the company gain in the tachycardia market, because it is compatible with upcoming pacemaker-cardioverter-defibrillators. This technological link is a good example of Medtronic's efforts to build upon its position in bradycardia to gain business elsewhere. Analysts believe that the strategy will be successful, enabling the company to secure the lead position in a $1 billion tachycardia market over the next three to five years.

FIGURE 27.1   Results of a $10,000 Investment in Medtronic, Inc., Common Stock with Dividends Reinvested from 1984 to 1993

	Average Share Price	Annual Dividends	Shares Bought from Dividends	Total # Shares Owned	Value of Shares Owned
1984	8⅝	$220	25	1,184	$10,212
1985	8⅝	236	27	1,211	10,445
1986	16⅞	266	15	1,226	20,688
1987	21½	306	14	1,240	26,660
1988	21	372	17	1,257	26,397
1989	27⅜	440	16	1,273	34,848
1990	37¾	522	13	1,286	48,546
1991	66½	617	9	1,295	86,117
1992	83⅞	725	8	1,303	109,289
1993	73⅝	886	12	1,315	96,817

Note: Medtronic, Inc.'s, fiscal year ends April 30.

Other business segments are expected to grow rapidly through the end of the 1990s. The company is negotiating to buy a small manufacturer of blood-salvaging equipment, which is used during major surgeries to reduce the need for transfused blood. These products complement Medtronic's blood oxygenators that replace the lungs during open-heart surgery. The new company should add some $40 million in annual sales initially, and its contribution is expected to rise as its offerings move into foreign markets. Medtronic's angioplasty catheters are benefiting from extra promotional support, and the company has several heart valves under development.

Prospects also are promising for neurological products, as a trend toward self-medicating is lifting demand for a patient-controlled drug pump. Medicare's decision to cover the cost of this device should help sales in 1994 and beyond.

On balance, analysts look for healthy sales growth, plus fairly stable profit margins, to support double-digit earnings gains through much of the 1990s.

Investment Results
Steadily growing sales and earnings have resulted in generous rewards for shareholders. A $10,000 investment made at the average

FIGURE 27.2   Selected Per-Share Data of Medtronic, Inc., from 1984
to 1993

	Earnings Per Share	Book Value	Average Price Per Share	Percentage of Profits Paid in Dividends	Average PE Ratio
1984	$ .76	$5.44	8⅝	25%	11.3
1985	1.07	6.07	8⅝	19	8.1
1986	1.31	6.88	16⅞	17	12.9
1987	1.58	7.43	21½	16	13.6
1988	1.75	8.84	21	17	12.0
1989	2.02	9.98	27⅜	17	13.6
1990	2.33	11.48	37¾	17	16.2
1991	2.71	13.40	66½	18	24.5
1992	3.32	14.55	83⅞	17	25.3
1993	4.06	16.12	73⅝	17	18.4

Note: Earnings and book value and the percentage of profits paid in dividends in 1993
are based on analysts' estimates.

price at which the shares traded in 1984 would have bought 1,159
shares. With annual dividends used to purchase additional shares, the
initial $10,000 would have grown to a value of $96,817 in 1993 (based
on the average share price in that year). Figure 27.1 shows the year-
by-year results of a $10,000 investment in Medtronic stock from 1984
to 1993. Brokerage commissions are not considered. All numbers take
into account two-for-one stock splits in 1989 and 1991.

The December 31, 1993, closing price of Medtronic, Inc., common
shares traded on the NYSE was 82⅛. The market value of $107,994
on that date was more than ten times the original $10,000 invested in
1986.

Figure 27.2 shows selected per-share data of Medtronic, Inc., during
the period from 1984 to 1993. The data has been adjusted for stock
splits in 1989 and 1991.

Earnings per share increased over the prior year in every year from
1984 to 1993. Book value per share also increased each year during
that period. The average PE ratio gradually increased during the period
from about 10 times earnings to more than 25 times earnings in 1992,
reflecting investors' expectations for continued future earnings growth
for the company. Remember that a high PE ratio often indicates that a

stock is vulnerable to adverse news. Uncertainty over health-care legislation was certainly a factor in the stock's price retreat during 1993.

Common Stock Quarterly Price Record
Following are the high and low prices of Medtronic, Inc., common stock during the 1992 and 1993 fiscal years, adjusted for a two-for-one stock split:

	1st Quarter	2nd Quarter	3rd Quarter	4th Quarter
1992				
High	$63¾	$78¾	$97	$88⅛
Low	54⅛	60¾	72¾	64⅛
1993				
High	$83¾	$100⅜	$103½	$91⅛
Low	68	73⅛	87⅝	53¼

As this chart shows, it is not necessary for a patient investor to pay top price for common shares. In every quarter during 1992 and 1993, investors could buy shares at a price substantially below the high price of the previous quarter. Buying shares carefully can have a long-term impact on your total investment return.

CREATING A STOCK PORTFOLIO IN THE MEDICAL-SUPPLIES INDUSTRY

A number of companies in the crowded and competitive medical-supplies industry warrant a look for long-term investors. With industry sales in the $100-billion range, large, publicly held companies vie for the growing revenues fueled by a health-conscious world. Industry sales recently have been growing at nearly 10 percent per year. A number of companies, such as Johnson & Johnson ($14 billion in sales), Abbott Laboratories ($9 billion in sales), McKesson Corporation ($12 billion in sales) and Baxter International ($9 billion in sales), control large segments of the market.

Following are a number of companies in the medical-supplies industry that analysts considered suitable for growth portfolios. Because the share prices of many stocks already reflect their growth potential, and the industry faces risks from health-care reform, investors should select stocks from this industry carefully.

Note: This is by no means an all-inclusive list of investment-worthy companies in the medical-supplies industry. Johnson & Johnson, for instance, is treated separately in Chapter 12, "Investing for Growth—Conservatively," and Cardinal Health, Inc., is reviewed in Chapter 13, "Investing for Growth- -Aggressively." Per-share information has been adjusted for any stock splits.

Company	1993 Earnings Per Share	12/31/93 Share Price	Dividend Yield	PE Ratio*
Abbott Laboratories	$1.69	29⅝	2.7%	17.5
Dentsply International, Inc.	1.81	44	Nil	24.3
Diagnostek, Inc.	.50	19	Nil	38
Invacare Corporation	1.50	27½	Nil	18.3
Nellcor, Inc.	1.50	24¾	Nil	16.5
Owens & Minor, Inc.	.90	23	0.8	25.5
Stryker Corporation	1.25	28¼	0.2	22.6

*December 31, 1993, share price divided by 1993 earnings per share.

What the Companies Do

Abbott Laboratories (ABT–NYSE) makes health-care products, including drugs, intravenous solutions, diagnostic tests, laboratory and hospital instruments, prepared infant formulas and nutritional products. The company also makes agricultural and chemical products. Abbott's brand names include Isomil, Similac, Murine, Selsun Blue and Sucaryl. Drug and nutritional products account for about 51 percent of sales and 56 percent of profits. Hospital and laboratory products contribute the balance of sales and profits. International business produces about 37 percent of sales and 28 percent of pretax profits. The company invests nearly 10 percent of sales into research and development. Sales grew from $3.1 billion in 1984 to $8.4 billion in 1993. Profits per share during the same period rose from $ .42 to $1.69. (Abbott Laboratories has about 49,000 employees and 83,000 shareholders.)

Per-Share Financial Summary

	1984	1993
Revenues	$3.23	$10.24
Earnings	.42	1.69
Dividends	.15	.68
Average Stock Price	5⅜	26⅞

The stock was split two-for-one in 1986, 1990 and 1992.

Dentsply International, Inc. (XRAY–OTC), develops, manufactures and markets a broad range of products for the dental market, and conventional X-ray systems, mammography systems and X-ray tubes for the medical X-ray market. The company's three principal product categories include dental, consumable and laboratory products (accounts for 60 percent of sales), dental equipment (28 percent of sales) and medical X-ray products (7 percent of sales). Foreign business contributes about 41 percent of total sales.

Dentsply International is the surviving corporation of the June 1993 merger with Gendex Corporation. The surviving company's common stock shares were offered initially to the public in August of 1987 at a price of 3⅞ per share (adjusted for a stock split in 1992). The stock sold at an average price of 43¼ in 1993. Sales have grown from $16 million in 1987 to $552 million in 1993. Per-share earnings have increased to $1.81 in 1993 from $.25 in 1987. (The company has about 4,400 employees and 9,000 shareholders.)

Per-Share Financial Summary

	1987	1993
Revenues	$2.75	$19.95
Earnings	.25	1.81
Dividends	Nil	Nil
Average Stock Price	3⅝	43¼

The stock was split two-for-one in 1992.

Diagnostek, Inc. (DXK–NYSE), is a leading manager of prescription-drug benefits and hospital pharmacy care. The company provides pharmaceuticals by mail, contracts pharmacy management services to hospitals and HMOs, and rents medical-imaging and diagnostic equipment to hospitals. Mail pharmacy services account for about 63 percent of sales and contract pharmacy services, 35 percent.

Diagnostek, Inc., had revenues of $1.2 million in 1985. Sales have increased without interruption to more than $400 million in 1993. During the same period, per-share earnings have grown from $.01 to

$ .50. The average price of the stock rose over the years from 1⅝ in 1985 to 12⅞ in 1993. (The company has about 1,800 employees and 1,000 shareholders.)

Per-Share Financial Summary

	1985	1993
Revenues	$.13	$20.18
Earnings	.01	.50
Dividends	Nil	Nil
Average Stock Price	1⅝	12⅞

Invacare Corporation (IVCR–OTC) designs, manufactures and distributes an extensive line of durable medical equipment and supplies for the home health-care and extended-care markets. Products include manual and motorized wheelchairs, home-care and nursing-home beds, medical oxygen concentrators, and cardiovascular equipment. The company has international operations in France, Germany, Mexico and the United Kingdom. Foreign sales account for 33 percent of the total. Invacare invests 1.7 percent of sales in research and development.

Invacare sales have risen from $90 million in 1984, the year of its initial public offering, to $365 million in 1993. Earnings per share also have prospered, going from a loss of $ .49 in 1984, a loss of $ .08 in 1985, to a profit of $ .26 in 1986 and $1.50 in 1993. From an IPO of $5.50 in 1984, the stock price has risen to an average of 24½ in 1993. (The company has about 2,900 employees and 1,500 shareholders.)

Per-Share Financial Summary

	1984	1993
Revenues	$7.99	$25.36
Earnings	d .49	1.50
Dividends	.01	Nil
Average Stock Price	3⅝	24½

A 100 percent stock dividend was paid in 1991.

Nellcor, Inc. (NELL–OTC), designs, produces and distributes monitoring instruments, detectors and related sensors and adaptors. Its products are used mainly in operating rooms, intensive care units, emergency transport and the home. Primary products include pulse oximeters, used to measure blood-oxygen saturation; sensors; multifunction monitors; and apnea (temporary cessation of breathing) monitors. The company's instruments monitor patients noninvasively.

International business accounts for about 17 percent of total sales. Nellcor invests about 10 percent of sales in research and development.

Nellcor, Inc.'s, IPO was in May of 1987 at $16 a share. The price fell a few months later reaching a low of $7 by the end of 1987 but has gradually moved up. Sales have grown from $81 million in 1987 to $218 million in 1993. Per-share earnings have been erratic, going from $ .68 in 1987 to as low as $ .56 in 1989, and reaching $1.50 in 1993. (The company has about 1,800 employees and 880 shareholders.)

Per-Share Financial Summary

	1987	1993
Revenues	$6.01	$13.06
Earnings	.68	1.50
Dividends	Nil	Nil
Average Stock Price	14⅝	25⅞

Owens & Minor, Inc. (OMI–NYSE), is a wholesaler of medical and surgical supplies to hospitals and other health-care institutions in 40 states. The company deals mainly with nonprofit hospitals through the umbrella group Voluntary Hospitals of America. It also distributes drugs to hospitals and alternate medical-care facilities in Florida. Owens & Minor operates 29 distribution centers located in 21 states.

Owens & Minor has enjoyed nearly steady sales growth over the years. Total sales have grown from $306 million in 1984 to $1.4 billion in 1993. Per-share earnings during that period have grown from $ .28 to $ .90. After adjusting for three-for-two stock splits in 1985, 1988, 1991, and 1993, the average annual price of the stock rose from 2¾ in 1984 to 17⅞ in 1993. (The company has about 1,450 employees and 9,800 shareholders.)

Per-Share Financial Summary

	1984	1993
Revenues	$16.11	$45.91
Earnings	.19	.60
Dividends	.05	.14
Average Stock Price	1⅞	11⅞

Stryker Corporation (STRY–OTC) develops, manufactures and markets surgical (accounts for 83 percent of sales) and medical devices (17 percent of sales). Surgical products include orthopedic implants, powered instruments, arthroscopy systems and other operating-room devices. Medical products are patient handling equipment, such as specialty stretcher and maternity beds, and physical-therapy services. Foreign sales account for about 31 percent of the total. The company invests nearly 7 percent of sales in research and development.

Stryker Corporation has enjoyed steady growth, from $84 million of sales in 1984 to $557 million in 1993. Earnings have grown from $ .16 per share in 1984 to $1.25 per share in 1993. Shareholders have benefited as well, with the share price going from an average of 2¾ in 1984 to 30⅜ in 1993. (The company has about 2,900 employees and 3,500 shareholders.)

Per-Share Financial Summary

	1984	1993
Revenues	$1.89	$11.52
Earnings	.16	1.25
Dividends	Nil	.07
Average Stock Price	2¾	30⅜

The stock was split three-for-two in 1985, two-for-one in 1987, three-for-two in 1989 and two-for-one in 1991.

SUMMARY

Many people have blamed new technology for fueling the growth of medical costs, while others have hailed it for reducing them. Depending on your perspective, both views can be correct. For instance, minimally invasive surgery has increased the number of people opting for surgery; at the same time, the cost per surgical procedure has been reduced. New products promise growth for medical-supply companies, but the uncertainties associated with health-care reform warn investors to be cautious. Overall, however, the future looks bright for innovative competitors in the industry.

CHAPTER 28

Recreation

Corporate empire builders historically have been attracted to entertainment companies, particularly film studios. Domestic conglomerates liked to round out their horizontal expansions by adding a movie distributor. Often lacking any synergies, the mergers were not always a huge success.

Today, the combinations generally have made more economic sense. Large Japanese home-electronics firms, for example, have sound reasons for wanting captive producers of entertainment software. During the period of high Japanese PE ratios, companies such as Sony and Matsushita had no competing U.S. bids when they offered to buy Columbia Pictures and MCA, with its Universal Studios. Business conditions also were preeminent in the recent acquisition of New Line Cinema by Turner Broadcasting.

Walt Disney Company, already a fully synergistic entertainment power, generally has expanded or duplicated existing operations. The company also has sought to acquire unusual talent, as in the absorption of the well-known independent film producer, Miramax. Walt Disney himself recognized early in his career as a successful animator and film producer the opportunity to enhance other endeavors with value based on the fame of the characters he created. The accuracy of his foresight was affirmed by the success of Disneyland and Walt Disney World. And the enormous success of Tokyo Disneyland inspired the Euro

Disney project in France. Euro Disney, however, has had more than its share of start-up problems because of in large part to a depressed European economy.

In keeping with the growing importance the public is placing on health and fitness, many companies in this industry emphasize active forms of recreation. The Disney theme parks offer active physical involvement. The audience has to get out of the house and go somewhere. And people generally are inclined to make the effort. While the initial motivation may have been to please the children, attractions such as Epcot Center plus cabaret entertainment and golf now offer adult diversion as well.

Other companies, such as Brunswick and Outboard Marine, which fell on hard times following a worldwide powerboat buying binge in the late 1980s, seem to be recovering. These companies take more specific aim at fulfilling the desire for active recreation. So far, their operating reports have not confirmed a rebound, but domestic economic indicators such as personal income and durable goods orders foretell much better times ahead for these boat makers.

Then there are the cruise lines, such as Royal Caribbean Cruises and Carnival Cruise Lines, which both envision a much bigger cruise market in their ambitious construction plans.

Investment Outlook

Most companies in the recreation industry fared better in 1993 than the prior year, and analysts see favorable earnings prospects in the near future. For investors seeking timely investment ideas, the recreation industry seems generally a good place to look.

★ Recommended Stock

Walt Disney Company
500 South Buena Vista Street
Burbank, CA 91521-7320
818-560-1000

Chairman and CEO: Michael D. Eisner
Number of shareholders: 408,000

Number of employees: 62,000
Where the stock trades: NYSE
Symbol: DIS

What the Company Does

The Walt Disney Company operates Disneyland in California and Walt Disney World in Florida. The Florida facility includes The Magic Kingdom, Epcot Center and Disney-MGM Studios. Through Buena Vista, Touchstone, Hollywood Pictures and Miramax, the company provides entertainment for theaters, television and video. Disney also licenses rights, publishes books and records music. The company owns The Disney Channel and station KCAL-TV in Los Angeles. It earns royalties from Tokyo Disneyland and owns 49 percent of Euro Disney SCA in France. Foreign sales account for about 17 percent of total revenues.

Reason for Recommendation

The Walt Disney Company has several strategic and financial objectives that guide management decision making in creating value for its shareholders. According to the company, its overriding objective is to sustain Disney as the world's premier entertainment company from a creative, strategic and financial standpoint. Another objective is to maintain and build on the integrity of the Disney name and franchise. To maintain the brand's image, the company goes to great lengths to preserve the fundamental values with which Disney products and services are most often associated: quality, imagination and guest service.

The company's financial objectives are to achieve 20 percent annual earnings growth over current five-year periods, beginning with 1991 as the base year, and through profitable operations and reinvestment of cash flow, 20 percent annual return on shareholders' equity.

A dynamic film business continues to generate sales and earnings records for Disney. On top of three years of exceptional progress in the important holiday season, this segment achieved a 45 percent operating income gain in the last quarter of 1993. Large contributions came from Aladdin video sales in America and movie showings in overseas markets. Earnings for the company as a whole surged 36 percent in the final 1993 quarter.

The company is negotiating solutions for the problems at Euro Disney. The company's $350 million charge in 1993 left it with a zero equity in the French project. Discussions were under way in early 1994 with Euro Disney's lenders to work out a financial restructuring that would lower interest expense. Analysts expect that more equity will

FIGURE 28.1   Results of a $10,000 Investment in Walt Disney Company
Common Stock with Dividends Reinvested from 1984
to 1993

	Average Share Price	Annual Dividends	Shares Bought from Dividends	Total # Shares Owned	Value of Shares Owned
1984	3¾	$213	56	2,722	$ 10,210
1985	5½	217	39	2,761	15,185
1986	10⅜	220	21	2,782	28,863
1987	15½	222	14	2,796	43.338
1988	15¼	279	18	2,814	42,913
1989	25⅛	281	11	2,825	70,978
1990	27¾	395	14	2,839	78,782
1991	27⅞	482	17	2,856	79,611
1992	36⅞	571	15	2,871	105,868
1993	41⅞	689	16	2,887	120,893

replace some debt and the company will absorb some Euro Disney
losses in the second half of fiscal 1994.

About 52 film releases by Disney's four studios provide the chance
for some film hits by the end of 1994. While the immediate future is
hazy, numerous projects to foster growth keep Disney a popular
investment.

Investment Results

The Walt Disney Company has rewarded its shareholders since 1984
with nearly uninterrupted annual increases in the price of its stock.
Investors were rewarded by the market's reaction to the company's
solid growth in sales and earnings. An investment of $10,000 in 1984
would have bought 2,666 shares at the average market price in that
year (adjusted for stock splits). Figure 28.1 shows the year-by-year
results of a $10,000 investment in Disney stock from 1984 to 1993.
Brokerage commissions are not considered. Numbers have been adjusted for four-for-one splits in 1986 and 1992.

The December 31, 1993, closing price of Walt Disney Company
common shares traded on the NYSE was $42⅝. The market value of
$123,058 on that date was more than 12 times the original $10,000
invested in 1984.

Figure 28.2 shows selected per-share data of Walt Disney Company
during the period from 1984 to 1993. The data has been adjusted for
stock splits.

FIGURE 28.2   Selected Per-Share Data of Walt Disney Company from
1984 to 1993

	Earnings Per Share	Book Value	Average Price Per Share	Percentage of Profits Paid in Dividends	Average PE Ratio
1984	$ .19	$ 2.14	3¾	38%	19.7
1985	.32	2.29	5½	23	17.2
1986	.46	2.71	10⅜	17	22.6
1987	.71	3.50	15½	11	21.8
1988	.95	4.43	15¼	10	16.1
1989	1.28	5.62	25⅛	9	19.6
1990	1.50	6.62	27¾	9	18.5
1991	1.20	7.43	27⅞	14	23.2
1992	1.52	8.97	36⅞	13	24.3
1993	1.63	9.39	41⅞	14	25.7

The stock was split four-for-one in 1986 and 1992.

Earnings per share rose steadily until a reversal in 1991, followed by a recovery in the next two years. Book value, on the other hand, increased steadily over the years as the company retained most of its earnings, paying out only a small portion in dividends. PE ratios have been relatively high since the early 1980s and moving up gradually, reflecting investor confidence.

Common Stock Quarterly Price Record

Following are the high and low prices of the Walt Disney Company common stock during the 1992 and 1993 fiscal years, adjusted for a four-for-one stock split in 1992:

	1st Quarter	2nd Quarter	3rd Quarter	4th Quarter
1992				
High	$30⅜	$39⅜	$41⅛	$37½
Low	25⅞	28½	34⅝	32¾
1993				
High	$45¼	$47⅞	$45⅛	$41⅜
Low	33¼	41¾	38¼	36

Note: Disney's fiscal year ends September 30.

In every quarter during 1992 and 1993, it was possible to buy shares at a price significantly below the high price of the prior quarter. In most quarters, the difference was substantial. Careful buying of shares can have a long-term positive impact on your total investment return.

CREATING A PORTFOLIO OF STOCKS IN THE RECREATION INDUSTRY

Following are a number of companies that are considered by some analysts to be favorably positioned for capital appreciation.

Company	1993 Earnings Per Share	12/31/93 Share Price	Dividend Yield	PE Ratio*
Carnival Cruise Lines, Inc.	$2.25	47⅜	1.2	21.1
Cedar Fair, L.P.	2.26	35	6.1	15.5
Electronic Arts, Inc.	.90 E	30	Nil	33.3
Harley-Davidson, Inc.	1.95	44⅛	0.5	22.6
WMS Industries	1.64	28¾	Nil	17.5

*December 31, 1993, share price divided by 1993 earnings per share.

What the Companies Do

Carnival Cruise Lines, Inc. (CCL–NYSE), is the world's largest cruise line based on passenger capacity. It operates 20 ships in the Caribbean, South Pacific and Mediterranean, and in Alaska. The cruise segment, accounting for 86 percent of sales, includes Carnival's nine ships, Holland America's six ships, Windstar Sail Cruises' three sailing ships, and Seabourn's two ships. Holland America Westours tour and hotel business contributes 14 percent of revenues. The company had an IPO of common shares in 1987. (The company has about 11,800 employees and 3,600 shareholders.)

Per-Share Financial Summary

	1987	1993
Revenues	$4.79	$11.00 E
Earnings	1.30	2.25
Dividends	Nil	.56
Average Stock Price	12⅞	40⅛

Cedar Fair, L.P. (FUN–NYSE) is a limited partnership, managed by Cedar Fair Management Company. It owns and operates four amusement/theme parks: Cedar Point in Sandusky, Ohio; Valleyfair in Shakopee, Minnesota; and Dorney Park and Wildwater Kingdom, both located near Allentown, Pennsylvania. As a limited partnership, the company is not subject to corporate income taxes. Distributions are treated as a nontaxable return of capital. The initial offering of limited partnership units was made in April of 1987. (The company has more than 5,000 seasonal and 450 full-time employees.)

Per-Unit Financial Summary

	1987	1993
Revenues	$4.86	$8.04
Earnings	.96	2.26
Distributions	.71	1.89
Average Unit Price	8⅛	31¾

Electronic Arts, Inc. (ERTS–OTC), provides interactive entertainment software for various hardware platforms, including IBM-compatible personal computers, Commodore, Apple, Nintendo, Sega and 3DO. The company develops along the lines of film-studio procedures. It markets its own products as well as labels of other software publishers in the manner of music, magazine and video distribution. Electronic Arts has a 21 percent ownership in 3DO Company. The company's IPO was made in September of 1989 at $2 per share and adjusted for two-for-one stock splits in 1992 and 1993. (The company has about 900 employees and 2,200 shareholders.)

Per-Share Financial Summary

	1989	1993
Revenues	$1.94	$8.78
Earnings	.17	.90
Dividends	Nil	Nil
Average Stock Price	2⅛	30⅞

Harley-Davidson, Inc. (HDI–NYSE), manufactures heavyweight custom and touring motorcycles and related products, which account for about 75 percent of its revenues. It also makes recreational and specialized commercial vehicles through its Holiday Rambler Corporation subsidiary, which provides the other 25 percent of sales. Harley-Davidson is the only U.S. manufacturer of motorcycles. It has 13 manufacturing and office facilities in the United States and

4 abroad. Foreign business accounts for about 20 percent of sales. Sales totaled $1.2 billion in 1993. The stock was listed for trading on the NYSE in 1986 and was split two-for-one in 1990 and 1992. (The company has about 5,800 employees and 13,000 shareholders.)

Per-Share Financial Summary

	1987	1993
Revenues	$11.91	$32.04
Earnings	.21	1.95
Dividends	Nil	.12
Average Stock Price	2⅝	38½

WMS Industries (WMS–NYSE) is the dominant manufacturer of pinball machines in the United States, with a 70 percent market share. It is also a leading producer of video arcade games. Amusement games account for about 79 percent of total sales. Revenues totaled $331 million in 1993. The stock was split two-for-one in 1992. (The company has about 3,800 employees and 2,000 shareholders.)

Per-Share Financial Summary

	1984	1993
Revenues	$3.82	$14.07
Earnings	d.99	1.31
Dividends	Nil	Nil
Average Stock Price	3⅛	25½

SUMMARY

Corporate empire builders have historically been attracted to entertainment companies, but often lacking any synergies, the mergers were not always a success. Today, the combinations generally have made more economic sense, with acquiring companies having sound reasons for wanting captive producers of entertainment products. In keeping with the growing importance the public is placing on health and fitness, many companies in this industry emphasize active forms of recreation. The Disney theme parks offer active physical involvement. And people usually are inclined to make the effort. Then there are the cruise lines, such as Royal Caribbean Cruises and Carnival Cruise Lines, which both envision a much bigger cruise market in their ambitious construction plans. Investors seeking timely investment ideas might take a good look at companies in the recreation industry.

CHAPTER 29

Retail Building Supply

The retail building-supply industry has been undergoing a transformation from small, stodgy stores to larger stores and more recently to very large superstores. Home Depot, first to utilize the retail building-supply superstore concept, is also the fastest growing company in this industry. In smaller markets, a different type of store is needed. Lowe's Companies has developed a superstore format for these markets.

Until the 1970s, retail outlets in this industry consisted of a lumberyard with an accompanying hardware store. Typically, their size ranged from 10,000 to 20,000 square feet. Later, a new generation of stores containing 40,000 to 60,000 square feet of space became the norm. But since 1990 or so, the new superstores have begun to appear. These operations may contain anywhere from 80,000 to 120,000 square feet.

With the sophisticated planning and management techniques required by superstores, companies have gained efficiency by setting up duplicate stores at different locations. It is becoming increasingly more difficult for independent operators to compete with the well-managed chains.

Home Depot remains the undisputed leader in the field as it builds a chain of warehouse superstores across the United States. The stores are efficiently run and popular with customers, who can leisurely examine the merchandise and serve themselves. Other top retailers following the Home Depot lead are Hechinger, with its "Home Quarters Warehouse," and Grossman's with "Contractors' Warehouse."

Investment Potential

The rapid growth and prosperous future anticipated for the most successful companies in this industry have caused them to carry high PE ratios. They must keep expanding to provide investors with worthwhile returns over the next several years. Growth prospects for companies carrying lower PE ratios such as Hechinger Company probably are less well defined than for the high fliers such as Home Depot and Lowe's Companies.

★ Recommended Stock

Lowe's Companies, Inc.
Box 1111
North Wilkesboro, NC 28656
919-651-4000

Chairman and CEO: Laurence A. Tisch
Number of Shareholders: 6,300
Number of Employees: 18,000
Where the stock trades: NYSE
Symbol: LOW

According to the May 1993 proxy statement, directors, officers and an employee stock ownership trust own 26 percent of the outstanding shares of common stock.

What the Company Does
Lowe's Companies Inc. is one of America's largest retailers, with total sales of more than $4.5 billion. The company sells building materials and hard goods through a chain of more than 300 stores in 20 states, mainly in the Southeast, with an average store size of 33,000 square feet. Each Lowe's store combines the merchandise, sales and service of a home-improvement center, a building-contractor supply business and a consumer durables retailer. Average store sales are about $12.6 million per year, of which 56 percent is to home center

customers, 30 percent to professional contractors and 14 percent to durables customers. Big stores average about $16.4 million in sales.

Reason for Recommendation

Lowe's has been a publicly owned company since 1961. The stock was listed on the NYSE in 1979, on the Pacific Stock Exchange in 1981 and on The Stock Exchange of London in 1981. Lowe's is a company in transformation, changing itself from a chain of small, tired home-improvement stores into a modern merchandiser of warehouse super-stores. The old units, with an average store size of 33,000 square feet, are being closed and replaced with 85,000-square-foot stores in the same communities. About 65 superstores were opened in 1993, with more than half representing enlargement and relocation of existing stores. The large stores account for about half of Lowe's 314 stores in place at the end of 1993. The company expected to open another 50 to 55 superstores in 1994, with most being relocations.

In the early 1990s, Lowe's adopted an "every-day-low-price" policy, causing its gross margin (sales less cost of goods sold) to fall between 1990 and 1992. But by changing its product mix, it raised its ratio of consumer sales to contractor sales. This move enabled the company to increase its gross margin to a healthy 23.5 percent. Its pricing remains competitive.

Despite substantial preopening costs, Lowe's has kept its overhead expenses under control. The result has been climbing profit margins. Analysts expect sales to grow about 17 percent to about $4.5 billion in fiscal 1993 (the fiscal year ended January 31, 1994). But earnings may soar 35 percent to $1.60 per share. In fiscal 1994, share earnings are expected to jump another 20 percent to $1.95 per share.

Lowe's management believes the future of the company is bright. Housing expenditures and investments increased every year of the past decade, and the majority of baby boomers are just now reaching their peak earning years. The home-center sector of the Lowe's market is growing at twice the rate of the gross national product, and when consumer durables are added, the market may approach $250 billion by the year 2000.

The retail building-supply industry is highly fragmented, with the top-ten home-improvement retailers (combined) accounting for less than a quarter of the total market opportunity. Lowe's predicts that by the year 2000, after further consolidation and shakeout, America will have roughly 2,000 home-improvement superstores. If the average

FIGURE 29.1 Results of a $10,000 Investment in Lowe's Companies, Inc., Common Stock Made in 1984

	Average Share Price	Annual Dividends	Shares Bought from Dividends	Total # Shares Owned	Value of Shares Owned
1984	5¼	$152	29	1,933	$10,148
1985	6½	173	26	1,959	12,733
1986	8	195	24	1,983	15,864
1987	6	218	36	2,019	12,114
1988	5⅛	242	47	2,066	10,588
1989	6⅝	247	37	2,103	13,932
1990	8½	273	32	2,135	18,147
1991	7½	298	39	2,174	16,305
1992	10⅜	326	31	2,205	22,876
1993	21	352	16	2,221	46,641

superstore does about $35 million in annual sales, those 2,000 stores will account for $70 billion—still less than half of the home-center market opportunity. Lowe's goal is to have 600 of those 2,000 super-stores and to be consistently profitable and constantly growing.

Investment Results

Lowe's Companies, Inc., has enjoyed a steady, if not spectacular growth in sales and earnings over the years. Following sluggish growth of the share price from 1984 to 1990, the stock reacted strongly to the company's efforts to transform itself to large home-improvement destination centers.

Figure 29.1 shows the ten-year results of a $10,000 investment in Lowe's Companies common stock from 1984 to 1993. All numbers have been adjusted for two-for-one stock splits in 1992 and 1994. It is assumed the stock was purchased at the average of the high and low prices in 1984. A $10,000 investment in 1984 would have purchased 1,904 shares, adjusted for the stock splits. Cash dividends have been applied to purchase additional shares. Brokerage commissions are not considered.

The December 31, 1993, closing price of Lowe's Companies on the NYSE was 29¾. The value of the original $10,000 investment on that date was $66,074.

FIGURE 29.2   Per-Share Financial Results of Lowe's Companies, Inc., from 1984 to 1993

	Earnings Per Share	Book Value	Sales	Average Per-Share Price	Average PE Ratio
1984	$ .43	$2.35	$11.65	5¼	12.2
1985	.41	2.75	13.97	6½	15.9
1986	.35	3.41	14.41	8	22.9
1987	.35	3.70	15.51	6	17.1
1988	.46	3.95	16.94	5⅛	11.1
1989	.50	4.33	17.79	6⅝	13.3
1990	.48	4.68	19.42	8½	17.7
1991	.37	4.59	20.97	7½	20.3
1992	.58	5.02	26.36	10⅜	17.9
1993	.90	5.91	30.70	21	23.3

Historical Financial Data

Sales of Lowe's Companies, Inc., grew from $1.6 billion in 1984 to more than $4.5 billion in 1993. In the same period, earnings have gone from $61.4 million to $131.8 million. Figure 29.2 shows important per-share data for the company during the period from 1984 to 1993. All yearly numbers relate to the company's fiscal years, which end on January 31, and have been adjusted for stock splits.

The PE ratio of Lowe's has been a reflection of investor optimism of the company's future earnings potential, rising in the early 1990s as the firm's transformation to large home-improvement distribution centers began to take hold. In early 1994, with the share price having risen to more than $36 per share, the earnings multiple had soared to 40 times the 1993 earnings, leaving the stock vulnerable to a price correction.

Common Stock Quarterly Price Record

Following are the high and low prices of Lowe's Companies, Inc., common stock during the fiscal years ending January 31, 1991, and 1992, adjusted for stock splits:

	1st Quarter	2nd Quarter	3rd Quarter	4th Quarter
1992				
High	$10⅞	$11⅞	$12¼	$14⅜
Low	8⅝	9⅛	8	9¼
1993				
High	$17¾	$20	$24¾	$31
Low	13¼	15	18⅜	23¼

In most quarterly periods during 1992 and 1993, fluctuating stock prices made it possible for a patient investor to purchase shares at a substantially lower cost than the high price of the prior quarter. Remember, careful timing of stock purchases can have an important effect on your long-term investment return.

CREATING A PORTFOLIO OF STOCKS IN THE RETAIL BUILDING-SUPPLY INDUSTRY

The biggest companies in this group have significant potential for growth. But with premium PE ratios, their riskiness is increased in the event that their aggressive growth plans come up against stumbling blocks. Following are companies in the retail building-supply industry that analysts believe also have potential for capital appreciation.

Company	1993 Earnings Per Share	12/31/93 Share Price	Dividend Yield	PE Ratio*
Hechinger Company	$ .59	9¾	1.4%	16.5
Home Depot, Inc. (The)	1.01	39½	0.4	39.1
Hughes Supply, Inc.	1.25	19½	0.6	15.6

*December 31, 1993, share price divided by 1993 earnings per share.

What the Companies Do

Hechinger Company (HECHA–OTC) operates a chain of specialty retail building-supply stores located primarily along the mid-Atlantic seaboard. The company has been an operator of full-service home-improvement/building-supply stores but in recent years has been transforming itself. It has been closing some of its company-name stores and renovating others, giving them a new hybrid format called Home Project Center. Sales totaled $2.1 billion in 1993. (The company has about 17,000 employees and 4,500 shareholders.)

Per-Share Financial Summary

	1984	1993
Revenues	$14.30	$49.86
Earnings	.74	.59
Dividends	.10	.16
Average Stock Price	11⅛	10⅜

The company's stock was split five-for-four in 1984, 1985 and 1986.

The Home Depot, Inc. (HD–NYSE), operates a chain of retail "warehouse" building-supply/home-improvement stores in Eastern Seaboard states from Connecticut to Florida, and in Texas, Arizona and California. Stores average 97,000 square feet and carry about 30,000 items. Sales totaled $9.2 billion in 1993. (The company has about 39,000 employees and 4,900 shareholders.)

Per-Share Financial Summary

	1984	1993
Revenues	$1.71	$20.56
Earnings	.06	1.01
Dividends	Nil	.12
Average Stock Price	2	42⅞

The company's stock was split three-for-two in 1987, 1989, 1990, 1991 and 1992, and was split four-for-three in 1993.

Hughes Supply, Inc. (HUG–NYSE), is a wholesale distributor of electrical, plumbing, heating and air-conditioning, and other materials and supplies to the construction industry and mechanical trades in Florida, Georgia and other Southeastern states. The company distributes about 95,000 products representing 6,000 manufacturers through wholesale outlets. Sales totaled $660 million in 1993. (The company has about 1,900 employees and 1,500 shareholders.)

Per-Share Financial Summary

	1984	1993
Revenues	$50.91	$143.83
Earnings	1.35	1.25
Dividends	.19	.15
Average Stock Price	14¼	16½

The company's stock was split three-for-two in 1988.

SUMMARY

The retail building-supply industry has been undergoing a transformation from small, stodgy stores to larger stores and more recently to very large superstores. Until the 1970s, retail outlets in this industry consisted of a lumberyard with an accompanying hardware store, ranging in size from 10,000 to 20,000 square feet. Since 1990 or so, the new superstores have begun to appear. These operations may contain anywhere from 80,000 to 120,000 square feet. Home Depot remains the undisputed leader in the field as it builds a chain of warehouse superstores across the United States. The rapid growth and prosperous future anticipated for the most successful companies in this industry have caused them to carry high PE ratios. They must keep expanding to provide investors with worthwhile returns over the next several years, or suffer share-price corrections from a disappointed investment community.

CHAPTER 30

Semiconductors

The semiconductor industry has continued to score record sales and profits. Virtually all makers of integrated circuits enjoyed unprecedented prosperity in 1993. Continuing progress in the near future seems all but inevitable. The risk in later years lies not so much in the state of the economy but in how companies in the industry manage the proceeds of their current prosperity. Overexpansion is the traditional consequence of good times. The rapid advance of technology that continues to open new applications for integrated circuits offers to make this industry less sensitive to the business cycle than in the past.

Some companies are accelerating their rate of growth; but earnings reports in other cases have missed widespread analyst expectations and resulted in abrupt and sometimes sharp reversals in stock prices. Investor disappointment sometimes comes simply because expectations are unrealistic in the first place. This happens easily in the high-technology group because the complex factors that drive industry growth are not simple to understand. Often, investors have nothing more to base decisions on than past trends.

The wave of prosperity that engulfed the semiconductor industry in the early 1990s resulted not so much from an improved economy but from the surge in personal computer sales that generated enormous demand for microprocessors (the "brains" of desktop and mobile computers). These remarkable devices also found markets in applications such as antilock brakes, which have shown tremendous growth in demand even when overall car sales had remained static. A surge in sales of semiconductors also was fed by the spread of cellular telephones and wireless radio, which required microprocessors specially designed for their use.

An indicator of microchip demand came from economists at Texas Instruments, Inc. In the first part of 1994, they had estimated that semiconductor needs would grow 17 percent in 1994, a substantial decline from the 29 percent advance in 1993. That forecast has since been increased to a 21 percent rise in chip sales for 1994, bringing the worldwide market size to $93 billion. The higher revision reflects strong orders in Texas Instruments' own semiconductor segment, which was up 36 percent in the first quarter of 1994. A less sharp increase was reported by Motorola, with 1994 first-quarter sales up 26 percent and orders up 15 percent.

Investment Outlook

The semiconductor industry appears on a course that will see its sales growing unabated for the next few years. Analysts believe, however, that if plant expansion gets out of hand, profits could be held back. But most stocks in this group should do well in the near-term, though long-term appreciation may be hampered by currently high prices, and there is susceptibility to market fluctuations.

★ *Recommended Stock*

Intel Corporation
2200 Mission College Boulevard
P.O. Box 58119
Santa Clara, CA 95052-8119
408-765-8080

Chairman: Gordon E. Moore
Number of shareholders: 32,500
Number of employment: 29,500
Where the stock trades: OTC: Nasdaq
Symbol: INTC

What the Company Does

Intel Corporation is a leading supplier of microcomputer components and modules. The company's major customers are computer and computer peripheral manufacturers worldwide. Intel also sells to *original equipment manufacturers* (OEMs), including makers of automobiles and a wide range of industrial and telecommunications equipment. Personal computer (PC) users buy Intel's PC enhancements, business communications products and networking products at retail stores around the world.

Intel was founded in 1968 to design and manufacture very complex silicon chips. The company's first products were semiconductor memory chips. In 1971, Intel introduced the world's first microprocessor, a development that changed not only the future of the company but in some ways much of the industrial world. Increasingly, Intel's business direction has been set by the directions that the microprocessor revolution has taken.

Reason for Recommendation

After 25 years in business, Intel is an industry leader. Today's powerful yet inexpensive computers are being connected to networks that allow many types of data to be shared. According to the company, Intel's mission is to supply the electronic building blocks for this new computer and communications industry, an industry in which many key products are built around technologies that Intel has helped pioneer, including PC architecture.

Revenues of $8.78 billion in 1993 were up 50 percent over the prior year; net profits more than doubled. The year's results reinforced Intel's position as the largest semiconductor manufacturer in the world. According to the market research firm Dataquest, Intel's estimated chip sales were more than 28 percent higher than those of its nearest competitor.

The company's microprocessor business boomed in 1993, with the introduction of powerful new products and increased demand for its mainstream processors. The Pentium processor, introduced in mid-1993, is the newest generation in Intel's compatible family of microprocessors. Since its introduction, it has enjoyed the fastest production ramp of any new processor generation in the company's history. By late 1994, Intel expects that about one-quarter of its microprocessor shipments to the PC market segment will be Pentium processors.

In its first 25 years of business, Intel has done well in an intensely competitive industry. The convergence of computing and communica-

FIGURE 30.1 Results of a $10,000 Investment in Intel Corporation Common Stock in 1984

	Average Share Price	Annual Dividends	Shares Bought from Dividends	Total # Shares Owned	Value of Shares Owned
1984	11⅜	Nil	0	879	$ 9,999
1985	8⅞	Nil	0	879	7,801
1986	8⅛	Nil	0	879	7,141
1987	14⅜	Nil	0	879	12,636
1988	14⅛	Nil	0	879	12,416
1989	14¾	Nil	0	879	12,965
1990	20	Nil	0	879	17,580
1991	24¼	Nil	0	879	21,315
1992	34½	$ 43	1	880	30,360
1993	58½	176	3	883	51,656

tions opens promising avenues for growth. In recent years, Intel has been moving resources into areas such as fax-modem boards, networking products, mobile computing and the recently announced ProShare personal conferencing products. The commercial availability of the company's advanced microprocessors will keep business growing while competitors work to establish credibility. Performance of new versions nearly doubles the capabilities of current designs. And once past the start-up phase, output from new state-of-the-art facilities in California and Ireland will make the new devices more profitable than the chips that they replace.

Investment Results

Over the years, Intel shareholders have prospered along with the company. Following two years of declining sales in 1985 and 1986, and operating at a loss in 1986, sales and earnings have moved steadily forward.

Figure 30.1 shows the results of a $10,000 investment in Intel Corporation common stock from 1984 to 1993. It is assumed that the stock was purchased at the average of the high and low prices in 1984. A $10,000 investment in 1984 would have purchased 879 shares, adjusted for a three-for-two stock split in 1987 and a two-for-one split in 1993. Cash dividends commenced in 1992. Brokerage commissions are not considered.

FIGURE 30.2   Per-Share Financial Results of Intel Corporation from
1984 to 1993

	Earnings Per Share	Book Value	Sales	Average Price Per-Share	Average PE Ratio
1984	$ .51	$ 3.98	$ 4.77	11⅜	22.3
1985	Nil	4.08	3.92	8⅞	N/A
1986	d.52	3.61	3.58	8⅛	N/A
1987	.49	3.88	5.66	14⅜	29.3
1988	1.26	5.76	7.96	14⅛	11.2
1989	1.18	6.91	8.47	14¾	12.5
1990	1.60	8.99	9.82	20	12.5
1991	1.91	10.83	11.72	24¼	12.7
1992	2.51	13.01	13.96	34½	13.7
1993	5.16	17.94	21.01	58½	11.3

On December 31, 1993, the closing price of Intel Corporation on
the NASDAQ market was 62. The value of the original $10,000
investment on that date was $54,746.

Historical Financial Data

Intel entered a dynamic phase of net-income expansion in 1987,
with profits arising from the ashes of a $183-million loss in 1986 to a
profit of $175 million in 1987 and then going on to net profits of more
than $2.2 billion in 1993. Sales rose from $1.9 billion in 1987 to nearly
$8.8 billion in 1993. Figure 30.2 shows important per-share data for
the company during the period from 1984 to 1993. All yearly numbers
relate to the company's fiscal years, ended December 25, and are
adjusted for stock splits.

The PE ratio has remained at fairly low levels during most of the
ten-year period. The market seems reluctant to believe that earnings
will continue their strong growth in the years ahead. If earnings
expand, and market optimism increases the PE multiple, shareholders
could enjoy rising share prices over the next few years.

Common Stock Quarterly Price Record

Following are the high and low prices of Intel Corporation common
stock during the fiscal years ending December 25, 1992, and 1993,
adjusted for a stock split in 1993:

	1st Quarter	2nd Quarter	3rd Quarter	4th Quarter
1992				
High	$34.25	$28.94	$33.31	$45.00
Low	24.38	23.50	27.56	31.25
1993				
High	$59.94	$58.75	$68.75	$73.25
Low	43.25	43.69	50.00	56.25

The price of Intel shares rose quite steadily during 1992 and 1993. Interesting note: In most quarters, it was possible to buy shares at prices substantially below the high of the previous quarter. Careful buying can help increase your long-term investment return.

CREATING A PORTFOLIO OF STOCKS IN THE SEMICONDUCTOR INDUSTRY

In four years, from 1990 to 1993, the semiconductor industry grew from about $28 billion to more than $42 billion. Industry sales are expected to reach $53 billion in 1995. The equities of many of the companies competing for this business hold promise for capital appreciation. Following is information on a number of highly regarded firms.

Company	1993 Earnings Per Share	12/31/93 Share Price	Dividend Yield	PE Ratio*
Applied Materials	$1.21	38¾	Nil	32.0
Linear Technology Corp.	.99	38¾	0.7%	39.1
Micron Technology, Inc.	1.00	18⅝	0.2	18.6
Motorola, Inc.	1.78	46⅛	0.7	25.9
Novellus Systems, Inc.	1.10	34¼	Nil	31.1

*December 31, 1993, share price divided by 1993 earnings per share.

What the Companies Do

Applied Materials, Inc. (AMAT–OTC), produces wafer-fabrication equipment for semiconductor makers. The company's product areas include chemical and physical vapor deposition, which is used to layer conducting or insulating films on silicon wafers; epitaxy, used to form a pure silicon layer on which circuits are constructed; etch, used to inscribe circuits on wafers; and ion implantation, used to alter conductivity of wafer regions. Sales totaled $1.08 billion in 1993. (The company has about 4,500 employees and 1,000 shareholders.)

Per-Share Financial Summary

	1984	1993
Revenues	$ 3.28	$13.44
Earnings	.26	1.21
Dividends	Nil	Nil
Average Stock Price	3⅞	28⅛

The company's stock was split two-for-one in 1986, 1992 and 1993.

Linear Technology Corp. (LLTC–OTC) manufactures and markets analog integrated circuits, including voltage converters, signal interface circuits, signal converters and filters. These devices are used to transform analog signals associated with continuous, real-world phenomena such as temperature or pressure into digital form for manipulation or storage as data. The company's products are used in laptop computers, cellular telephones, medical devices and factory automation. Sales totaled $150 million in 1993. The stock was first offered to the public in May of 1986 at s split-adjusted price of $4 per share. (The company has about 870 employees and 600 shareholders.)

Per-Share Financial Summary

	1986	1993
Revenues	$ .70	$ 4.23
Earnings	.04	.99
Dividends	Nil	.15
Average Stock Price	3⅞	30⅛

Micron Technology, Inc. (MU–NYSE), makes and markets semiconductor components, board-level products and system-level products used in the computer, telecommunications and office-automation industries. The company also manufactures computers. Its major products include: one- and four-megabit DRAMs based on CMOS; a family of static RAMs; and one- and two-megabit video RAMs. Foreign business accounts for about 30 percent of the total. Sales totaled $828 million in 1993. The company's stock was split five-for-two in 1994. (The company has about 4,900 employees and 2,500 shareholders.)

Per-Share Financial Summary

	1984	1993
Revenues	$1.96	$ 8.26
Earnings	.30	1.00
Dividends	Nil	.02
Average Stock Price	10⅞	16⅜

Motorola, Inc. (MOT–NYSE), is a leading manufacturer of electronic equipment and components. In the communications sector, it produces mobile radios and paging systems. Its semiconductor business makes a broad line of integrated circuits and discrete products. And in its general systems area, the company produces cellular telephones and infrastructure equipment, and computers. Motorola also makes electronic equipment for government, automotive and industrial markets. Foreign markets account for about 54 percent of the business. Sales totaled $16.9 billion in 1993. The company's stock was split three-for-one in 1984 and two-for-one in 1993 and 1994. (The company has about 120,000 employees and 21,500 shareholders.)

Per-Share Financial Summary

	1984	1993
Revenues	$11.65	$30.44
Earnings	.74	1.78
Dividends	.15	.22
Average Stock Price	9½	39⅛

Novellus Systems, Inc. (NVLS–OTC), designs, manufactures, markets and services equipment used in the fabrication of integrated circuits. The company's three product lines are used to deposit a variety of insulating films and tungsten on silicon wafers through the chemical and physical vapor-deposition processes. Foreign sales account for about 44 percent of the business. Sales totaled $113 million in 1993. The company completed its initial public stock offering in August of 1988 at $4 per share, adjusted for a two-for-one split in 1990. (The company has about 370 employees and 300 shareholders.)

Per-Share Financial Summary

	1988	1993
Revenues	$2.13	$8.01
Earnings	.25	1.10
Dividends	Nil	Nil
Average Stock Price	3⅝	25½

SUMMARY

The semiconductor industry recently has achieved record sales and profits. Virtually all makers of integrated circuits enjoyed unprecedented prosperity in 1993. Continuing progress in the near future seems all but inevitable. The rapid advance of technology that continues to open new applications for these devices offers to make this industry less sensitive to the business cycle than in the past. The prosperity that engulfed the semiconductor industry in the early 1990s resulted not so much from an improved economy but from the surge in personal computer, cellular telephones and wireless radio sales that generated enormous demand for microprocessors. The semiconductor industry appears on a course that will see its sales growing unabated for the next few years.

CHAPTER 31

Telecommunications Equipment

Three firms dominate the $2-billion-plus telecommunications equipment industry, which enjoyed a banner year in 1993. ADC Telecommunications, Inc., Andrew Corporation and DSC Communications Corporation all have seen their revenues increase steadily in recent years. Profits rebounded sharply for the industry as customers resumed their long-dormant capital-spending programs in response to the generally improving economic climate. On average, the group's equities more than doubled in price during 1993. In addition to growing profits, they benefited from major announcements by telecommunication-services companies concerning the building of America's Information Superhighway.

Bell Atlantic announced in 1993 that it would spend about $15 billion over ten years to make its telephone and cable networks compatible for sending all kinds of voice, video and data traffic. Another of the "Baby Bells," U.S. West, agreed to make a $2.5 billion investment in Time Warner, Inc., the nation's second-largest cable company. More mergers or joint ventures among telephone, CATV and other media companies are in the works, as technological breakthroughs and regulatory changes accelerate the race to offer consumers all types of interactive services. Pacific Telesis Corporation, the regional Bell company headquartered in San Francisco, announced that it was going to spend $16 billion to rewire the West Coast with fiber-optic, all-digital systems that would be able to deliver telephone calls, data and entertainment programming to homes and offices. MCI Communications announced in early 1994 a plan to invest more than $20 billion to create and provide new services via SONET fiber-optic technology to teleconsumers, businesses, research facilities and government customers.

All this activity should create a windfall for telecommunications equipment makers. Industry analysts have estimated that industry profits would rise by about 60 percent in 1994 and continue compounding over the next few years at a 20 percent to 25 percent annual rate. Strong overseas growth prospects, particularly in markets such as China, republics of the former Soviet Union and South America will help fuel this growth.

Investment Outlook

Telecommunications equipment stocks performed uncommonly well in 1993. The shares of ADC Telecommunications (my recommended company), Andrew Corporation and DSC Communications are expected to continue to move ahead. But move into these stocks cautiously. The high valuations put on these shares by investors makes them vulnerable to any bad news. New positions in the stocks should be taken when market corrections provide buying opportunities, or as part of a long-term program of constant dollar investing.

★ Recommended Stock

ADC Telecommunications, Inc.
4900 West 78th Street
Minneapolis, MN 55435
612-938-8080

Number of shareholders: 1,600
Number of employees: 2,300
Where the stock trades: OTC
Symbol: ADCT

What the Company Does
ADC Telecommunications, Inc., designs, manufactures and markets a wide variety of transmission, networking and broadband connectivity

products sold to telephone-operating companies, interexchange carriers, other common carriers, broadcast and cable TV networks, private network users and original equipment manufacturers. A majority of the company's sales are made by a direct sales force. Sales offices are located throughout the United States, Canada, Europe, the Pacific Basin, Australia and Central and South America.

The company pursues a strategy of diversity in products and market areas. Investments are spread across a number of product lines rather than being concentrated in a single venture. Markets for its products are selected on the basis of the company's ability to secure and defend a leadership position.

Reason for Recommendation

Since 1977, ADC Telecommunications, Inc., never has had an unprofitable year. Under very able management, the company has seen its sales grow steadily over the years, from $76 million in 1983 to $366 million in 1993. Net profits during the same period have grown from $5.5 million to $31.6 million.

According to the company's 1993 annual report, 55 percent of sales came from broadband connectivity, 26 percent from networking and 19 percent from transmission products. ADC's strategies for 1994 and beyond include an increasing focus on nontraditional markets such as cable TV and cellular communications, increasing their international presence and increasing fiber-optic and electronic product offerings. The company believes it possesses the tools to address the emerging multimedia markets. While implementation risks exist, the company feels that the risks are appropriate for the expanded opportunities afforded by the multimedia markets.

ADC Telecommunications set financial records in 1993: its highest annual order, revenue, gross profit, operating income, net income and earnings per-share levels. In the last quarter, the company had more than $100 million in revenues, also a record. The transmission division enjoyed a more than 20 percent increase in revenues for its newer fiber-transmission systems, nearly doubled its video-transmission-equipment revenues and commercially released a number of new products. The networking division increased net sales of its public network access equipment by more than 40 percent and initiated commercial sales of its CityCell microcell product.

The company's 1993 product sales mix maintained a gross margin at a relatively constant percentage of net sales compared to 1992, with a balance of product development and business growth requirements,

FIGURE 31.1   Results of a $10,000 Investment in ADC
Telecommunications Common Stock Made in 1984

	Average Share Price	Annual Dividends	Total Shares Owned	Value of Shares Owned
1984	2¾	$0	3,636	$10,000
1985	3¾	0	3,636	13,635
1986	6¼	0	3,636	22,725
1987	8	0	3,636	29,088
1988	8⅜	0	3,636	30,451
1989	7½	0	3,636	27,270
1990	10¼	0	3,636	37,269
1991	16	0	3,636	58,176
1992	17⅞	0	3,636	64,993
1993	31¼	0	3,636	113,625

coupled with expense control efforts. Net income for 1993, at $31.6 million, or $1.15 per share, represented a 50 percent increase over 1992 net income and a 16 percent return on equity.

Analysts expect continued growth in sales and earnings, assuming that economic activity continues to retain, if not pick up, strength. ADC Telecommunications was off to a very strong start in 1994, with best-ever first quarter results. Net sales were up 16 percent over the prior year's first quarter, while net income was up 27 percent.

Telecommunications companies should continue to increase capital expenditures, pushing ADC Telecommunication's profits up in the years just ahead.

Investment Results

The share price of ADC Telecommunications stock has moved generally upward since 1984, growing from an average price of 2¾ in 1984 to 31¼ in 1993. Prices have been adjusted to account for stock splits in 1986, 1987 and 1993. The company has paid no dividends to shareholders, choosing instead to reinvest its earnings back into the business. Shareholders apparently have benefited from the company's strategy through the increasing value of the stock.

Figure 31.1 shows the ten-year results of a $10,000 investment in ADC Telecommunications common stock from 1984 to 1993. It is assumed the stock was purchased at the average of the high and low prices in 1984. A $10,000 investment in 1984 would have purchased

FIGURE 31.2 Per-Share Financial Results of ADC Telecommunications, Inc., from 1984 to 1993

	Earnings Per Share	Book Value	Sales	Average Per-Share Price	Average PE
1984	$ .13	$1.56	$ 3.39	2¾	22.2
1985	.30	1.87	4.84	3¾	12.5
1986	.46	2.33	5.56	6¼	13.6
1987	.59	2.92	6.43	8	13.6
1988	.65	3.57	6.86	8⅜	12.9
1989	.63	4.18	7.43	7½	11.9
1990	.87	5.04	9.78	10¼	11.8
1991	.83	5.90	10.94	16	19.3
1992	.78	6.69	11.63	17⅞	22.9
1993	1.15	7.96	13.22	31¼	27.2

3,636 shares, adjusted for stock splits. Brokerage commissions are not considered.

ADC Telecommunication's stock was split three-for-two in 1986 and 1987 and two-for-one in 1993.

The December 31, 1993, closing price of ADC Telecommunications, Inc., on the Nasdaq National Market was 35⅝. The value of the original $10,000 investment on that date was $129,532.

Historical Financial Data

ADC Telecommunications has delivered a solid record of growth. From total sales of just more than $23 million in 1977, the company grew to $87 million in 1984 and $366 million in 1993. Earnings have kept pace, growing from $900,000 in 1977 to $31.6 million in 1993. Figure 31.2 sets forth important per-share data for the company during the period from 1984 to 1993. All yearly numbers relate to the company's fiscal years, which end on October 31.

In the past few years, investors have been willing to pay a higher multiple of earnings for the stock than in most earlier years. The average PE ratio remained in the 12 to 13 times earnings range from 1985 to 1990. Then the market began bidding up the price of ADC stock, with the stock selling at an average of 19.3 times per-share earnings in 1991, 22.9 times earnings in 1992 and 27.2 times earnings in 1993. This expansion of the PE ratio reflects investor optimism about earnings growth for ADC in the future. It also should be a warning sign to investors about the stock's vulnerability to any bad news that may affect the company, which could lead to a price correction.

Common Stock Quarterly Price Record

Following are the high and low prices of ADC Telecommunications, Inc., common stock during the fiscal years ending October 31, 1992, and 1993, adjusted for the stock split in 1993:

	1st Quarter	2nd Quarter	3rd Quarter	4th Quarter
1992				
High	$15.50	$14.50	$18.25	$19.00
Low	10.25	11.88	12.88	16.13
1993				
High	$24.75	$23.50	$31.25	$44.00
Low	18.13	18.63	20.13	29.25

As this chart shows, it is not necessary for a patient investor to pay top price for common shares. In both years, the stock hit its high price in the fourth quarter and its low in the first quarter. In most quarters, the highs and lows were above those of previous quarters, not unexpected in a stock that was rising so quickly. Interesting note: In every quarterly period, patient investors were able to buy the stock at a price below the high of the previous quarter.

CREATING A PORTFOLIO OF STOCKS IN THE TELECOMMUNICATIONS/ EQUIPMENT INDUSTRY

Other companies in the relatively small telecommunications/equipment industry have had a difficult time in recent years. Sales for Andrew Corporation remained stagnant until 1990, when they bounced up. Earnings growth has been constant since 1986. Sales of Cobra Electronics Corporation have declined steadily since 1989, and the company has operated at a loss since 1990. Only DSC Communications Corporation, the largest company in the group, has had a major turnaround and has bright prospects for the future. Sales, erratic until 1991, have since jumped from $461 million in that year to more than

$700 million in 1993. Earnings have gone from a loss of $108 million in 1991 to a profit of more than $70 million in 1993.

Following are four other publicly held companies in the telecommunications/equipment industry. Few companies in the group have been able to post consistent sales and earnings gains in recent years.

Company	1993 Earnings Per Share	12/31/93 Share Price	Dividend Yield	PE Ratio*
Andrew Corporation	$1.09	38½	Nil	35.3
Cobra Electronics Corporation	d.53	2⅝	Nil	NMF
DSC Communications Corporation	1.49	61½	Nil	41.3
Porta Systems Corporation	d1.08	10⅛	Nil	NMF

d = deficit
NMF not meaningful

*December 31, 1993, share price divided by 1993 earnings per share.

What the Companies Do

Andrew Corporation (ANDW–OTC) is a major worldwide supplier of electronic communications products and systems. The Commercial Products division makes microwave, cellular and satellite station antennas, towers and coaxial cable. This division accounted for 74 percent of 1993 sales. The Government Products group provides radar and navigational systems for defense and other markets, and the Network Products division designs and develops image processors, interfaces and converters for communication. Foreign operations contribute about 41 percent of total sales. Revenues totaled $430 million in 1993. (The company has about 2,900 employees and 1,100 shareholders.)

Per-Share Financial Summary

	1984	1993
Revenues	$7.24	$17.10
Earnings	.69	1.09
Dividends	Nil	Nil
Average Stock Price	11⅜	21

The stock was split two-for-one in 1993 and three-for-two in 1994.

Cobra Electronics Corporation (COBR-OTC) designs and markets consumer electronics, mostly manufactured in the Far East. The company's product lines include cordless telephones, telephone answering machines, CB radios, radar and laser detectors and radio scanners sold under the Cobra name. Other products include clock radios sold under the Lloyd's trademark and professional tape recorders sold under the Marantz trademark. Cobra's main customers are wholesalers, discount stores and mass merchants. Sales totaled $98 million in 1993. (The company has about 240 employees and 1,500 shareholders.)

Per-Share Financial Summary

	1984	1993
Revenues	$18.39	$15.86
Earnings	d2.44	d.53
Dividends	Nil	Nil
Average Stock Price	5¾	3¼

d = deficit

The company's stock was split three-for-two in 1987.

DSC Communications Corporation (DIGI–OTC), formerly Digital Switch, designs, manufactures, markets and services telecommunications systems and products for domestic and international long-distance carriers, local exchange carriers and private network customers. Sales totaled $730 million in 1993. (The company has about 4,000 employees and 3,500 shareholders.)

Per-Share Financial Summary

	1984	1993
Revenues	$ 9.05	$13.28
Earnings	1.40	1.49
Dividends	Nil	Nil
Average Stock Price	26⅛	47

Porta Systems Corporation (PSI–AMEX) designs, manufactures and markets telecommunications protection and testing equipment. The United States and Puerto Rico account for 33 percent of revenues; the United Kingdom, 31 percent; and other foreign countries, 36 percent. Major customers include British Telecom, Telefonos de Mexico, and NYNEX. Sales totaled $68 million in 1993. (The company has about 850 employees and 800 shareholders.)

Per-Share Financial Summary

	1984	1993
Revenues	$5.39	$9.84
Earnings	.19	d1.08
Dividends	Nil	Nil
Average Stock Price	10¾	11⅛

SUMMARY

The $2 billion-plus telecommunications/equipment industry enjoyed a banner year in 1993. ADC Telecommunications, Inc., Andrew Corporation and DSC Communications Corporation all have reported steady revenue increases in recent years. Profits rebounded sharply for the industry as customers resumed their long-dormant capital-spending programs in response to the generally improving economic climate. Industry analysts have estimated that industry profits would rise by about 60 percent in 1994 and continue compounding over the next few years at a 20 percent to 25 percent annual rate. Strong overseas growth prospects, particularly in markets such as China, republics of the former Soviet Union and South America will help fuel this growth.

APPENDIX

Companies with Dividend Reinvestment Plans (DRIPs)

This directory lists companies that offer dividend reinvestment plans (DRIPs). If share purchases are offered at a discount, that information is noted under the name of the company. *Dividend* indicates that the discount applies to shares purchased from reinvested dividends. *Cash* indicates that the discount applies to shares purchased from optional cash payments. *New Issue Shares* indicates that the discount applies to the purchase of shares bought directly from the company.

Options available to investors are coded as follows:

A = Participants can make optional cash payments in addition to reinvesting dividends.

B = Participants can specify a portion of shares for dividend reinvestment and receive cash dividends on the balance.

C = Participants can make optional cash payments without being required to reinvest dividends.

Company	Telephone	Options	Min./Max. Optional Cash Purchase
AAR Corporation	404-953-8300	C	$25–$5,000/qtr.
Abbott Laboratories	617-575-2900	C	$10–$5,000/qtr.

Company	Telephone	Options	Min./Max. Optional Cash Purchase
Acme-Cleveland Corporation	216-737-5742	C	$10–$5,000/qtr.
Aetna Life and Casualty Company	203-273-3945	A	$50–$5,000/mo.
AFLAC, Inc.	800-235-2667	B,C	$20–$5,000/mo.
Air Products & Chemicals, Inc.	215-481-8101	C	$25–$20,000/yr.
Albany International	518-445-2284	B,C	$10–$5,000/mo.
Allegheny Ludlum Corporation	412-394-2813	A	$25–$3,000/qtr.
Allegheny Power System, Inc.	212-752-2121	B,C	$50–$10,000/qtr.
ALLIED Group, Inc.	515-280-4211	B,C	$25–$5,000/mo.
Allied Signal, Inc.	800-255-4332	B,C	$25–$5,000/mo.
Aluminum Company of America	412-553-4708	B,C	$25–$5,000/mo.
AMAX, Inc.	800-243-4000	B,C	$100–$5,000/qtr.
Amcast Industrial Corporation	513-298-5251	A	$25–$1,000/qtr.
AMCORE Financial, Inc.	815-961-7098	B,C	$10–$3,000/qtr.
Amerada Hess Corporation	800-647-4273	A,B	$50–$5,000/qtr.
American Brands, Inc.	203-698-5440	A	$100–$10,000/qtr.
American Business Products, Inc.	404-953-8300	A	$10–$1,000/mo.
American Colloid Company	708-392-4600	B,C	$25–$5,000/qtr.
American Cyanamid Company	201-831-3586	A	$10–$1,000/mo.
American Electric Power Co., Inc.	800-237-2667	B,C	$0–$5,000/qtr.
American Express Company Dividend: 3%	212-640-5693	B,C	$50–$5,000/mo.
American Filtrona Corporation	804-346-2401	C	$25–$1,000/mo.
American General Corporation	800-446-2617	B,C	$25–$6,000/qtr.
American Greetings Corporation	216-252-7300	none	N/A

Company	Telephone	Options	Min./Max. Optional Cash Purchase
American Home Products Corporation	212-878-6139	B,C	$50–$10,000/mo.
American Recreation Centers	916-852-8005	C	$10–$500/mo.
American Telephone & Telegraph	800-348-8288	A,B	$100–$50,000/yr.
American Water Works Company, Inc. Dividend: 5% Cash: 5%	609-346-8290	B	N/A
Ameritech	800-233-1342	B,C	$50–$50,000/yr.
Amoco Corporation	800-638-5672	A	$10–$5,000/mo.
AMP, Inc.	717-780-4869	B,C	$50–$5,000/mo.
AmSouth Bancorporation	205-583-4439	B,C	$10–$5,000/qtr.
AmVestors Financial Corporation	913-232-6945	A	$25–$2,500/qtr.
Anheuser-Busch Companies	314-577-2309	A	$25–$5,000/mo.
Aon Corporation	800-446-2617	A	$20–$1,000/mo.
Apache Corporation	713-296-6504	A,B	$50–$5,000/qtr.
Aquarion Company Dividend: 5%	800-526-0801	C	$10–$5,000/mo.
ARCO Chemical	215-359-3382	A	$10–$3,000/qtr.
Arkla, Inc.	318-429-2925	A	$10–none
Armstrong World Industries, Inc.	717-396-2029	A	$50–$3,000/qtr.
Arrow Financial Corporation	518-745-1000	C	$0–$10,000/qtr.
Arvin Industries, Inc.	312-461-2549	A	$25–$1,000/mo.
Asarco, Inc.	800-524-4458	A	$25–$1,000/mo.
Ashland Coal	304-526-3750	A	$10–$20,000/yr.
Associated Banc-Corporation	800-236-2722	B	N/A
Atlanta Gas Light Company	404-584-3819	B,C	$25–$5,000/mo.
Atlantic Energy, Inc.	609-645-4507	C	$0–$200,000/yr.
Atlantic Richfield Company	212-791-6422	B,C	$10–$60,000/yr.

Company	Telephone	Options	Min./Max. Optional Cash Purchase
Atmos Energy Corporation Dividend: 3%	800-382-8667	B,C	$25–$60,000/yr.
Avery Dennison Corporation	818-304-2032	A	$25–$3,000/mo.
Avnet, Inc.	516-466-7000	A	$10–none
Avon Products, Inc.	212-456-6786	A	$10–$5,000/mo.
Baker Hughes, Inc.	713-439-8668	A	$10–$1,000/qtr.
Baldwin Technology	617-575-2900	none	N/A
Ball Corporation Dividend: 5%	317-747-6170	C	$25–$2,000/mo.
Baltimore Bancorporation Dividend: 5% Cash: 5%	800-435-7016	B,C	$100–$10,000/mo.
Baltimore Gas & Electric Company	800-258-0499	B,C	$10–$6,000/qtr.
Banc One Corporation	800-753-7107	A	$10–$5,000/qtr.
Bancorporation Hawaii, Inc. Dividend: 5%	808-537-8239	B,C	$25–$5,000/qtr.
Bancorporation of Mississippi, Inc.	601-680-2000	A	$25–$1,000/qtr.
Bangor Hydro-Electric Company	207-990-6936	B,C	$25–$25,000/yr.
Bank of Boston Corporation Dividend: 3%	617-929-5445	B,C	$25–$5,000/mo.
Bank of Granite Corporation	704-396-3141	none	N/A
Bank of New York Company, Inc.	800-524-4458	C	$25–none/mo.
BankAmerica Corporation Dividend: 1% Cash: 1%	800-642-9880	B,C	$100–$10,000/mo.
Bankers Trust New York Corporation	800-221-4096	B,C	$25–$5,000/mo.
Banta Corporation	414-287-3920	A	$10–$1,000/mo.

Company	Telephone	Options	Min./Max. Optional Cash Purchase
Bard (CR), Inc.	908-277-8221	A,B	$10–$2,500/mo.
Barnes Group, Inc.	203-583-7070	A	$10–$10,000/qtr.
Barnett Banks, Inc.	904-791-7093	A,B	$25–$10,000/mo.
Bausch & Lomb, Inc.	617-575-2900	A	$25–$5,000/mo.
Baxter International, Inc.	708-948-2886	B,C	$25–$25,000/yr.
Bay State Gas Company New Issue Shares: 3%	508-836-7313	B,C	$10–$2,000/mo.
BayBanks, Inc.	617-482-1040	C	$10–$1,000/mo.
BB&T Financial Corporation Dividend: 5%	919-399-4248	B,C	$25–$2,000/mo.
Becton, Dickinson & Company	212-791-6422	A	$25–$3,000/mo.
Bell Atlantic Corporation	800-631-2355	A,B	$100–$50,000/qtr.
BellSouth Corporation	800-631-6001	A,B	$50–$100,000/yr.
Bemis Company, Inc.	612-376-3011	C	$25–$10,000/qtr.
Beneficial Corporation	302-792-4753	C	$10–$1,000/mo.
Berkshire Gas Company	413-442-1511	B,C	$15–$3,000/qtr.
Black & Decker Corporation	212-791-6422	A	$10–$3,000/mo.
Black Hills Corporation	605-348-1700	A	$100–$3,000/qtr.
Block (H&R), Inc.	816-932-8468	A	$25–$2,000/mo.
Blount, Inc. Dividend: 5%	205-244-4000	B,C	$10–$25,000/yr.
BMJ Financial Corporation Dividend and Cash: 0% to 10%	609-291-2841	B,C	$100–varies/mo.
Boatman's Bancshares, Inc.	314-466-7720	C	$100–$10,000/qtr.
Bob Evans Farms	614-491-2225	A	$10–none
Boise Cascade Corporation	208-384-7056	A	$10–none
Borden, Inc.	800-524-4458	C	$10–$10,000/qtr.
Boston Bancorporation	800-524-4458	A	$100–$5,000/qtr.

Company	Telephone	Options	Min./Max. Optional Cash Purchase
Boston Edison Company	617-424-2658	B,C	$0–$5,000/qtr.
Bowater, Inc.	203-656-7206	B,C	$100–$5,000/mo.
Braintree Savings Bank	617-843-9100	B,C	$100–$5,000/qtr.
Briggs & Stratton Corporation	414-259-5480	A	$25–$5,000/qtr.
Briston-Myers Squibb Company	212-546-3309	A	$100–$5,000/mo.
British Airways PLC	212-648-3212	A	$10–$60,000/yr.
British Petroleum Company	800-428-4237	A	$20–$15,000/qtr.
Brooklyn Union Gas Company	718-403-3334	B,C	$10–$5,000/mo.
Brown Group, Inc.	314-854-4122	C	$25–$1,000/mo.
Brown-Forman Corporation	502-774-7688	C	$50–$3,000/qtr.
Browning-Ferris Industries, Inc.	713-870-7893	B,C	$25–$60,000/yr.
Brunswick Corporation	708-470-4293	A	$10–$1,000/mo.
Brush Wellman, Inc.	216-486-4200	A	$10–$5,000/qtr.
BSB Bancorporation, Inc.	607-779-2552	C	$10–$5,000/mo.
Cabot Corporation	617-575-2900	A,B	$10–$5,000/mo.
Cadmus Communications Corporation	804-287-5680	A	$25–$3,000/qtr.
California Financial Holding Company	800-524-4458	C	$100–$10,000/qtr.
California Water Service Company	408-451-8200	B	N/A
Campbell Soup Company	609-342-5919	A,B	$25–$1,000/mo.
Capital Holding Corporation	512-560-2391	B,C	$10–$5,000/mo.
Carlisle Companies, Inc.	315-474-2500	C	$10–$3,000/qtr.
Carolina Freight Corporation	704-435-6811	A	$0–none

Company	Telephone	Options	Min./Max. Optional Cash Purchase
Carolina Power & Light Company	800-662-7232	A,B	$20–$2,000/mo.
Carpenter Technology Corporation	212-791-6422	A	$10-3,000/qtr.
Cascade Natural Gas Corporation	206-624-3900	C	$25–$3,000/qtr.
Caterpillar, Inc.	309-675-4621	A	$10–$5,000/mo.
CB&T Financial Corporation	304-367-2375	A	$25–none
CBI Industries, Inc.	708-572-7366	C	$25–$3,000/qtr.
CBS, Inc.	212-975-4321	A	$25–$1,000/mo.
CCB Financial Corporation	800-829-8432	A	$10–$1,500/mo.
Centel Corporation	800-446-2617	A,B	$25–$5,000/qtr.
Centerbank	203-573-6630	A	$25–$1,000/qtr.
Centerior Energy Corporation	800-433-7794	B,C	$10–$40,000/qtr.
Central & South West Corporation	800-527-5797	B,C	$10–$5,000/qtr.
Central Bancshares of the South	205-933-3960	C	$25–$1,000/mo.
Central Fidelity Banks, Inc.	804-697-6942	B,C	$25–$10,000/mo.
Central Holding Company	800-257-1770	B,C	$25–$2,000/mo.
Central Hudson Gas & Electric	800-428-9578	B,C	$25–$10,000/qtr.
Central Jersey Bancorporation	908-294-4121	A,B	$10–$1,500/qtr.
Central Louisiana Electric Company	800-253-2652	B,C	$25–$5,000/mo.
Central Maine Power Company	800-695-4267	B,C	$10–$40,000/yr.
Central Vermont Public Service	802-747-5406	C	$50–$2,000/mo.
Centura Banks, Inc.	800-633-4236	C	$25–$2,500/mo.
Century Telephone Enterprises	800-833-1188	A,B	$25–$5,000/qtr.
Champion International Corporation	203-358-7000	A	$10–$5,000/mo.

Company	Telephone	Options	Min./Max. Optional Cash Purchase
Charter One Financial, Inc.	800-442-2001	A	$10–$5,000/qtr.
Chase Manhattan Corporation Dividend: 5% Cash: 3%	800-526-0801	B,C	$100–varies/mo.
Chemed Corporation	513-762-6900	C	$10–$1,000/mo.
Chemical Banking Corporation	800-647-4273	none	N/A
Chemical Financial Corporation	216-737-5745	A	$10–$3,000/qtr.
Chemical Waste Management	312-461-2543	C	$25–$2,000/mo.
Chesapeake Corporation	804-697-1166	A	$10–$5,000/qtr.
Chesapeake Utilities Corporation	302-734-6716	A	$10–$5,000/qtr.
Chevron Corporation	800-547-9794	C	$25–$1,000/mo.
Chrysler Corporation	313-956-3007	A,B	$25–$24,000/yr.
Chubb Corporation	908-580-3579	A	$10–$3,000/qtr.
CIGNA Corporation	215-761-3516	B,C	$10–$5,000/mo.
CILCORP, Inc.	800-622-5514	B,C	$25–$5,000/qtr.
Cincinnati Bell	800-345-6301	C	$0–$5,000/mo.
Cincinnati Financial Corporation	513-870-2000	C	$25–$1,000/mo.
Cincinnati Gas & Electric Company	513-287-1940	B,C	$25–$40,000/yr.
Cincinnati Milacron, Inc.	513-841-8782	C	$25–$1,000/mo.
CIPSCO, Inc.	312-427-2953	A,B	$10–$50,000/qtr.
Citizens Bancorporation	301-206-6243	A	$25–$3,750/qtr.
Citizens Banking Corporation	313-257-2593	A	$25–$5,000/qtr.
CLARCOR, Inc.	212-791-6422	C	$25–$3,000/mo.
Cleveland-Cliffs, Inc.	216-694-5459	A	$10–$2,000/mo.
Clorox Company	510-271-2927	B,C	$10–$60,000/yr.
CMS Energy Corporation	517-788-1867	C	$25–$60,000/yr.
CNB Bancshares, Inc.	812-464-3400	A,B	$25–$5,000/qtr.
Coca-Cola Company	404-676-2777	B,C	$10–$60,000/yr.

Company	Telephone	Options	Min./Max. Optional Cash Purchase
Coca-Cola Enterprises	404-676-7052	B,C	$10–$60,000/yr.
Colgate-Palmolive Company	212-310-2575	B,C	$20–$60,000/yr.
Colonial BancGroup (Ala.)	205-240-5182	A,B	$10–$3,000/qtr.
Colonial Gas Company Dividend: 5%	508-458-3171	B,C	$10–$5,000/qtr.
Colorado National Bankshares Dividend: 5%	303-629-1968	B,C	$50–$1,000/mo.
Comerica	800-551-6161	A	$10–$3,000/qtr.
Commercial Intertech Corporation	216-746-8011	A	$30–$5,000/qtr.
Commonwealth Edison Company	800-950-2377	B,C	$25–$3,000/qtr.
Commonwealth Energy System	800-447-1183	C	$10–$5,000/qtr.
Communications Satellite Corporation	202-863-6200	A	$25–$1,000/qtr.
Community Bank System, Inc.	315-445-2282	C	$25–$2,000/qtr.
ConAgra, Inc.	402-595-4000	A	$25–$5,000/qtr.
Connecticut Energy Corporation	203-382-8156	B,C	$50–$6,000/qtr.
Connecticut Natural Gas Corporation	203-727-3203	A,B	$25–$5,000/qtr.
Connecticut Water Service, Inc. Dividend: 5%	203-669-8636	A,B	$100–$3,000/qtr.
Consolidated Edison Company of N.Y.	800-221-6664	A,B	$20–$3,000/qtr.
Consolidated Natural Gas Company	412-227-1183	B,C	$25–$5,000/qtr.
Consolidated Rail Corporation	215-209-5099	B,C	$0–$4,000/yr.
Consumers Water Company	800-292-2925	A,B	$10–$50,000/yr.
Cooper Industries	212-791-6422	B,C	$25–$24,000/yr.

Company	Telephone	Options	Min./Max. Optional Cash Purchase
CoreStates Financial Corporation Dividend: 3%	215-973-2836	B,C	$50–$5,000/mo.
Coming, Inc.	312-461-4834	A	$10–$5,000/mo.
CPC International, Inc.	201-894-2460	A,B	$10–$12,000/yr.
CPI Corporation	314-231-1575	A	$10–$10,000/qtr.
Crane Company	203-363-7239	B,C	$10–$5,000/mo.
Crestar Financial Corporation Dividend: 5%	804-782-5769	A	$10–$10,000/qtr.
Crompton & Knowles Corporation	203-353-5400	A	$30–$3,000/qtr.
CRSS, Inc.	713-552-2000	A,B	$10–$10,000/qtr.
CSX Corporation	800-521-5571	C	$25–$1,500/mo.
Cummins Engine Company, Inc.	800-446-2617	A	$10–$6,000/qtr.
Curtice-Burns Foods, Inc.	716-383-1850	A	$25–$5,000/mo.
Cyprus Minerals Company	303-643-5046	A	$50–$3,000/mo.
Dana Corporation	419-535-4633	A	$25–$2,000/mo.
Dauphin Deposit Corporation	717-255-2369	A	$50–$1,000/mo.
Dayton Hudson Corporation	800-446-2617	B,C	$10–$1,000/mo.
Dean Foods Company	708-678-1680	A	$25–$3,000/qtr.
Deere & Company	309-765-4539	A	$50–$10,000/mo.
Delmarva Power & Light Company	800-365-6495	B,C	$0–$100,000/yr.
Delta Air Lines, Inc.	404-715-2391	A	$25–$10,000/yr.
Delta Natural Gas Company	606-744-6171	A,B	$25–$3,000/qtr.
Detroit Edison Company	313-237-8757	A	$20–$5,000/qtr.
Dexter Corporation	203-627-9051	C	$25–$3,000/qtr.
Dial Corporation	800-453-2235	A	$10–$3,000/mo.
Dominion Bankshares Corporation	703-563-6226	A	$50–$5,000/qtr.
Dominion Resources, Inc.	800-552-4034	B,C	$0–$50,000/qtr.

Company	Telephone	Options	Min./Max. Optional Cash Purchase
Donaldson Company, Inc.	800-551-6161	A	$10–$1,000/mo.
Donnelley (R. R.) & Sons Company	312-326-7189	B,C	$10–$60,000/yr.
Dow Chemical Company	517-636-1463	A	$10–$25,000/qtr.
Dow Jones & Company	212-416-2600	A,B	$25–$1,000/mo.
DPL, Inc.	800-322-9244	C	$25–$1,000/qtr.
DQE Company	800-247-0400	B,C	$10–$15,000/qtr.
Dresser Industries, Inc.	214-740-6888	A	$25–$1,000/mo.
Dreyfus Corporation	800-524-4458	none	N/A
Du Pont de Nemours (E. I.)	800-526-0801	A	$20–$5,000/qtr.
Duke Power Company	800-488-3853	B,C	$25–$6,000/mo.
Duriron Company	513-476-6183	A	$25–$3,000/qtr.
Eastern Company	203-729-6183	B,C	$25–$3,000/qtr.
Eastern Enterprises	800-524-4458	C	$10–$3,000/qtr.
Eastern Utilities Associates Dividend: 5%	617-357-9590	B,C	$0–$5,000/qtr.
Eastman Kodak Company	800-253-6057	B,C	$0–$60,000/yr.
Eaton Corporation	216-737-5745	B,C	$10–$60,000/yr.
Ecolab, Inc.	212-791-6422	B,C	$10–$60,000/yr.
EG&G, Inc.	617-431-4143	C	$10–$1,000/mo.
Elco Industries, Inc.	815-397-5151	C	$25–$1,000/mo.
EMC Insurance Group, Inc.	515-280-2836	B,C	$100–$9,000/qtr.
Emerson Electric Company	314-553-2197	A	$25–$2,500/qtr.
Empire District Electric Company	417-623-4700	C	$50–$3,000/qtr.
Energen Corporation	800-654-3206	B,C	$25–$5,000/qtr.
EnergyNorth, Inc. Dividend: 5%	603-625-4000	A,B	$50–$2,500/qtr.
Engelhard Corporation	908-205-6065	A	$10–$3,000/mo.
Engraph, Inc.	404-329-0332	A	$25–$5,000/qtr.
Enron Corporation	713-853-5455	A	$10–$2,000/mo.

Company	Telephone	Options	Min./Max. Optional Cash Purchase
ENSERCH Corporation	214-651-8700	A	$10–$15,000/qtr.
Equifax, Inc.	404-888-5003	A	$10–$5,000/qtr.
Equitable Resources, Inc.	412-553-5892	A	$10–$3,000/qtr.
Essex County Gas Company Dividend: 5%	508-388-4000	B,C	$0–$5,000/qtr.
E-Systems, Inc.	214-661-1000	B,C	$25–$5,000/qtr.
Ethyl Corporation	312-461-6834	C	$25–$1,000/mo.
E'Town Corporation Dividend: 5% Cash: 5%	908-654-1234	C	$100–$2,000/mo.
Excel Bancorportion, Inc.—Quincy	617-575-2900	A	$50–$1,000/qtr.
Exxon Corporation	214-444-1157	A,B	$50–$8,000/mo.
F&M National Corporation (Virginia) Dividend: 5%	703-665-4387	B,C	$25–$5,000/qtr.
Fay's, Inc.	315-451-8000	B,C	$25–$5,000/mo.
Federal National Mortgage Assn.	800-647-4273	A	$10–$1,000/mo.
Federal Paper Board Company, Inc.	201-391-1776	A	$10–$3,000/qtr.
Federal Signal Corporation	708-954-2000	A,B	$25–$3,000/qtr.
Federal-Mogul Corporation	800-257-1770	B,C	$10–$25,000/yr.
Ferro Corporation	216-575-2658	B,C	$10–$3,000/mo.
Fifth Third Bancorporation	513-762-8613	C	$25–$1,000/mo.
Figgie International, Inc.	800-345-1505	A	$10–$5,000/qtr.
Fina, Inc.	212-791-6422	A	$10–$1,000/mo.
First Alabama Bancshares, Inc.	205-832-8450	A	$20–$3,000/mo.
First Bancorporation of Ohio	216-384-7347	A	$30–$1,000/qtr.

Company	Telephone	Options	Min./Max. Optional Cash Purchase
First Bank System, Inc. Dividend: 3%	612-973-0334	B,C	$25–$5,000/qtr.
First Central Financial Corporation	718-921-8283	A	$100–$750/mo.
First Chicago Corporation Dividend: 3%	312-732-4812	B,C	$25–$5,000/mo.
First Colonial Bankshares Corp.	312-419-9891	C	$25–$3,000/mo.
First Commerce Corporation Dividend: 5%	504-582-2917	A,B	$50–$3,000/qtr.
First Commercial Corporation Dividend: 5%	501-371-6666	B,C	$25–$2,000/qtr.
First Eastern Corporation Dividend: 5%	717-826-4682	B,C	$35–$5,000/qtr.
First Empire State Corporation	716-842-5445	A	$10–$1,000/qtr.
First Fidelity Bancorporation Dividend: 5%	800-524-4450	A	$50–$60,000/yr.
First Financial Holdings, Inc.	803-724-0800	A	$25–$2,000/mo.
First Harrisburg Bancorporation	717-232-6660	A,B	$25–$250/qtr.
First Interstate Bancorporation Dividend: 3% Cash: 3%	800-522-6645	B,C	$100–varies/mo.
First Michigan Bank Corporation Dividend: 5%	616-396-9325	A,B	$100–$500/qtr.
First Midwest Bancorporation, Inc. Dividend: 3%	312-427-2953	B,C	$100–$5,000/qtr.
First Mississippi Corporation	601-948-7550	A	$25–$3,000/mo.

Company	Telephone	Options	Min./Max. Optional Cash Purchase
First National Bancorporation (GA)	706-503-2114	B	N/A
First National Bank Corporation (MI)	313-225-2996	B,C	$50–$5,000/qtr.
First Northern Savings Bank (WI)	414-437-7101	A,B	$25–$3,000/qtr.
First of America Bank Corporation Dividend: 5%	800-782-4040	C	$25–$25,000/qtr.
First Security Corporation (UT)	801-350-5292	B,C	$50–$5,000/mo.
First Tennessee National Corporation	901-523-5630	B,C	$25–$5,000/qtr.
First Union Corporation Dividend: 2% Cash: 2%	704-374-6782	A	$25–$15,000/qtr.
First Virginia Banks, Inc.	703-241-3669	A	$25–$5,000/qtr.
First Western Bancorporation, Inc.	412-652-8550	A,B	$25–$5,000/qtr.
Firstar Corporation	414-765-4985	A,B	$50–$10,000/mo.
Firstbank of Illinois Company	217-753-7371	B,C	$25–$3,000/qtr.
Fleet/Norstar Financial Group, Inc. Dividend: 5% Cash: 3%	401-278-5149	A	$10–$2,500/mo.
Fleming Companies, Inc. Dividend: 5%	405-841-8127	A,B	$25–$5,000/qtr.
Florida Progress Corporation	800-352-1121	B,C	$10–$100,000/yr.
Florida Public Utilities	407-838-1729	B,C	$25–$2,000/qtr.
Flowers Industries, Inc.	912-226-9110	A,B	$25–$3,000/mo.
Food Lion, Inc.	800-633-4236	A	$10–$2,500/mo.

Company	Telephone	Options	Min./Max. Optional Cash Purchase
Foote, Cone & Belding	800-446-2617	C	$25–$1,000/mo.
Ford Motor Company	212-613-7147	A	$10–$1,000/mo.
Foster Wheeler Corporation	800-526-0801	A	$10–none/mo.
Fourth Financial Corporation	316-261-4155	B	N/A
FPL Group, Inc.	407-694-4704	B,C	$100–$100,000/yr.
Franklin Resources	415-312-3033	C	$50–$10,000/qtr.
Freeport-McMoran, Inc.	504-582-4490	A	$10–$1,000/mo.
Fuller (H. B.) Company	612-647-3666	A	$10–$6,000/qtr.
Fulton Financial Corporation	800-626-0255	A,B	$25–$1,000/mo.
Gannett Company, Inc.	703-284-6962	B,C	$10–$5,000/mo.
GATX Corporation	312-621-6200	A	$25–$3,000/mo.
GenCorp	216-869-4453	A	$10–$3,000/qtr.
General Electric Company	203-326-4040	B,C	$10–$10,000/mo.
General Mills, Inc.	800-245-5703	A,B	$10–$3,000/qtr.
General Motors Corporation Dividend: 3% Cash: 3%	212-791-3909	B,C	$25–$2,500/mo.
General Public Utilities Corporation	201-263-6600	A	$50–$6,000/qtr.
General Reinsurance Corporation	203-328-5000	B,C	$10–$10,000/qtr.
General Signal Corporation	203-329-4321	C	$25–$10,000/qtr.
Genuine Parts Company	404-953-1700	A	$10–$3,000/qtr.
Georgia Pacific Corporation	404-521-5210	B,C	$25–$5,000/mo.
Gerber Products Company	616-928-2000	B,C	$25–$3,000/qtr.
Giant Food, Inc.	800-934-5449	A	$10–$1,000/qtr.

Company	Telephone	Options	Min./Max. Optional Cash Purchase
Glaxo Holdings PLC ADR	800-524-4458	B,C	$50–$5,000/mo.
Goodrich (B. F.) Company	216-374-2613	C	$25–$1,000/mo.
Goodyear Tire & Rubber Company	216-796-3457	B,C	$10–$15,000/qtr.
Gorman-Rupp Company	419-755-1322	C	$20–$1,000/mo.
Goulds Pumps, Inc.	800-937-5449	A	$10–$5,000/mo.
Grace (W. R.) & Company	800-647-4273	A,B	$1–$99,999/qtr.
Graco, Inc.	612-623-6701	A	$25–$1,000/qtr.
Great Falls Gas Company	406-791-7500	none	N/A
Great Western Financial Corporation Dividend: 3%	818-775-3741	B,C	$100–$10,000/qtr.
Green Mountain Power Corporation Dividend: 5%	802-660-5785	B,C	$50–$6,000/qtr.
Grenada Sunburst System Corporation	601-960-2602	B	N/A
Grumman Corporation	516-575-5287	C	$25–$10,000/qtr.
GTE Corporation	800-225-5160	B,C	$25–$5,000/qtr.
Guardsman Products, Inc.	616-957-2600	A	$200–$3,000/qtr.
Gulf States Utilities Company	800-231-9266	B,C	$25–$9,000/qtr.
Handleman Company	800-257-1770	A	$10–$3,000/mo.
Handy & Harman	212-661-2400	A	$10–$60,000/yr.
Hanna (M. A.) Company	800-688-4259	B,C	$25–$3,000/mo.
Hannaford Brothers Company	207-883-2911	B,C	$25–$2,000/mo.
Harcourt General, Inc.	617-232-8200	C	$25–$2,500/qtr.
Harland (John H.) Company	800-568-3476	A	$25–$3,000/qtr.
Harleysville Group, Inc.	215-256-5392	A,B	$10–$3,000/qtr.

Company	Telephone	Options	Min./Max. Optional Cash Purchase
Harris Corporation	800-542-7792	A	$10–$5,000/qtr.
Harsco Corporation	717-763-7064	A	$10–none/mo.
Hartford Steam Boiler	617-575-2900	A	$10–$1,000/mo.
Hartmarx Corporation	312-372-6300	C	$25–$1,000/mo.
Haverfield Corporation	216-226-0510	C	$20–$1,000/mo.
Hawaiian Electric Industries, Inc.	808-532-5841	C	$25–$25,000/qtr.
Heinz (H. J.) Company	800-253-3399	C	$25–$1,000/qtr.
Hercules, Inc.	800-647-4273	A	$10–$2,000/mo.
Hershey Foods Corporation	717-534-7527	A,B	$50–$20,000/yr.
Hexcel Corporation Dividend: 5%	510-828-4200	B	N/A
Hibernia Corporation Dividend: 5%	504-586-5552	B,C	$100–$3,000/mo.
Home Depot, Inc. (The)	800-633-4236	A	$10–$4,000/mo.
Homestake Mining Company	800-442-2001	A	$25–$5,000/qtr.
Honeywell, Inc.	612-870-6887	A	$25–$3,000/mo.
Hormel (George A.)	800-551-6161	A	$25–$1,000/mo.
Houghton Mifflin Company	617-725-5128	A	$25–$3,000/qtr.
Household International, Inc. Dividend: 2.5%	312-461-5754	C	$100–$5,000/qtr.
Houston Industries, Inc.	800-231-6406	B,C	$50–$6,000/qtr.
Hubbell, Inc.	212-613-7147	B,C	$100–$1,000/qtr.
HUBCO, Inc.	201-348-2326	A	$10–$2,000/qtr.
Huntington Bancshares, Inc. Dividend: 5%	614-463-3878	A	$50–$5,000/qtr.
IBP, Inc.	402-241-2559	A	$10–$1,000/mo.
Idaho Power Company	800-635-5406	B,C	$10–$15,000/qtr.
IES Industries	800-247-9785	C	$25–$5,000/mo.
Illinois Power Company	800-800-8220	C	$25–$5,000/qtr.
IMCERA Group, Inc.	800-446-2617	A	$10–$1,000/mo.

Company	Telephone	Options	Min./Max. Optional Cash Purchase
Imperial Bancorporation	800-522-6645	none	N/A
Inco, Ltd. Dividend: 5%	212-612-5846	B,C	$30–$10,000/qtr.
Independence Bancorporation (PA) Dividend: 5%	215-453-3005	C	$50–$3,000/qtr.
Independence Bancorporation (NJ)	201-825-2676	B,C	$500–$2,000/qtr.
Independent Bank Corporation (MA) Dividend: 5%	617-982-6457	B,C	$25–varies/yr.
Indiana Energy, Inc.	317-321-0440	B,C	$25–$3,000/qtr.
Ingersoll-Rand Company	800-524-4458	C	$10–$3,000/qtr.
Inland Steel Industries, Inc.	312-461-4075	C	$25–$10,000/qtr.
Insteel Industries, Inc.	704-383-5183	A	$10–none/mo.
Integra Financial Corporation	412-644-8400	C	$100–$5,000/qtr.
Intel Corporation	800-442-2001	A	$25–$15,000/qtr.
Intermark, Inc.	619-459-1000	A	$10–$1,000/mo.
International Business Machines	212-791-4208	A,B	$10–$25,000/qtr.
International Multifoods Corporation	800-468-9716	B,C	$10–$60,000/yr.
International Paper Company	914-397-1500	B,C	$25–$20,000/yr.
Interpublic Group of Companies, Inc.	212-791-6422	A	$10–$3,000/qtr.
Interstate Power Company	319-582-5421	B,C	$25–$3,000/qtr.
Iowa-Illinois Gas & Electric Company	800-373-4443	B,C	$25–$5,000/qtr.
IPALCO Enterprises, Inc.	317-261-8394	B,C	$25–$3,000/mo.
ITT Corporation	201-601-4202	A	$50–$60,000/yr.
IWC Resources Corporation	317-263-6358	B,C	$25–$5,000/qtr.

Company	Telephone	Options	Min./Max. Optional Cash Purchase
Jefferson Bankshares, Inc. Dividend: 5%	804-972-1115	A	$30–$1,500/qtr.
Jefferson-Pilot Corporation	800-829-8432	A	$20–$1,000/mo.
Johnson & Johnson	212-791-6422	B,C	$25–$50,000/yr.
Johnson Controls, Inc.	414-228-2363	A,B	$50–$15,000/qtr.
Joslyn Corporation	312-454-2900	C	$25–$2,000/mo.
Jostens, Inc.	800-551-6161	A	$25–$1,000/mo.
Justin Industries, Inc.	817-336-5125	C	$25–$1,000/mo.
Kaman Corporation	800-647-4273	A	$25–$5,000/qtr.
Kellogg Company	800-323-6138	A,B	$25–$25,000/yr.
Kemper Corporation Dividend: 5%	708-540-2000	A	$25–$5,000/qtr.
Kennametal, Inc. Dividend: 5%	412-539-5204	C	$25–$3,000/qtr.
Kerr-McGee Corporation	800-624-9541	A	$10–$1,000/mo.
Key Centurion Bancshares, Inc.	800-633-4236	B,C	$25–$2,000/qtr.
KeyCorp	518-486-8254	C	$10–$10,000/mo.
Keystone Financial, Inc.	718-921-8200	C	$100–$5,000/qtr.
Keystone Heritage Group, Inc.	717-274-6845	A	$10–$2,000/qtr.
Keystone International, Inc.	713-937-5301	A,B	$50–$5,000/qtr.
Kimberly-Clark Corporation	800-442-2001	A,B	$25–$3,000/qtr.
K-Mart Corporation	313-643-1040	A	$25–$100,000/yr.
KN Energy, Inc.	303-989-1740	B,C	$5–$6,000/qtr.
Knight-Ridder, Inc.	305-376-3938	A	$25–$1,000/mo.
Kollmorgen Corporation	617-575-2404	C	$25–$1,000/mo.
Kuhlman Corporation	606-224-4300	C	$10–$3,000/qtr.
KU Energy	606-288-1188	A,B	$20–$10,000/qtr.
Kysor Industrial Corporation	616-779-2200	A	$10–$12,000/yr.

Company	Telephone	Options	Min./Max. Optional Cash Purchase
La-Z-Boy Chair Company	313-241-4414	C	$25–$1,000/mo.
Laclede Gas Company	800-456-9852	none	N/A
Lafarge Corporation Dividend: 5%	800-633-4236	none	N/A
Lakeland First Financial Group	201-584-6666	A	$100–$2,000/qtr.
Lance, Inc.	704-554-1421	A	$10–$1,000/mo.
LG&E Energy Corporation	502-627-2000	B,C	$25–$40,000/yr.
Liberty National Bancorporation (KY)	502-566-1771	A,B	$25–$5,000/qtr.
Lilly (Eli) & Company	800-833-8699	C	$25–$25,000/yr.
Limited (The), Inc.	800-446-2617	A	$30–$6,000/qtr.
Lincoln National Corporation	219-455-2056	B,C	$25–$1,700/mo.
Lincoln Telecommunications Company	402-476-5277	C	$100–$3,000/qtr.
Liz Claiborne, Inc.	212-791-6422	A	$25–$1,000/mo.
Loctite Corporation	617-575-2900	A,B	$25–$1,000/mo.
Louisiana-Pacific Corporation	503-221-0800	A	$25–$12,000/yr.
Lowe's Companies, Inc.	919-651-4631	A	$10–$1,000/mo.
Luby's Cafeterias, Inc.	512-654-9000	B	$20–$5,000/qtr.
Lukens, Inc.	215-383-2601	A	$50–$6,000/mo.
Lyondell Petrochemical Company	800-524-4458	A	$25–$10,000/qtr.
MacDermid, Inc.	203-575-5813	A,B	$50–none/qtr.
Madison Gas & Electric Company	800-356-6423	A,B	$10–$3,000/qtr.
Magna Group, Inc.	618-233-2120	C	$25–$5,000/mo.
MAPCO, Inc.	212-701-7607	A	$10–$3,000/qtr.
Marion Merrell Dow, Inc.	212-791-6422	A	$0–$3,000/qtr.
Mark Twain Bancshares, Inc.	314-889-0708	B,C	$10–$2,000/mo.

Company	Telephone	Options	Min./Max. Optional Cash Purchase
Marsh & McLennan Companies, Inc.	800-457-8968	A	$10–$3,000/qtr.
Marsh Supermarkets, Inc.	317-594-2647	B,C	$100–$5,000/mo.
Martin Marietta Corporation	212-791-6422	B,C	$50–$100,000/yr.
MASSBANK Corporation	617-942-8120	B,C	$50–$1,500/qtr.
May Department Stores Company	800-524-4458	A	$25–none/mo.
Maytag Company	515-791-8344	C	$25–$5,000/mo.
McCormick & Company, Inc.	800-424-5855	A,B	$100–$3,000/qtr.
McDermott International, Inc.	800-446-2617	B,C	$25–$15,000/qtr.
McDonald's Corporation	800-621-7825	A	$50–$75,000/yr.
McGraw-Hill, Inc.	212-512-4150	A	$10–$1,000/qtr.
McKesson Corporation	415-983-9470	B,C	$10–$60,000/yr.
MCN Corporation	800-257-1770	B,C	$25–$50,000/yr.
MDU Resources Group, Inc.	701-222-7621	B,C	$50–$5,000/qtr.
Mead Corporation	513-495-3710	C	$25–$2,000/mo.
Media General, Inc. Dividend: 5%	804-649-6619	B,C	$25–$5,000/mo.
Medusa Corporation	216-371-4000	B,C	$10–$5,000/qtr.
Mellon Bank Corporation Dividend: 3% Cash: 3%	412-236-8000	C	$100–varies/mo.
Mercantile Bancorporation, Inc.	314-241-4002	A	$10–$3,000/mo.
Mercantile Bankshares Corporation Dividend: 5%	401-237-5211	A	$25–$5,000/qtr.
Merck & Company, Inc.	908-594-6627	C	$25–$50,000/yr.
Mercury Finance Company	708-564-3720	none	N/A

Company	Telephone	Options	Min./Max. Optional Cash Purchase
Meridian Bancorporation, Inc. Dividend: 5%	215-655-2438	A,B	$10–$4,000/qtr.
Merrill Lynch & Company, Inc.	800-637-3766	A	$0–none; anytime
Merry Land & Investment Company Dividend: 5%	706-722-6756	B	N/A
Metropolitan Financial Corporation	612-928-5000	A,B	$50–$2,500/qtr.
Michigan National Corporation	800-426-5754	C	$25–$5,000/mo.
Middlesex Water Company	908-634-1500	B,C	$25–$25,000/qtr.
Midwest Resources, Inc.	800-247-5211	A	$100–$5,000/mo.
Millipore Corporation	617-275-9200	C	$25–$3,000/qtr.
Minnesota Mining & Manufacturing	800-468-9716	A	$10–$10,000/qtr.
Minnesota Power & Light Company	800-535-3056	B,C	$10–$10,000/qtr.
Mobil Corporation	703-846-3901	A,B	$10–$5,000/mo.
Mobile Gas Service Corporation	205-476-2720	B	N/A
Modine Manufacturing Company	414-636-1361	A	$10–$5,000/mo.
Monsanto Company	314-694-5353	A	$10–$3,000/qtr.
Montana Power Company	800-245-6767	B,C	$10–$15,000/qtr.
Morgan (J. P.) & Company Dividend: 3%	212-791-6422	B,C	$50–$5,000/mo.
Morrison Knudsen Corporation	208-386-5000	A	$25–$1,000/qtr.
Motorola, Inc.	312-461-2339	A,B	$25–$5,000/qtr.
Nalco Chemical Company	708-305-1000	B,C	$50–$15,000/qtr.

Company	Telephone	Options	Min./Max. Optional Cash Purchase
Nash Finch Company	612-832-0534	A,B	$10–$1,000/mo.
Nashua Corporation	603-880-2323	A	$100–$5,000/qtr.
National City Corporation Dividend: 3% Cash: 3%	216-575-2532	B,C	$20–varies/mo.
National Commerce Bancorp (TN)	404-588-7822	A,B	$100–$10,000/qtr.
National Community Banks (NJ) Dividend: 5% Cash: 5%	201-357-7164	C	$40–$8,000/mo.
National Data Corporation	800-633-4236	A	$25–$1,000/qtr.
National Fuel Gas Company	212-541-7533	C	$25–$5,000/mo.
National Medical Enterprises, Inc.	310-998-8434	A	$10–$1,000/mo.
National Service Industries, Inc.	919-770-6000	A	$10–$4,000/mo.
National-Standard Company	616-683-8100	C	$10–$3,000/mo.
NationsBank Corporation Dividend: 5%	704-386-7804	A	$20–$3,000/qtr.
NBD Bancorporation, Inc.	313-225-3578	A	$10–$10,000/qtr.
NBSC Corporation	803-778-8213	A	$25–$3,000/qtr.
Neiman-Marcus Group	617-575-2900	C	$25–$2,500/qtr.
Nevada Power Company	800-344-9239	B,C	$25–$5,000/qtr.
New England Electric System	508-366-9011	B,C	$25–$5,000/mo.
New Jersey Resources Corporation	800-438-1230	C	$25–$30,000/yr.
New York State Electric & Gas Corp.	800-225-5643	C	$10–$5,000/qtr.
New York Times Company	212-791-6422	A	$10–$3,000/qtr.
Newell	800-446-2617	B,C	$10–$30,000/yr.

Company	Telephone	Options	Min./Max. Optional Cash Purchase
Niagara Mohawk Power Corporation	315-428-6750	B,C	$25–$50,000/yr.
NICOR, Inc.	708-305-9500	B,C	$25–$5,000/mo.
NIPSCO Industries, Inc.	800-348-6466	A	$25–$5,000/qtr.
Nordson Corporation	216-892-1580	A	$10–$4,000/qtr.
Norfolk Southern Corporation	804-629-2600	A	$10–$3,000/qtr.
North Carolina Natural Gas Corp. Dividend: 5%	919-483-0315	C	$25–$3,000/qtr.
North Fork Bancorporation, Inc.	212-791-6422	B,C	$200–varies/mo.
Northeast Utilities	800-999-7269	B,C	$100–$25,000/mo.
Northern States Power Company	612-330-5560	B,C	$10–$10,000/qtr.
Northrop Corporation	212-613-7147	A	$100–$1,000/mo.
Northwest Illinois Bancorporation	800-288-9541	A	$100–$10,000/qtr.
Northwest Natural Gas Company	503-220-2591	B,C	$25–$5,000/qtr.
Northwestern Public Service Company	800-245-6977	B,C	$10–$2,000/mo.
Norwest Corporation	612-667-9799	B,C	$25–$30,000/qtr.
Nucor Corporation	704-374-2697	A	$10–$1,000/mo.
NUI Corporation Dividend: 5%	908-781-0500	B,C	$25–$3,000/qtr.
NYNEX Corporation	212-370-7500	B,C	$0–$5,000/qtr.
Occidental Petroleum Corporation	800-622-9231	A,B	$50–$1,000/mo.
Ohio Casualty Corporation	513-867-3904	A,B	$10–$5,000/mo.
Ohio Edison Company	800-736-3403	B,C	$10–$40,000/yr.
Oklahoma Gas & Electric Company	800-395-2662	A,B	$25–$1,000/qtr.
Old Kent Financial Corporation	616-771-5482	A	$100–$1,000/qtr.

Company	Telephone	Options	Min./Max. Optional Cash Purchase
Old National Bancorporation (IN) Dividend: 3% Cash: 2.5%	812-464-1434	B,C	$100–$3,500/qtr.
Old Republic International Corp.	212-791-6422	B,C	$100–$5,000/qtr.
Olin Corporation	212-613-7147	A	$50–$5,000/mo.
Omnicare, Inc.	513-762-6967	A	$10–$1,000/mo.
One Valley Bancorp of West Virgina	304-348-7023	A	$25–$3,000/qtr.
Oneida, Ltd. Dividend: 5%	312-461-7763	B	N/A
ONEOK, Inc.	918-588-7159	A,B	$25–$5,000/qtr.
Orange and Rockland Utilities, Inc.	212-613-7147	B,C	$25–$5,000/qtr.
Otter Tail Power Company	218-739-8481	A	$10–$2,000/mo.
Outboard Marine Corporation	617-575-2900	A	$10–$3,000/qtr.
Pacific Enterprises	800-722-5483	A	$25–$25,000/qtr.
Pacific Gas & Electric Company	800-367-7731	none	N/A
Pacific Telesis Group	415-394-3074	B,C	$50–$50,000/yr.
Pacific Western Bancshares, Inc. New Issue Shares: 5%	800-522-6645	B,C	$25–$3,000/6 mo.
Pacificorp	800-233-5453	B,C	$25–$25,000/qtr.
Paine Webber Group, Inc.	212-713-2722	A	$10–$3,000/qtr.
Pall Corporation	516-484-5400	B,C	$10–$5,000/mo.
Panhandle Eastern Corporation	800-225-5838	B,C	$25–$60,000/yr.
Paramount Communications, Inc.	212-373-8100	C	$100–$3,500/mo.
Parker-Hannifin Corporation	216-531-3000	A	$10–$1,000/mo.
Penney (J. C.) Company, Inc.	800-842-9470	B,C	$20–$10,000/mo.

Company	Telephone	Options	Min./Max. Optional Cash Purchase
Pennsylvania Enterprises, Inc.	717-829-8843	A,B	$10–$5,000/qtr.
Pennsylvania Power & Light Company	800-345-3085	C	$0–$5,000/qtr.
Pennzoil Company	713-546-4000	A	$40–$6,000/qtr.
Pentair, Inc.	800-551-6161	A	$10–$3,000/qtr.
Peoples Bancorporation of Worcester	800-937-5449	B,C	$100–$12,500/qtr.
Peoples Energy Corporation	800-228-6888	A	$25–$3,000/mo.
Pep Boys—Manny, Moe and Jack	215-227-9208	A,B	$100–$10,000/qtr.
PepsiCo, Inc.	212-613-7147	B,C	$10–$60,000/yr.
Perkin-Elmer Corporation	203-762-1485	B	N/A
Pfizer, Inc.	212-573-3087	A	$10–$10,000/mo.
Phelps Dodge Corporation	602-234-8100	A	$10–$2,000/qtr.
Philadelphia Electric Company	800-626-8729	B,C	$0–$50,000/yr.
Philadelphia Suburban Corporation Dividend: 5%	215-527-8000	B	N/A
Philip Morris Companies, Inc.	800-442-0077	B,C	$10–$60,000/yr.
Phillips Petroleum Company	800-356-0066	A	$10–$10,000/mo.
Piccadilly Cafeterias, Inc. Dividend: 5%	504-293-9440	B,C	$100–$5,000/qtr.
Piedmont Natural Gas Dividend: 5%	704-364-3120	B,C	$25–$3,000/mo.
Pinnacle West Capital Corporation	800-457-2983	B,C	$10–$5,000/qtr.
Pioneer Hi-Bred International, Inc.	617-575-2900	C	$25–$1,000/mo.
Pitney Bowes, Inc.	203-356-5000	B,C	$100–$3,000/qtr.
PNC Financial Corporation	800-982-7652	A,B	$50–$1,000/mo.

Company	Telephone	Options	Min./Max. Optional Cash Purchase
Polaroid Corporation	617-577-3963	A	$10–$3,000/qtr.
Portland General Corporation	503-464-8599	B,C	$25–$5,000/mo.
Portsmouth Bank Shares, Inc.	603-436-6630	none	N/A
Potlatch Corporation	415-576-8806	A	$25–$1,000/mo.
Potomac Electric Power Company	800-527-3726	C	$25–$5,000/mo.
PPG Industries, Inc.	412-434-3312	A	$10–$3,000/qtr.
Premier Industrial Corporation	216-391-8300	A	$10–$5,000/qtr.
Preston Corporation	212-613-7147	A	$25–$2,500/qtr.
Procter & Gamble Company	800-742-6253	none	N/A
PSI Resources, Inc.	800-446-2617	B,C	$25–$7,000/mo.
Public Service Company of Colorado Dividend: 3%; New Issue Shares: 3%	303-294-2617	A,B	$25–$100,000/yr.
Public Service Co. of North Carolina Dividend: 5%	704-864-6731	A,B	$25–$6,000/qtr.
Public Service Enterprise Group	800-242-0813	B,C	$25–$100,000/yr.
Puget Sound Power & Light Company	206-462-3719	C	$25–$20,000/yr.
Quaker Oats Company	800-344-1198	B,C	$10–$30,000/yr.
Quaker State Corporation	814-676-7806	A	$10–$3,000/qtr.
Quanex Corporation	800-231-8176	A	$10–$1,000/mo.
Quantum Chemical Corporation	212-949-5000	A	$25–$3,000/mo.
Questar Corporation	801-534-5885	B,C	$50–$15,000/qtr.
Ralston Purina Company	314-982-3000	B,C	$10–$25,000/yr.
Raymond Corporation	607-656-2466	A	$10–$3,000/mo.
Raytheon Company	617-575-2900	A	$10–$5,000/qtr.

Company	Telephone	Options	Min./Max. Optional Cash Purchase
Regional Bancorporation, Inc.	617-395-7700	B,C	$100–$1,000/qtr.
Reynolds & Reynolds Company	513-443-2000	A	$100–$1,000/qtr.
Reynolds Metals Company	800-526-0801	A	$25–$3,000/qtr.
Rhone-Poulenc Rorer, Inc.	215-454-3850	A,B	$25–$3,000/qtr.
Rite Aid Corporation	212-701-7608	A,B	$25–$25,000/yr.
Roadway Services, Inc.	216-258-2467	A	$10–$3,000/mo.
Roanoke Electric Steel	919-770-6000	none	N/A
Rochester Gas & Electric Corporation	716-546-2700	B,C	$10–$5,000/mo.
Rochester Telephone Corporation	800-836-0342	B,C	$25–$5,000/mo.
Rockwell International Corporation	412-565-7120	A	$10–$1,000/mo.
Rollins Environmental Services, Inc.	800-525-7686	A	$25–$2,500/mo.
Rollins, Inc.	800-568-3476	none	N/A
Rollins Truck Leasing Corporation	800-525-7686	A	$25–$2,500/mo.
Roosevelt Financial Group, Inc.	314-532-6200	A	$25–$1,000/qtr.
Rose's Stores, Inc.	919-770-6000	B,C	$10–$3,000/qtr.
Rouse Company	410-992-6546	C	$50–none/qtr.
RPM, Inc.	216-273-5090	C	$25–$5,000/mo.
Rubbermaid, Inc.	216-264-6464	A	$10–$3,000/qtr.
Russell Corporation	205-329-4832	A	$10–$2,000/mo.
Ryder System, Inc.	305-593-4053	B,C	$25–$60,000/yr.
Rykoff-Sexton, Inc.	213-622-4131	A	$50–$500/qtr.
Safety-Kleen Corporation	708-697-8460	A	$25–$5,000/mo.
Salomon, Inc.	212-791-6422	A	$10–$3,000/qtr.
San Diego Gas & Electric Company	800-522-6645	B,C	$25–$5,000/qtr.

Company	Telephone	Options	Min./Max. Optional Cash Purchase
Santa Fe Pacific Corporation	212-791-6422	A	$10–$1,000/mo.
Sara Lee Corporation	312-558-8450	A	$10–$5,000/qtr.
Savannah Foods & Industries, Inc.	912-651-4901	A	$10–$3,000/qtr.
SCANA Corporation	800-763-5891	B,C	$25–$3,000/qtr.
SCE Corporation	800-347-8625	B,C	$0–$10,000/mo.
Schering-Plough Corporation	201-822-7477	B,C	$25–$36,000/yr.
Schwab (Charles)	312-461-2288	B,C	$25–$5,000/mo.
Scott Paper Company	800-752-0771	A	$10–$3,000/qtr.
Seafield Capital Corporation	816-842-7000	A,B	$25–$5,000/qtr.
Sears, Roebuck & Company	212-791-3357	A	$25–$3,000/mo.
Selective Insurance Group	201-948-1762	B,C	$100–$1,000/qtr.
Sherwin Williams Company	216-737-2736	A	$10–$2,000/mo.
Sierra Pacific Resources	800-662-7575	C	$25–$5,000/qtr.
SIFCO Industries, Inc.	216-575-2532	A	$20–$3,000/qtr.
Signet Banking Corporation Dividend: 5%	800-451-7392	C	$10–$10,000/mo.
Simpson Industries, Inc.	313-540-6200	C	$10–$1,000/mo.
Smith (A. O.) Corporation	414-359-4150	A	$0–$5,000/qtr.
SmithKline Beecham PLC	800-428-4237	B,C	$10–$60,000/yr.
Smucker (J. M.) Company	216-682-3000	B,C	$20–$1,500/mo.
Snap-on-Tools	800-524-0687	A,B	$100–$5,000/qtr.
Society Corporation	800-542-7792	B,C	$25–$5,000/qtr.
Society for Savings Bancorporation	617-575-2900	B,C	$100–$2,500/mo.
Sonat, Inc.	212-613-7147	A	$25–$6,000/qtr.
Sonoco Products Company	803-383-7740	A	$10–$500/mo.

Company	Telephone	Options	Min./Max. Optional Cash Purchase
South Jersey Industries, Inc. Dividend: 3% Cash: 3%	609-561-9000	B,C	$25–$3,000/qtr.
Southeastern Michigan Gas	800-255-7647	C	$25–$5,000/qtr.
Southern California Water Company	714-394-3710	B	N/A
Southern Company	404-668-3168	B,C	$25–$6,000/qtr.
Southern Indiana Gas & Electric	800-227-8625	A	$25–$5,000/mo.
Southern National Corporation	919-671-2273	A	$25–$5,000/mo.
Southern New England Telecom	203-771-2058	C	$0–$3,000/qtr.
SouthTrust Corporation	205-254-6764	B,C	$25–$5,000/mo.
Southwest Gas Corporation	800-331-1119	A	$25–$25,000/yr.
Southwest Water Company Dividend: 5%	818-918-1231	B,C	$25–$3,000/qtr.
Southwestern Bell Corporation	314-235-6380	B,C	$50–$5,000/yr.
Southwestern Electric Service Co. Dividend: 5%	214-741-3125	A,B	$25–$3,000/qtr.
Southwestern Energy Company	312-407-4880	C	$25–$1,000/mo.
Southwestern Public Service Company	806-378-2841	B,C	$25–$3,000/qtr.
Sprint Corporation	913-624-2541	B,C	$25–$5,000/qtr.
SPX Corporation	616-724-5572	C	$25–$10,000/qtr.
St. Joseph Light & Power Company	816-233-8888	A	$100–$75,00/qtr.
St. Paul Bancorporation	312-804-2283	A	$50–$1,500/qtr.
St. Paul Companies, Inc.	612-221-7788	A,B	$10–$60,000/yr.
Standard Commercial Corporation	919-291-5507	B,C	$25–$3,000/mo.

Company	Telephone	Options	Min./Max. Optional Cash Purchase
Standard Products Company	216-281-8300	A	$50–$3,000/qtr.
Stanhome, Inc.	413-562-3631	A	$10–$5,000/qtr.
Stanley Works (The)	800-288-9541	A	$25–$5,000/mo.
Star Banc Corporation	513-632-4610	C	$50–$5,000/qtr.
State Street Boston Corporation	617-575-2900	A	$10–$1,000/mo.
Stone & Webster, Inc.	800-647-4273	C	$50–$1,500/mo.
Stride Rite Corporation	617-575-2900	C	$10–$1,000/mo.
Suffolk Bancorporation New Issue Shares: 3%	516-727-5667	B,C	$300–$5,000/qtr.
Summit Bancorporation (New Jersey) Dividend: 5% Cash: 5%	201-701-2512	B,C	$50–$5,000/mo.
Sun Company, Inc.	800-888-8494	A	$0–$10,000/qtr.
Sundstrand Corporation	815-226-2136	C	$25–$3,000/mo.
SunTrust Banks, Inc.	800-568-3476	A	$10–$60,000/yr.
Super Valu Stores, Inc.	612-450-4075	A	$10–$3,000/qtr.
Susquehanna Bancshares, Inc.	717-626-4721	A	$100–$2,500/qtr.
Synovus Financial Corporation	404-649-2387	A	$0–$6,000/qtr.
Sysco Corporation	713-584-1390	none	N/A
Tambrands, Inc.	914-696-6060	A,B	$25–$24,000/yr.
TCF Financial Corporation	612-370-1789	B,C	$25–$5,000/qtr.
TECO Energy, Inc.	813-228-1326	B,C	$25–$5,000/qtr.
Telephone and Data Systems, Inc. Dividend: 5%	312-630-1900	B,C	$10–$5,000/qtr.
Temple-Inland, Inc.	800-446-2617	A	$25–$1,000/qtr.
Tenneco, Inc. Dividend: 3%	800-446-2617	B,C	$50–$5,000/mo.
Texaco, Inc.	800-283-9785	A	$50–$120,000/yr.

Company	Telephone	Options	Min./Max. Optional Cash Purchase
Texas Utilities Company Dividend: 5%	800-828-0812	C	$25–$3,000/qtr.
Textron, Inc.	212-791-6422	B,C	$25–$1,000/mo.
Thomas & Betts Corporation	908-707-2363	A	$10–$3,000/qtr.
Thomas Industries, Inc.	502-893-4600	B,C	$25–$3,000/mo.
Tidewater, Inc.	800-647-4273	A	$25–$5,000/qtr.
Time Warner, Inc. Dividend: 5%	212-484-6971	B,C	$25–$10,000/qtr.
Times Mirror "A"	213-237-3955	A,B	$250–$10,000/qtr.
Timken Company Dividend: 5%	216-471-3376	B	N/A
TNP Enterprises Company	817-731-0099	B,C	$25–$5,000/qtr.
Torchmark Corporation	312-407-2258	B,C	$100–$6,000/qtr.
Toro Company	612-450-4004	A	$10–$1,000/mo.
Total Petroleum (North America) Dividend: 5%	303-291-2003	B	N/A
Transamerica Corporation	800-446-2617	B,C	$10–$5,000/mo.
Travelers Corporation Dividend: 5%	203-277-2819	B,C	$5–$5,000/mo.
Tribune Company	312-222-4144	B,C	$50–$2,000/mo.
TRINOVA	800-446-2617	A	$10–$20,000/yr.
TRW, Inc.	216-291-7654	A	$10–$2,000/qtr.
Twin Disc, Inc.	414-634-1981	A	$10–$2,000/mo.
Tyco Laboratories, Inc.	412-236-8143	A	$25–$1,000/mo.
U.S. Bancorporation (Oregon)	503-275-6472	B,C	$25–$6,000/qtr.
U.S. Trust Corporation	212-425-4500	A	$30–$1,000/mo.
U.S. West, Inc.	800-537-0222	A,B	$0–$50,000/yr.
UGI Corporation Dividend: 5%	215-337-1000	A,B	$25–$3,000/qtr.
UJB Financial Corporation	609-987-3442	A	$10–$10,000/qtr.

Company	Telephone	Options	Min./Max. Optional Cash Purchase
Union Bank Dividend: 5%	213-239-0672	A,B	$25–$3,000/qtr.
Union Camp Corporation	201-628-2000	A	$25–$15,000/yr.
Union Carbide Corporation	203-794-2212	C	$25–$1,000/mo.
Union Electric Company	314-554-3502	C	$0–$60,000/yr.
Union Pacific Corporation	212-791-6422	B,C	$10–$60,000/yr.
Union Planters Corporation Dividend: 5%	901-523-6980	B,C	$100–$2,000/qtr.
United Carolina Bancshares Corp.	919-642-1140	A	$25–$5,000/mo.
United Cities Gas Company Dividend: 5%	615-373-0104	A,B	$25–$10,000/qtr.
United Illuminating Company	203-777-7050	A,B	$10–$10,000/qtr.
United Mobile Homes, Inc. Dividend: 5% Cash: 5%	908-542-4927	B,C	$500–$15,000/qtr.
United States Shoe Corporation	513-527-7480	A	$25–$25,000/yr.
United Water Resources, Inc. Dividend: 5% Cash: 5%	201-767-2811	B,C	$25–$3,000/qtr.
UNITIL Corporation Dividend: 5%	603-772-0775	B,C	$25–$5,000/qtr.
Universal Corporation	804-254-1303	A,B	$10–$1,000/mo.
Universal Foods Corporation	414-347-3827	A,B	$25–$1,500/mo.
Unocal Corporation	800-647-4273	A	$25–$1,000/mo.
Upjohn Company	800-323-1849	B,C	$25–$6,000/qtr.
Upper Peninsula Energy Corporation	906-487-5020	C	$50–$5,000/qtr.
USF&G Corporation	301-547-3000	B,C	$0–$5,000/qtr.
USLICO Corporation	703-875-3600	A	$100–$2,500/qtr.

Company	Telephone	Options	Min./Max. Optional Cash Purchase
USLIFE Corporation	212-709-6230	A,B	$25–$4,000/qtr.
UST Corporation Dividend: 10% Cash: 10%	617-726-7262	B,C	$100–varies/qtr.
UST, Inc.	203-622-3656	B,C	$10–$10,000/mo.
USX–Marathon Group	412-433-4815	C	$50–$10,000/mo.
USX–U.S. Steel	412-433-4815	C	$50–$10,000/mo.
UtiliCorp United, Inc. Dividend: 5%	800-487-6661	C	$0–$10,000/qtr.
Valley Bancorporation (Wisconsin)	414-738-3829	A,B	$10–$25,000/qtr.
Valley National Bancorporation (NJ)	201-777-1800	A	$50–$2,000/mo.
Valley Resources Dividend: 5%	617-774-3119	B,C	$25–$5,000/mo.
Varian Associates, Inc.	617-575-2900	C	$10–$1,000/mo.
Vermont Financial Services Corp.	802-257-7151	A	$0–$3,000/qtr.
VF Corporation	215-378-1151	A	$10–$3,000/qtr.
Vulcan Materials Company	212-791-6422	A	$10–$3,000/qtr.
Wachovia Corporation	919-770-5787	A,B	$20–$2,000/mo.
Walgreen Company	312-461-5535	A	$10–$5,000/qtr.
Warner-Lambert Company	201-540-3498	A	$10–$1,000/mo.
Washington Energy Company Dividend: 5%	206-622-6767	C	$25–$3,000/qtr.
Washington Gas Light Company	202-624-6688	B,C	$25–$10,000/qtr.
Washington Mutual Savings Bank	206-461-3184	C	$100–$5,000/qtr.
Washington National Corporation	708-570-3208	B,C	$25–$5,000/qtr.
Washington Water Power Company	800-727-9170	C	$0–$100,000/yr.
Waste Management, Inc.	708-572-8826	C	$25–$2,000/mo.

Company	Telephone	Options	Min./Max. Optional Cash Purchase
Weis Markets, Inc.	717-286-4571	A	$10–$3,000/qtr.
Wells Fargo & Company Dividend: 3% Cash: 3%	800-446-2617	B,C	$150–$250,000/mo.
Wendy's International, Inc.	614-764-3251	B,C	$20–$20,000/yr.
West One Bancorporation	208-383-7245	C	$25–$2,500/qtr.
WestAmerica Bancorporation	415-257-8011	A	$25–$400/mo.
Westinghouse Electric Corporation	412-244-3654	A,B	$100–$5,000/mo.
Westvaco Corporation	212-318-5288	A,B	$0–$5,000/qtr.
Weyerhaeuser Company	800-647-4273	B,C	$100–$5,000/qtr.
Whirlpool Corporation	312-461-2543	A	$10–$3,000/qtr.
Whitman Corporation	708-818-5015	B,C	$10–$60,000/yr.
WICOR, Inc.	800-236-3453	A	$100–$5,000/mo.
Wilmington Trust Company	302-651-1448	B,C	$10–$5,000/qtr.
Winn-Dixie Stores, Inc.	904-783-5433	A	$10–$10,000/mo.
Wisconsin Energy Corporation	800-558-9663	C	$25–$8,000/mo.
Wisconsin Public Service Corporation	800-236-1551	B,C	$25–$5,000/mo.
Wisconsin Southern Gas Company, Inc.	414-248-8861	C	$50–$2,000/qtr.
Witco Corporation	212-791-6422	A	$10–$20,000/yr.
Woolworth Corporation	212-791-6422	B,C	$20–$60,000/yr.
Worthington Industries, Inc.	800-441-2001	B,C	$50–$5,000/qtr.
WPL Holdings, Inc.	800-356-5343	B,C	$20–$3,000/mo.
Wrigley (Wm.) Jr. Company	312-644-2121	A	$50–$5,000/mo.
Xerox Corporation	800-828-6396	B,C	$10–$5,000/mo.

Company	Telephone	Options	Min./Max. Optional Cash Purchase
York Financial Corporation Dividend: 10%	717-846-8777	B,C	$25–$2,500/qtr.
Zero Corporation	213-629-7000	C	$25–$8,000/mo.
Zions Bancorporation	801-524-4849	A,B	$10–$5,000/qtr.
Zurn Industries, Inc.	814-452-2111	A	$10–$3,000/qtr.

GLOSSARY

account executive A brokerage firm employee, also called registered representative, who advises and handles orders for clients and has the legal powers of an agent.

accumulated dividend The dividend due, but not paid, usually to holders of cumulative preferred stock. It is carried on the books of the corporation as a liability until paid.

acquisition One company taking over controlling interest in another company.

active market Heavy volume of trading in a particular stock, commodity or bond. This usually results in a narrower spread between bid and asked prices than when trading is quiet.

adjusted basis The base price from which to calculate capital gains or losses on the sale of a security. The cost of commissions is deducted when net proceeds are used for tax purposes. To arrive at the adjusted basis, the price must be adjusted to account for any stock splits that have occurred since the initial purchase.

adjusted debit balance (ADB) Formula for determining the position of a margin account, as required under Regulation T of the Federal Reserve Board.

against the box Refers to a short sale by the holder of a long position in the same security. When a stock is sold short against the box, it is a short sale, but only in effect, because the stock may be delivered from the seller's own account.

alien corporation   A company incorporated under the laws of a foreign country regardless of where it operates.

all or none   A buy or sell order marked to signify that no partial transaction is to be executed.

allotment   The amount of securities assigned to each of the participants in an investment banking syndicate formed to underwrite and distribute a new issue.

alpha   A mathematical estimate of the amount of return expected from an investment's inherent values, such as the rate of growth in its earnings per share, as distinct from its return caused by movements in the market. An alpha of 1.25 indicates that a stock is projected to rise 25 percent in price in a year when the return on the market is expected to be zero.

American Depositary Receipts (ADRs)   Receipts for the shares of a foreign-based corporation held in the vault of a U.S. bank and entitling the shareholder to all dividends and capital gains, thus eliminating the need to buy shares of those foreign-based companies in overseas markets.

American Stock Exchange (AMEX)   The stock exchange located at 86 Trinity Place in New York City. Stocks and bonds traded on the AMEX generally are those of small to medium-sized companies.

American Stock Exchange Composite Index   A market-capitalization-weighted index of the prices of the stocks traded on the American Stock Exchange.

analyst   A person in a brokerage house, mutual fund group or bank trust department who studies companies and makes buy-or-sell recommendations on the securities of particular companies and industry groups.

annual meeting   A yearly meeting when managers of a company report to stockholders on the year's results, and the board of directors stands for election for the next year.

annual report   A record of a corporation's financial condition that must be distributed to stockholders each year under Securities and Exchange Commission regulations. The report includes a description of the company's operations, plus its balance sheet and income statement.

annual total return   The capital gain or loss plus the sum of dividend disbursements during a 12-month period.

appreciation   The increase in the value of an asset such as a stock, bond or option.

arbitrage   The profiting from differences in price when the same security, currency or commodity is traded on two or more markets.

arbitration   An alternative to suing in court to settle disputes between customers and their brokers and between brokerage firms.

ascending tops   A chart pattern that traces a security's price over a period of time and shows that each peak in a security's price is higher than the preceding peak. The upward movement is considered bullish, meaning that the upward trend is likely to continue.

asked price   The price at which a security or commodity is offered for sale on an exchange or in the over-the-counter market. It is usually the lowest round lot price at which a dealer will sell.

asset play   A stock market term for a stock that is attractive because the current price does not fully reflect the value of the company's assets.

at the close   An order to buy or sell a security within the final 30 seconds of trading. Execution of such orders cannot be guaranteed.

at the market   An order to buy or sell a security at the best available price.

at the opening   A customer's order to buy or sell a security at the price that applies when an exchange opens. If not executed at that time, the order is automatically canceled.

authorized shares   The maximum number of shares that a company may legally create under the terms of its articles of incorporation.

average   An appropriately weighted and adjusted mean of selected securities designed to represent market behavior in general or for important segments of the market. Among the most familiar averages are the Dow Jones Industrials and the Standard & Poor's 500.

average down   A strategy to lower the average price paid for a company's shares by buying shares at the current price and then buying additional shares if the price should decline.

balance sheet   A financial report showing the status of a company's assets, liabilities, and owners' equity on a given date.

basis point   The smallest measure used in quoting yields on bonds and notes. One basis point is 0.01 percent of yield. Thus, a bond's yield that changes from 7.54 percent to 8.44 percent is said to have gone up 90 basis points.

basis price   The price an investor uses to calculate capital gains when selling a stock or bond.

bear   A person who thinks the market will fall.

bear market   A prolonged period of falling prices.

beta   A coefficient measuring a stock's volatility in relation to the rest of the stock market. The Standard & Poor's 500 Stock Index has a beta coefficient of 1. Any stock with a higher beta is more volatile than the market, and any with a lower beta can be expected to rise and fall more slowly than the market.

bid and asked   A bid is the highest price a prospective buyer is prepared to pay for a security at a particular time, while asked is the lowest price a seller is willing to take for the same security.

big board   Popular term for the New York Stock Exchange.

Black Monday   October 19, 1987, when the Dow Jones Industrial Average fell a record 508 points following sharp drops the week before.

block   A large quantity of stock or a large dollar amount of bonds held or traded.

blue chip   Common stock of a well-known established company that has a long record of profit growth and dividend payment and a reputation for high-quality management, products and services.

blue-sky laws   Laws passed by various states to protect investors against securities fraud.

boiler room   A place where high-pressure salespeople use banks of telephones to call lists of potential investors to sell speculative, sometimes fraudulent, securities.

bond   An interest-bearing or discounted government or corporate security that obligates the issuer to pay the bondholder a specified sum of money, usually at specific intervals, and to repay the principal amount of the loan at maturity.

bond rating   A method of evaluating the possibility of default by a bond issuer.

bond ratio   A leverage ratio measuring the percentage of a company's capitalization represented by bonds. It is calculated by dividing the total bonds due after one year by the same figure plus all equity.

book   The record maintained by a specialist of buy-and-sell orders in a given security.

book value   Net asset value of a company's securities.

bottom   Support level for market prices of any type of securities.

bottom fisher   An investor who is looking for stocks that have fallen to their bottom prices before turning up.

breadth of the market   The percentage of stocks participating in a particular market move.

breakout   The rise in a security's price above a resistance level (usually its previous high) or the drop below a level of support (usually the previous lowest price). A breakout is expected to signify a continuing move in the same direction.

broker   A person who acts as an agent for a buyer or seller of securities, usually charging a commission, and who must be registered with the exchange where the securities are traded.

bull   A person who thinks prices will rise.

bull market   A prolonged rise in the prices of stocks, bonds or commodities. A bull market is characterized by high trading volume and usually lasts at least a few months.

business cycle   Recurrence of periods of expansion and contraction in economic activity with effects on inflation, growth and employment.

buy-and-hold strategy   A strategy that calls for accumulating shares in a company over the years, allowing an investor to pay favorable long-term capital-gains tax on profits, and that needs much less attention than a more active trading strategy.

buying on margin   Buying securities with credit through a margin account held with a broker.

call An issuer's right to redeem bonds or preferred stock before maturity.

call feature A part of the agreement a bond issuer makes with a buyer, called the indenture, which describes the schedule and price of redemptions before maturity. Most corporate and municipal bonds can be called after ten years. Government bonds usually cannot be called.

call protection The length of time during which a security cannot be redeemed by the issuer.

capital gain The difference between an asset's purchase price and selling price, when the difference is positive.

capitalization *See* market capitalization.

capital stock Common and preferred stock authorized by a company's charter and having par value, stated value or no par value.

cash equivalents Instruments or investments of such high liquidity and safety that they are virtually as good as cash. Examples would include money market funds and Treasury bills.

cash ratio The ratio of cash and marketable securities to current liabilities.

cats and dogs Speculative stocks that have short histories of sales, earnings, and dividend payments.

chartist A technical analyst who charts the patterns of stocks, bonds and commodities to make buy-and-sell recommendations to clients.

churning Excessive trading of a customer's account. Churning is illegal under SEC and exchange rules, but is difficult to prove.

closed-end fund A type of fund that has a fixed number of shares. Unlike open-end mutual funds, it does not stand ready to issue and redeem shares on a continuous basis. Closed-end funds generally are listed on major stock exchanges.

closing price The price of the last transaction completed during a day of trading on a stock exchange.

combined financial statement A financial statement that combines the assets, liabilities, net worth and operating figures of two or more affiliated companies.

commercial paper Short-term obligations with maturities ranging from 2 to 270 days issued by banks, corporations and other borrowers.

commission The fee paid to a broker for executing a trade based on the number of shares traded or the dollar amount of the trade.

common stock Units of ownership of a public corporation, usually with the right to vote and to receive dividends.

common stock ratio The percentage of a corporation's total capitalization represented by common stock.

company risk The risk that has to do with the unique characteristics of any one stock and the industry in which it operates. It represents about 70 percent of the total risk faced by securities investors.

compound annual return The annual return that is earned on principal plus the return that was earned earlier. If $100 is deposited in an interest-bearing account at 10 percent, the investor will be credited with $110 at the end of the first year and $121 at the end of the second year. The extra $1 is earned on the $10 interest from the first year. Returns can also be compounded on a daily, quarterly, half-yearly or other basis.

confirmation   A formal memorandum from a broker to a customer giving details of a securities transaction.

consolidated financial statement   A financial statement that combines all assets, liabilities and operating accounts of a parent company and its subsidiaries.

constant dollar plan   A system of accumulating assets by investing a fixed amount of dollars in securities at set intervals. Also called dollar cost averaging.

consumer price index   A measure of change in consumer prices, as determined by a monthly survey of the U.S. Bureau of Labor Statistics.

conversion price   The dollar value at which convertible bonds, debentures or preferred stock can be converted into common stock.

conversion ratio   The relationship that determines how many shares of common stock will be received in exchange for each convertible bond or preferred share when the conversion takes place.

convertibles   Preferred stocks or bonds that are exchangeable for a set number of another form of securities (usually common stock) at a prestated price.

corporate bond   A debt instrument issued by a private corporation, as distinct from a governmental agency or municipality.

corporation   A legal entity chartered by a U.S. state or the federal government. It has limited liability (owners can lose only what they invest), easy transfer of ownership through the sale of shares of stock and continuity of existence.

correction   A reverse movement in the price trend of a security or index.

cost basis   The original price of an asset, used in determining capital gains.

coupon   The interest rate on a debt security that the issuer promises to pay to the holder until maturity, expressed as an annual percentage of face value.

covered option   An option contract backed by the shares underlying the option.

covered writer   The seller of covered options.

crash   A precipitate drop in stock prices and economic activity, usually brought on by a loss in investor confidence following periods of high inflation.

credit rating   A formal evaluation of a company's credit history and capability of repaying obligations.

cumulative preferred   Preferred stock whose dividends accumulate until paid out, if they have been omitted for any reason.

cumulative voting   A voting method that allows shareholders to cast all their votes for one candidate, rather than apportioning their votes equally among candidates. It improves minority stockholders' chances of naming representatives on the board of directors.

current assets   Cash, accounts receivable, inventory and other assets that are likely to be converted into cash, sold, exchanged or expensed, usually within a year.

current coupon bond   A corporate, federal or municipal bond with a coupon within half a percentage point of current market rates.

current market value   Present worth of a customer's portfolio at today's market price, as listed in a brokerage statement.

current maturity   The interval between the present time and the maturity date of a bond issue.

current ratio   Current assets divided by current liabilities.

current yield   The annual interest on a bond divided by the market price.

cyclical stock   A stock that tends to rise when the economy turns up and fall when the economy turns down, such as those of the housing, automobile and paper industries.

date of record   The date on which a shareholder must own shares to be entitled to a dividend. Also called the record date.

day order   An order to buy or sell securities that expires unless executed or canceled the day it is placed. All orders are day orders unless indicated to be good-till-canceled.

debenture   A general debt obligation backed only by the integrity of the borrower and documented by an agreement called an indenture.

debit balance   Money a margin customer owes a broker for loans to purchase securities.

debt instrument   A written promise to repay a debt, such as a bill, note, bond, banker's acceptance, certificate of deposit or commercial paper.

debt-to-equity ratio
1. Total liabilities divided by total shareholders' equity.
2. Total long-term debt divided by total shareholders' equity.

deep discount bond   A bond selling for a discount of more than about 20 percent from its face value.

default   The failure of a debtor to make timely payments of interest and principal as they come due or to meet some other provision of a bond indenture.

delayed opening   The postponement of the start of trading in a stock until a huge imbalance of buy-and-sell orders is overcome.

delisting   The removal of a company's security from an exchange because the firm did not abide by some regulation or the stock does not meet certain financial ratios or sales levels.

depression   An economic condition characterized by falling prices, reduced purchasing power, an excess of supply over demand, rising unemployment, deflation, public fear and caution and a general decrease in business activity.

dilution The effect on earnings per share and book value per share if all convertible securities were converted and all warrants or stock options were exercised.

discount bond A bond selling below its redemption value.

discount broker A brokerage firm that executes orders to buy and sell securities at commission rates lower than those charged by full-service brokers.

discretionary account An account giving a broker the power to buy and sell securities without the customer's prior knowledge or consent.

diversification Spreading risk by placing assets in several categories of investments, such as stocks, bonds, mutual funds, etc.

dividend A distribution of earnings to shareholders, paid in the form of cash, stock, scrip, or even company products or property.

dividend payout ratio The percentage of earnings paid to shareholders in cash.

dividend reinvestment plan Automatic reinvestment of shareholder dividends in more shares of the company's stock.

dollar cost averaging A method of accumulating assets by investing a fixed amount of dollars in securities at set intervals.

domestic corporation A corporation doing business in the U.S. state in which it was incorporated.

Dow Jones Industrial Average A price-weighted index of 30 actively traded blue-chip stocks.

dual-purpose fund An exchange-listed closed-end mutual fund that has two classes of shares. Preferred shareholders receive all the income (dividends and capital gains), while common shareholders receive all the capital gains.

earnings per share The portion of a company's profit allocated to each outstanding share of common stock.

equity The excess of securities over debit balance in a margin account.

equity financing Raising money by issuing shares of common or preferred stock.

equivalent taxable yield Comparison of the taxable yield on a corporate bond and the tax-free yield on a municipal bond.

exdividend Interval between the announcement and the payment of the next dividend. An investor who buys shares during that interval is not entitled to the dividend.

exdividend date The date on which a stock goes exdividend, usually about three weeks before the dividend is paid to stockholders of record.

execution Transacting a trade. A broker who buys or sell shares has executed an order.

exercise price   The price at which the stock underlying a put or call option can be sold (put) or purchased (call) over the specified period.

exstock dividends   The interval between the announcement and payment of a stock dividend. An investor who buys shares during that interval is not entitled to the announced stock dividend.

exwarrants   Stock sold with the buyer no longer entitled to the warrant attached to the stock.

face value   The value of a bond, note, mortgage, or other security as given on the certificate or instrument.

Fannie Mae   Nickname for the Federal National Mortgage Association.

federal deficit   The federal shortfall that results when the government spends more in a fiscal year than it receives in revenue.

federal funds rate   The interest rate charged by banks with excess reserves at the Federal Reserve district bank to banks needing overnight loans to meet reserve requirements.

Federal National Mortgage Association (FNMA)   A publicly owned, government-sponsored corporation chartered in 1938 to purchase mortgages from lenders and resell them to investors.

fill   To execute a customer's order to buy or sell a stock, bond or commodity.

fill or kill   An order to buy or sell a security, which is canceled if not executed immediately.

first call date   The first date specified in the indenture of a corporate or municipal bond contract on which part or all of the bond may be redeemed at a set price.

fiscal year   An accounting period covering 12 consecutive months, 52 consecutive weeks, 13 four-week periods or 365 consecutive days, after which the books are closed and profit or loss is determined.

Fitch Investors Service, Inc.   A New York- and Denver-based rating firm that rates corporate and municipal bonds, preferred stock, commercial paper and other obligations.

fixed income investment   A security that pays a fixed rate of return.

flash   A tape display designation used when volume on an exchange is so heavy that the tape runs more than five minutes behind.

flat market   A market characterized by horizontal price movement, usually accompanied by low activity.

floor broker   A member of an exchange who is an employee of a member firm and executes orders on the floor of the exchange for customers.

formula investing   An investment technique based on a predetermined timing or asset-allocation model that eliminates emotional decisions.

fractional share   A unit of stock less than one full share, often used if a shareholder is in a dividend reinvestment plan and the dividends being reinvested are insufficient to buy a full share at the stock's current price.

Freddie Mac   Nickname for the Federal Home Loan Mortgage Corporation.

full coupon bond   A bond with a coupon rate that is near or above current market interest rates.

full-service broker   A broker who provides a wide range of services to customers, including advice on which securities to buy and sell.

fully invested   Said of an investor or a portfolio when funds in cash or cash equivalents are minimal and assets are totally committed to other investments.

fully valued   Said of a stock that has reached a price at which analysts think the underlying company's earning power has been recognized by the market.

Ginnie Mae   Nickname for the Government National Mortgage Association and the certificate issued by that agency.

going long   Buying a stock or bond for investment or speculation.

going public   Phrase used when a private company first offers its shares to the public.

going short   Selling a stock that the seller does not have by borrowing it from a broker, hoping to purchase other shares of it at a lower price.

good-till-canceled order (GTC)   A customer's order to buy or sell a security, usually at a specified price, that remains in effect until executed or canceled.

greater fool theory   A theory that even though a stock or the market as a whole is fully valued, speculation is justified because there are enough fools to push it further upward.

hedging   A strategy used to offset investment risk.

high flier   A high-priced and highly speculative stock that moves up and down sharply over a short period of time.

holder of record   Owner of a company's securities as recorded on the books of the issuing company or its transfer agent as of a particular date.

hot issue   Newly issued stock that is in great public demand.

income shares   One of two kinds or classes of stock issued by a dual-purpose fund, holders of which receive all the interest and dividends produced by the portfolio.

index   A statistical composite that measures changes in the economy or in financial markets, often expressed in percentage changes from one period to another.

index fund   A mutual fund whose portfolio matches that of a broad-based index and whose performance mirrors the market as a whole.

indexing   Weighting one's portfolio to match a broad-based index such as Standard & Poor's 500 to match its performance.

indicated yield   The coupon or dividend rate as a percentage of the current market price.

individual retirement account (IRA)   A personal, tax-deferred retirement account that an employed person can set up.

inflation A rise in the prices of goods and services. Too much money chasing too few goods.

inflation rate The rate of change in prices in an inflationary period.

initial public offering A corporation's first offering of stock to the public.

inside information Corporate affairs that have not yet been made public. Insiders, such as officers of a company, are not allowed to trade on such information.

inside market Bid and asked quotes between dealers trading for their own inventories.

insider A person with access to corporate information before it is announced to the public.

insolvency Inability to pay debts when due.

interim dividend A dividend declared and paid before annual earnings have been determined, usually quarterly.

inverted yield curve An unusual situation where short-term interest rates are higher than long-term rates.

investment banker A firm, acting as underwriter or agent, that serves as intermediary between an issuer or securities and the investing public.

investment company A firm that invests the pooled funds of small investors in securities appropriate for its stated investment objectives.

junk bond A bond with a credit rating of BB or lower by rating agencies.

Keogh plan A tax-deferred pension account for employees of unincorporated businesses or for persons who are self-employed.

last sale The most recent trade in a particular security.

leg A sustained trend in stock market prices.

leverage In securities, a means of enhancing return or value without increasing investment. An example of leverage is buying securities on margin.

limited discretion An agreement between the broker and the customer that allows the broker to make certain trades without consulting the customer.

limit order An order to buy or sell a security at a specific price or better.

limit price The price set in a limit order.

listed security A stock or bond that has been accepted for trading by one of the organized and registered securities exchanges in the United States.

listing requirements Rules that must be met before a stock is listed for trading on an exchange.

locked in Unable to take advantage of preferential tax treatment on the sale of a security because the required holding period has not elapsed.

long position Ownership of a security, or an investor's ownership of securities held by a brokerage firm.

long-term debt Liability due in one year or more.

long-term financing Liabilities not repayable in one year and all equity.

low The bottom price paid for a security over the past year or since trading in the security began.

make a market Maintain firm bid-and-offer prices in a particular security by standing ready to buy or sell round lots at publicly quoted prices.

margin The amount a customer deposits with a broker when borrowing from the broker to buy securities.

margin account A brokerage account allowing a customer to buy securities with money borrowed from the broker.

margin call A demand that a customer deposit enough money or securities to bring a margin account up to the initial margin or minimum maintenance requirements.

margin requirement The minimum amount that a customer must deposit in the form of cash or eligible securities in a margin account as spelled out in Regulation T of the Federal Reserve Board.

marketable securities Securities that may be easily sold.

market capitalization The value of a corporation as determined by the market price of its issued and outstanding common stock, calculated by multiplying the number of outstanding shares by the current market price per share.

market price The last reported price at which a security was sold on an exchange, or the combined bid and asked prices for securities traded over the counter.

market timing Decisions on when to buy or sell securities in light of economic factors or technical indications such as the direction of stock prices and the volume of trading.

market value The current market price of a security.

market value-weighted index An index whose components are weighted according to the total market value of their outstanding shares.

maturity date The date on which the principal amount of a debt instrument becomes due and payable.

minority interest The interest of shareholders who, in the aggregate, own less than half the shares in a corporation.

money market The market for short-term debt instruments such as commercial paper, negotiable certificates of deposits, banker's acceptances, Treasury bills and discount notes of federal agencies.

money market fund An open-ended mutual fund that invests in short-term debt instruments and pays money market rates of interest.

money supply The total stock of money in the economy, consisting primarily of currency in circulation and deposits in savings and checking accounts.

most active list Stocks with the most shares traded on a given day.

moving average An average of security or commodity prices constructed on a period as short as a few days or as long as several years and showing trends for the latest interval.

municipal bond A debt obligation of a state or local government entity.

mutual fund   A fund operated by an investment company that raises money from shareholders and invests it in stocks, bonds, options, commodities or money market securities.

naked option   An option for which the buyer or seller has no underlying security position.

narrow market   A securities market characterized by light trading and greater fluctuations in prices than would be the case if trading were active.

NASD   The National Association of Securities Dealers.

Nasdaq   The National Association of Securities Dealers Automated Quotation system. It is owned and operated by the National Association of Securities Dealers.

National Association of Securities Dealers (NASD)   A nonprofit organization whose members include nearly all investment banking houses and firms dealing in the over-the-counter market.

national market system   A system of trading over the counter stocks under the sponsorship of the NASD and Nasdaq.

negative yield curve   A situation in which yields on short-term securities are higher than those on long-term securities of the same quality.

net change   The difference between the last trading price on a security from one day to the next.

net current assets   The difference between current assets and current liabilities.

net income per share of common stock   The amount of profit or earnings allocated to each share of common stock after all costs, taxes, allowances for depreciation and possible losses have been deducted.

new issue   A stock or bond being offered to the public for the first time, the distribution of which is covered by Securities and Exchange Commission rules.

New York Stock Exchange   The oldest (1792) and largest stock exchange in the United States, located at 11 Wall Street in New York City.

Nikkei Index   An index of 225 leading stocks traded on the Tokyo Stock Exchange.

no-load fund   A mutual fund offered by an open-end investment company that imposes no sales charge (load) on its shareholders.

noncallable   Preferred stock or a bond that cannot be redeemed at the option of the issuer.

noncumulative   a preferred stock issue in which unpaid dividends do not accrue.

no-par-value stock   Stock with no set (par) value specified in the corporate charter or on the stock certificate.

normal trading unit   The standard minimum size of a trading unit for a particular security; also called a round lot. For stocks, the normal trading unit is 100 shares.

odd lot   A securities trade made for less than the normal trading unit, or round lot. For stocks, any purchase or sale of less than 100 shares.

offer   The price at which someone who owns a security offers to sell it; also known as the asked price.

offering date   The date on which a distribution of stocks or bonds will first be available for sale to the public.

offering price   The price per share at which a new or secondary distribution of securities is offered for sale to the public.

open order   A buy or sell order for securities that has not yet been executed or canceled; a good-till-canceled order.

option   A transaction agreement tied to stocks, commodities or stock indexes. A call option gives its buyer the right to buy 100 shares of the underlying security at a fixed price before a specified date in the future. A put option gives its buyer the right to sell.

option holder   Someone who has bought a call or put option but has not yet exercised or sold it.

option premium   The amount per share paid by an option buyer to an option seller for the right to buy (call) or sell (put) the underlying security at a particular price within a specified period.

option writer   A person or financial institution that sells put and call options.

order   An instruction to a broker or dealer to buy or sell securities or commodities.

order ticket   A form completed by a registered representative of a brokerage firm after receiving order instructions from a customer.

OTC margin stock   The shares of certain large firms traded over the counter that qualify as margin securities under Regulation T of the Federal Reserve Board.

outstanding stock   Stock held by shareholders and shown on corporate balance sheets under the heading of capital stock issued and outstanding.

overbought   Description of a security or a market that recently has experienced an unexpectedly sharp price rise and is vulnerable to a price drop.

oversold   description of a stock or market that has experienced an unexpectedly sharp price decline and is due for an imminent price rise.

oversubscribed   An underwriting term describing a new stock issue for which there are more buyers than available shares.

over the counter (OTC)   A market in which securities transactions are conducted through a telephone and computer network connecting dealers in stocks and bonds, rather than on the floor of an exchange.

overvalued   Description of a stock whose current price is not justified by its price/earnings ratio or the earnings outlook for the company.

paid-in capital   Capital received from investors in exchange for stock, as distinguished from capital generated from earnings.

paper profit or loss   Unrealized capital gain or loss in an investment or portfolio. Such a gain or loss becomes realized only when the security is sold.

par   The nominal or face value of a security.

parent company   A company that owns or controls subsidiaries through ownership of voting stock.

participating preferred stock   Preferred stock that gives the holder the right to participate with the common stockholder in additional distributions of earnings under specified conditions.

par value   *See* par.

passive investing   Investing in a mutual fund that replicates a market index, such as the S&P 500 Index, thus assuring investment performance equivalent to the market as a whole.

pass-through security   A security, representing pooled debt obligations repackaged as shares, that passes income from debtors through the intermediary to investors.

payment date   The date on which a declared stock dividend or a bond interest payment is scheduled to be paid.

payout ratio   The percentage of a firm's profits that is paid out to shareholders in the form of dividends.

penny stock   A stock that typically sells for less than $1 a share, although it may rise to as much as $10 a share after the initial public offering because of heavy promotion.

pink sheets   A daily publication of the National Quotation Bureau that details the bid and asked prices of thousands of over-the-counter stocks.

plus tick   An expression used when a security has been traded at a higher price than the previous transaction in that security.

point   A change of $1 in the market price of a stock.

portfolio   A combined holding of more than one stock, bond, commodity, cash equivalent, or other asset by an individual or institutional investor.

position   An investor's stake in a particular security or market.

positive yield curve   A situation in which interest rates are higher on long-term debt securities than on short-term debt securities of the same quality.

preferred stock   A normally nonvoting class of capital stock that pays dividends at a specified rate and that has preference over common stock in the payment of dividends and the liquidation of assets.

preliminary prospectus   The first document released by an underwriter of a new issue to prospective investors, often called a red herring.

premium   The price a put-or-call-option buyer must pay to a put-or-call seller (writer) for an option contract.

price-earnings (PE) ratio   The price of a stock divided by its earnings per share over a 12-month period.

price-weighted index   An index in which component stocks are weighted by their price, giving higher priced stocks greater impact on the index than those at lower prices.

primary distribution   The sale of a new issue of stocks or bonds.

principal amount   The face value of a bond that must be repaid at maturity, as distinguished from the interest.

program trading   Computer-driven buying or selling of baskets of 15 or more stocks by index arbitrage specialists or institutional traders.

prospectus   A formal written offer to sell securities that sets forth the plan for a proposed business enterprise or mutual fund, or the facts about an existing one that an investor needs to make an informed decision.

public offering   An offering to the investment public of new securities at a price agreed on between the issuers and the investment bankers.

public offering price   The price at which a new issue of securities is offered to the public by underwriters.

put option   A contract that grants the right to sell at a specified price a specific number of shares by a certain date.

quick ratio   Cash, marketable securities and accounts receivable divided by current liabilities.

quotation   The highest bid and lowest offer (asked) price currently available on a security.

quoted price   The price at which the last sale and purchase of a particular security took place.

rally   A marked rise in the price of a security or market after a period of decline or sideways movement.

realized profit (or loss)   The profit or loss resulting from the sale or other disposal of a security.

record date   The date on which a shareholder must officially own shares to be entitled to the dividend.

redemption   Repayment of a debt security or preferred stock issue, at or before maturity, at par or at a premium price.

registered representative   An employee of a stock exchange member broker/dealer who acts as an account executive for customers.

registration   A process by which securities that are to be sold to the public are reviewed by the Securities and Exchange Commission.

reinvestment privilege   The right of a shareholder to reinvest dividends to buy more shares in the company or mutual fund.

resistance level   A price ceiling at which technical analysts note persistent selling of a security.

retail investor   An investor who buys securities on his or her own behalf.

retained earnings   Net profits kept to accumulate in a business after dividends are paid.

return   Profit on a securities investment, usually expressed as an annual percentage rate.

reverse split A procedure by which a corporation reduces the number of shares outstanding. The total number of shares will have the same market value after the reverse split as before, but each share will be worth more.

rights offering An offering of common stock to existing shareholders who hold rights that entitle them to buy newly issued shares at a discount from the price at which shares will later be offered to the public.

round lot The generally accepted unit of trading on a securities exchange, usually 100 shares for stock.

scrip A temporary document issued by a corporation that represents a fractional share of stock resulting from a split, exchange of stock or spin-off.

SEC The Securities and Exchange Commission.

secondary distribution The public sale of previously issued securities held by large investors.

seller's market A situation in which there is more demand for a security than there is available supply. As a result, prices tend to rise.

selling climax A sudden plunge in security prices as those who hold stocks or bonds panic and decide to dump their holdings all at once.

selling short The sale of a stock, not owned by the seller, in the hope of buying it back later at a lower price. The stock is borrowed by the seller at the time of the short sale.

settlement date The date by which an executed order must be settled, either by a buyer paying for the securities with cash or by a seller delivering the securities and receiving the proceeds from them.

share Unit of equity ownership in a corporation.

short covering The actual purchase of securities by a short seller to replace those borrowed at the time of a short sale.

short interest The total amount of shares of stock that have been sold short and have not yet been repurchased.

short position Stock shares that an individual has sold short and has not repurchased as of a particular date.

specialist A member of a stock exchange who maintains a fair and orderly market in one or more securities.

special situation An undervalued stock that should soon rise in value because of an imminent favorable turn of events.

speculation The assumption of risk in anticipation of gain but recognizing a higher-than-average possibility of loss.

split An increase in a corporation's number of shares of stock outstanding without any change in the shareholders' equity or the aggregate market value at the time of the split.

stock The ownership of a corporation represented by shares that are a claim on the corporation's earnings and assets.

stock dividend The payment of a corporate dividend in the form of stock rather than cash.

stock exchange An organized marketplace in which stocks and bonds are traded by members of the exchange, acting both as agents and principals.

stockholder of record A common or preferred stockholder whose name is registered on the books of a corporation as owning shares as of a particular date.

stock indexes and averages Indicators used to measure and report value changes in representative stock groupings.

stock symbol Letters used to identify listed companies on the securities exchanges on which they trade.

stop loss A customer order to a broker that sets the sell price of a stock below the current market price. It is used to protect profits or to prevent further losses if the stock drops.

street name A phrase describing securities held in the name of a broker or another nominee instead of a customer.

support level The price level at which a security tends to stop falling because there is more demand than supply.

suspended trading A temporary halt in trading in a security in advance of a major news announcement or to correct an imbalance of buy and sell orders.

tape A service that reports prices and size of transactions on major exchanges.

tax basis The price at which a security was purchased, plus brokerage commissions.

tax-exempt security An obligation, often called a municipal bond, whose interest is exempt from federal, state and/or local taxation.

technical analysis Research into the demand and supply for securities and commodities based on trading volume and price studies.

technical rally A short rise in securities' prices within a general declining trend.

thin market A market in which there are few bids to buy and few offers to sell.

tick Upward or downward price movement in a security's trades.

ticker The system that produces a running report of trading activity on the stock exchanges, called the ticker tape.

ticker tape A device that relays the stock symbol and the latest price and volume on securities as they are traded to investors around the world.

tight market The market in general or for a particular security characterized by active trading and narrow bid-offer price spreads.

topping out A term denoting a market or a security that is at the end of a period of rising prices and is expected to stay on a plateau or to decline.

total return The annual return on an investment including price change and income from dividends or interest.

trade date The day on which a security trade actually takes place.

treasury direct   A system through which an investor can invest in U.S. Treasury securities through Federal Reserve Banks, bypassing banks or broker-dealers and avoiding their fees.

treasury stock   Stock reacquired by the issuing company and available for retirement or resale.

triple witching hour   The last trading hour on the third Friday of March, June, September and December, when options and futures on stock indexes expire concurrently.

uncovered option   An option contract for which the owner does not hold the underlying security.

undermargined account   A margin account that has fallen below the margin or minimum maintenance requirements.

undervalued   A security selling below its liquidation value or the market value analysts believe it deserves.

underwriter   An investment banker who agrees to purchase a new issue of securities from an issuer and distribute it to investors.

unissued stock   Shares of a corporation's stock authorized in its charter but not issued.

unlisted security   A security that is not listed on an organized exchange and is traded in the over-the-counter market.

unpaid dividend   A dividend that has been declared by the board of directors of a corporation but has not reached its payment date.

unrealized profit (or loss)   A profit or loss that has not become actual because the security has not been sold.

unregistered stock   A stock or bond that is not registered with the SEC and therefore cannot be sold in the public market.

uptick   A transaction executed at a price higher than the preceding transaction in that security. Also called a plus tick.

uptrend   An upward direction in the price of a security or the market.

volume   The total number of bonds or stock shares traded in a particular period.

warrant   A type of security that entitles the holder to buy a proportionate amount of common stock at a specified price for a period of years or in perpetuity.

wire house   A brokerage firm whose branch offices are linked by a communications system that permits the rapid dissemination of prices, information and research relating to securities and financial markets.

writer   A person who sells put-and-call option contracts and therefore collects premium income.

yield   The percentage rate of return paid on a security, calculated by dividing its annual dividend or interest income by its cost to the investor.

zero-coupon security   A security that makes no periodic interest payments but instead is sold at a deep discount from its face value.

INDEX